Racism on the Internet

Yaman Akdeniz

Council of Europe Publishing

Cover photo ©Shutterstock
Cover design and layout: Documents and Publication Production Department (SPDP), Council of Europe Publishing
Council of Europe Publishing
F-67075 Strasbourg Cedex
http://book.coe.int

ISBN 978-92-871-6634-0
© Council of Europe, December 2009
Printed at the Council of Europe

Contents

1. Introduction

Racism was a pressing social problem long before the emergence of the digital age. The advancement of digital communication technologies such as the Internet has, however, added a new dimension to this problem by providing individuals and organisations with modern and powerful means to support racism and xenophobia. The use of the Internet as an instrument for the widespread dissemination of racist content is outlined in this introductory chapter. A typology of racist content on the Internet will also be provided.

There is no generally agreed definition of "hate speech" or "racist content". Generally, speech that incites or promotes hatred towards individuals, on the basis of their race, colour, ethnicity, gender, nationality, religion, sexual preference, disability, and other forms of individual discrimination can constitute "hate speech". In 1997, a Council of Europe recommendation on hate speech stated that the term "hate speech" should be understood as covering "all forms of expression which spread, incite, promote or justify racial hatred, xenophobia, anti-Semitism or other forms of hatred based on intolerance, including intolerance expressed by aggressive nationalism and ethnocentrism, discrimination and hostility against minorities, migrants and people of immigrant origin".[1] The European Court of Human Rights refers to "all forms of expression which spread, incite, promote or justify hatred based on intolerance (including religious intolerance)"[2] as "hate speech" but "only statements which promote a certain level of violence qualify as hate speech".[3] Racism, on the other hand, is described by the European Commission against Racism and Intolerance (ECRI) as "the belief that a ground such as race, colour, language, religion, nationality or national or ethnic origin justifies contempt for a person or a group of persons, or the notion of superiority of a person or a group of persons".[4] It should, however, be noted

---

1. Council of Europe, Committee of Ministers, Recommendation No. R (97) 20.

2. *Gündüz v. Turkey*, Application No. 35071/97 judgment of 4 December 2003, para. 40. See further European Commission for Democracy through Law (Venice Commission), Report on the relationship between freedom of expression and freedom of religion: the issue of regulation and prosecution of blasphemy, religious insult and incitement to religious hatred, adopted by the Venice Commission at its 76th Plenary Session (Venice, 17-18 October 2008), CDL-AD(2008)026, at www.venice.coe.int/docs/2008/CDL-AD(2008)026-e.pdf.

3. Ibid.

4. European Commission against Racism and Intolerance (ECRI) General Policy Recommendation No. 7 on national legislation to combat racism and racial discrimination, adopted by ECRI on 13 December 2002.

that "such speech does not necessarily imply the expression of 'hate' or emotions. Racial discourse may be concealed in statements that at first sight appear rational or routine".[5]

However, disagreements and variations exist on these definitions, and the content of "hate speech" or "racist content" could be broader based upon cultural, political, moral and religious differences around the world, and perhaps more evidently within the European region. Such differences, combined with historical, legal, and constitutional background, often lead into the adoption of different legal measures to deal with such content, and variations also exist with regards to what constitutes criminal conduct. While states such as France, Germany, Austria, and Belgium criminalise the denial of the Jewish Holocaust, other European states such as the United Kingdom, Ireland, and Italy do not have similar criminal provisions.

Racism and the dissemination of ideas based on hatred and racial superiority were a pressing social problem prior to the emergence of the information age and digital communications. Long before the Internet entered our homes, racist groups made use of other communication tools including the telephone networks as far back as the 1970s. For example, the Western Guard Party, a white supremacist neo-Nazi group based in Toronto, Canada, had a telephone answering machine which was used to propagate hatred,[6] and was the subject matter of a long legal dispute in the late 1980s.[7] The advancement of digital communication technologies such as the Internet has, however, added a new dimension to this problem by providing individuals and organisations "with modern and powerful means to support racism and xenophobia".[8]

Historically, concerns about "digital hate" date back to the mid 1980s and relate to the documented use of computers, computer bulletin boards and networks to disseminate racist views and content.[9] According to the Simon Wiesenthal

---

5. See Council of Europe Steering Committee for Human Rights (CDDH), Committee of Experts for the Development of Human Rights (DH-DEV), Working Group A, Report on "hate speech", document GT-DH-DEV A(2006)008, Strasbourg, 9 February 2007, at www.coe.int/t/e/human_rights/, para. 4.

6. Canadian Human Rights Commission, *Hate on the Net* (Ottawa: Association for Canadian Studies, Spring 2006) at 4, at www.chrc-ccdp.ca/pdf/HateOnInternet_bil.pdf .

7. *Canada (Human Rights Commission) v. Taylor* [1990] 3 S.C.R. 892 (Prohibition on telephone hate messages in section 13(1) of the Canadian Human Rights Act, S.C. 1976-77, c. 33 was justifiable). See also *Canada (Human Rights Commission) v. Canadian Liberty Net* [1998] 1 S.C.R. 626 and *Canada (Human Rights Commission) v. Heritage Front* [1994] F.C.J. No. 2010 (T.D.) (QL).

8. Council of Europe, Committee of Ministers, Explanatory Report of the Additional Protocol to the Convention on Cybercrime, concerning the criminalisation of acts of a racist and xenophobic nature committed through computer systems, (2002) at para. 3, at http://conventions.coe.int/.

9. See "'Neo-Nazis Inspire White Supremacists', *The Washington Post* (26 December 1984) (dissemination of racist comments through computer bulletin boards in North America). See also Anti-Defamation League, Report, "Computerized Networks of Hate" (January 1985).

Center's "Online Terror and Hate: The First Decade" report,[10] George Dietz, a West Virginia neo-Nazi, was already using the original computer bulletin boards systems (BBS) in 1983, and Dietz's postings served as a model for later websites. Louis Beam's Aryan Liberty Net was subsequently launched in the US BBS in 1984, as well as the militia movement.[11] In Germany, the "right-wing extremist organisations first used bulletin board systems and other electronic communication systems in the early 1990s".[12] The BBS movement quickly jumped on the Internet in the mid 1990s and white supremacist website StormFront was launched in 1995 in the US by former Ku Klux Klan member Don Black with the intention of creating a community around the white power movement, while Ernst Zündel's Holocaust Denial website was launched during 1998 in Canada.

New methods of dissemination of anti-Semitic and revisionist propaganda about the Holocaust (including video games, computer programs and the Minitel system in France) were noted by a United Nations Secretary-General report in 1994,[13] and the growing use of modern electronic media in international communications between right-wing radical groups (computer disks, databanks, etc.) was recorded in 1995.[14] Officially the use of electronic mail and the Internet was first observed as a growing trend amongst racist organisations to spread racist or xenophobic propaganda in 1996.[15] The UN Special Rapporteur on contemporary forms of racism, racial discrimination, xenophobia and related intolerance in his 1997 report declared that:

> The Internet has become the new battleground in the fight to influence public opinion. While it is still far behind newspapers, magazines, radio and television in the size of its audience, the Internet has already captured the imagination of people with a message, including purveyors of hate, racists and anti-Semites.[16]

---

10. The Simon Wiesenthal Center, iReport: "Online Terror and Hate: The First Decade", May 2008, at www.wiesenthal.com/ireport.

11. Ibid.

12. Council of Europe, Octopus Programme, *Organised Crime in Europe: The Threat of Cybercrime: Situation Report 2004* (Strasbourg, 2005), Council of Europe Publishing, p. 138.

13. Secretary-General, *Elimination Of Racism And Racial Discrimination*, UN GA, 49th Sess., UN Doc. A/49/677 (1994).

14. Maurice Glélé-Ahanhanzo, Implementation of the Programme of Action for the Second Decade to Combat Racism and Racial Discrimination – Report of the UN Special Rapporteur on contemporary forms of racism, racial discrimination, xenophobia and related intolerance, CHR Res. 1994/64, UN ESCOR, 51st Sess., UN Doc. E/CN.4/1995/78 (1995).

15. Secretary-General, Elimination of Racism and Racial Discrimination: Measures to combat contemporary forms of racism, racial discrimination, xenophobia and related intolerance, UN GA, 51st Sess., UN Doc. A/51/301 (1996).

16. Maurice Glélé-Ahanhanzo, Implementation of the Programme of Action for the Second Decade to Combat Racism and Racial Discrimination – Report of the UN Special Rapporteur on contemporary forms of racism, racial discrimination, xenophobia and related intolerance, CHR Res. 1996/21, UN ESCOR, 53rd Sess., UN Doc. E/CN.4/1997/71 (1997).

Although the majority of online racist content was disseminated through North America in the mid 1990s, it was accurately predicted that this would change with the rapid growth of Internet use around the globe. Easy and inexpensive access to the Internet, as well as the development of the World Wide Web, provided new and ready opportunities for publishing and this extended to material of a racist and xenophobic nature.[17] Flyers and pamphlets that had traditionally been distributed locally by hand and had limited visibility could be distributed and accessed globally through the Internet. In fact, the "slow, insidious effect of a relatively isolated bigoted commentary ... has now changed to a form of communication having a widespread circulation"[18] around the globe.

Quantifying the nature of online hate

There is strong documented evidence to show that racist organisations and individuals are currently using the Internet to disseminate racist content. Furthermore, since the 11 September terrorist attacks in the United States, terrorist organisations have started to make use of the Internet for spreading propaganda[19] and inciting violence.[20] The resurrection of Nazi ideology in Europe[21] and violent radicalisation[22] across the world are also partially blamed on Internet publications as information and publications associated with such movements are easily and freely available on the Internet.

While there was only a single racist website in April 1995, the Simon Wiesenthal Center estimated that there were more than 5 000 websites in 2005 in a variety of languages which promote racial hatred and violence, anti-Semitism and xenophobia around the world.[23] The Center's study, entitled "Digital Terrorism & Hate

---

17. See generally Kenneth S. Stern, *Hate and the Internet* (2004), American Jewish Committee, at www. ajc.org.
18. *Warman v. Harrison* [2006] CHRT 30 at para. 46. See further *Canada (Human Rights Commission) v. Canadian Liberty Net* [1998] 1 S.C.R. 626.
19. See generally Gabriel Weimann, *Terror on the Internet: The New Arena, the New Challenges* (Washington: US Institute of Peace, 2006).
20. See *Threats to international peace and security caused by terrorist acts*, SC Res. 1617, UN ESCOR, 2005, UN Doc. S/RES/1617. See also Anti-Defamation League, *JIHAD Online: Islamic Terrorists and the Internet* (2002), at www.adl.org/internet/ jihad_online.pdf.
21. Council of Europe, PA, 2006 Ordinary Sess. (Second Part), *Combating the resurgence of Nazi ideology*, Texts Adopted, Res. 1495 (2006). See also Council of Europe, PA, 2003 Ordinary Sess. (Fourth Part), *Racist, xenophobic and intolerant discourse in politics*, Texts Adopted, Res. 1345 (2003).htm. See further Council of Europe, PA, 2003 Ordinary Sess. (Fourth Part), Report of the Committee on Legal Affairs and Human Rights, Documents, Doc. 9904 (2003). All of these texts can be found at http://assembly.coe.int/.
22. Council of the European Union, *The European Union Strategy for Combating Radicalisation and Recruitment to Terrorism*, 14347/05 JAI 414 ENFOPOL 152 COTER 69, Brussels (25 November 2005).
23. Canada NewsWire, "Digital Terrorism & Hate 2005 Report Shows 25 Per Cent Increase In Hate Sites", 7 October 2005.

2005", reported a 25% increase in such websites compared to 2004 indicating that the problem of racism and xenophobia over the Internet was growing. The estimated number of websites which promote racial hatred and violence reached over 6 000 in May 2006 according to the "Digital Terrorism & Hate 2006" report.[24] A 17% increase was witnessed during 2007 with the estimated number of websites reaching almost 7 000.[25] In May 2008, in a report entitled "Online Terror and Hate: The First Decade",[26] the Simon Wiesenthal Center identified 8 000 websites and Internet postings that carried racist content as well as terrorist propaganda. This represented a 30% increase over the Center's 2007 findings. The Center's 2008 report provides an interactive snapshot into the many spheres of the global problem of Internet hate, exposing the inner workings of such notorious groups as al-Qaeda, Hamas, Hezbollah, Combat 18 and the Ku Klux Klan among others. While assessing the growing number of websites and forums that are associated with known racist and terrorist organisations the report states that "the Internet's unprecedented global reach and scope combined with the difficulty in monitoring and tracing communications make the Internet a prime tool for extremists and terrorists".[27] More recently, in May 2009, the Simon Wiesenthal Center in a report entitled "Facebook, YouTube +: How Social Media Outlets Impact Digital Terrorism and Hate" claimed that the number of websites and Internet postings carrying racist content, and terrorist propaganda surpassed 10 000.[28]

The nature of online hate

> While anti-Semitism is a prevalent theme among online extremists, no group is immune from attack and at the same time, no group is immune from having online extremists in their midst. Catholics, Muslims, Hindus, homosexuals, women, immigrants are some of the most targeted groups.[29]

Several controversial publications of a racist nature, or publications which encourage violence, are currently disseminated through a number of websites, blogs, and newsgroups. For example, a considerable number of websites disseminate

---

24. The Simon Wiesenthal Center, "Digital Terrorism & Hate 2006", available through www.wiesenthal. com.

25. The Simon Wiesenthal Center, "Digital Terrorism & Hate 2007", available through www.wiesenthal. com. See further the *Vancouver Sun* (British Columbia), "Hate mongers flock to the net; More than 7 000 websites said to be 'direct-marketing' racism and violence", 11 August 2007.

26. The Simon Wiesenthal Center, iReport: "Online Terror and Hate: The First Decade", May 2008, at www.wiesenthal.com/ireport.

27. Ibid.

28. Release of Simon Wiesenthal Center, "Facebook, YouTube +: How Social Media Outlets Impact Digital Terrorism and Hate" (New York Tolerance Center 5/13/09). Press release available through www.wiesenthal.com.

29. Ibid., pp. 8-9.

anti-Semitic materials[30] including the fraudulent document known as the *Protocols of the Elders of Zion*[31] "which purports to be the actual blueprint by Jewish leaders to take over the world".[32] Although several other controversial publications of a racist nature or that encourage violence are available over the Internet, none are as widely available as this anti-Semitic forgery which "refuses to die".[33] The *Protocols of the Elders of Zion* was first published in Russia in 1905 and is available through a number of websites including Hamas Online (website of the Palestinian Sunni Islamist militant organisation) and is still a bestseller in print format in many Muslim countries.[34] There are also several websites which deny the existence of the Holocaust or which try to minimise or justify the Nazi atrocities of the Second World War. The distribution of literature which promoted such ideas was largely limited until the mid 1990s but since then several, including the infamous Zundelsite, came to existence, and pamphlets such as *Did Six Million Really Die?* are freely available to download from these websites.

During the mid 1990s Andrew MacDonald's *The Turner Diaries*,[35] which has been considered by the US Justice Department and the FBI as the bible of right-wing militia groups, was also made available widely over the Internet and is believed to have provided the blueprint for the Oklahoma City bombing. Similarly, the *Encyclopaedia of the Afghan Jihad*, a manual of Jihad in 10 or 11 volumes, details how to make and use explosives and firearms, and how to plan and carry out assassinations and other terrorist acts. The *Encyclopaedia* is regarded as the "blueprint for terror" and is also available over the Internet in Arabic,[36] and it bore a "dedication to Osama bin Laden, among others, and suggested Big Ben and the Eiffel Tower as targets for attack, the prosecution alleged. The manual urged that plans 'should be laid out' to hit buildings such skyscrapers, ports, airports, nuclear plants and football stadiums, the prosecution said, and it talked about attacking large congregations of people at Christmas."[37] Other often-cited publications of

---

30. See UK Parliamentary Committee Against Antisemitism, *Report of the All-Party Parliamentary Inquiry into Antisemitism* (London: The Stationery Office Limited, 2006), at http://thepcaa.org/.
31. Sergius Nilus, *The Protocols of the Meetings of the Learned Elders of Zion With Preface and Explanatory Notes* (Honolulu: University Press of the Pacific, 2003).
32. Will Eisner, *The Plot: The Secret Story of the Protocols of the Elders of Zion* (New York: W.W. Norton & Company, 2005). See further Norman Cohn, *Warrant for Genocide: The Myth of the Jewish World Conspiracy and the Protocols of the Elders of Zion* (Serif Publishing, 2005); and Hadassa Ben-Itto, *The Lie That Wouldn't Die: The Protocols of the Elders of Zion* (Mitchell Vallentine & Company, 2005).
33. Edward Rothstein, "The Anti-Semitic Hoax That Refuses to Die", *The New York Times*, 21 April 2006.
34. Phillip Adams, "Mel Gibson's affliction seems hereditary", *The Australian*, 8 August 2006.
35. Andrew MacDonald, *The Turner Diaries: A Novel* (Fort Lee, N.J.: Barricade Books, 1996).
36. The US Department of Justice made available an English version as a PDF document a few years back. See *The Register*, "Download al Qaeda manuals from the DoJ, go to prison?" 30 May 2008, at www.theregister.co.uk/2008/05/30/notts_al_qaeda_manual_case/.
37. "Abu Hamza trial: Islamic cleric had terror handbook, court told", *The Guardian*, London, 12 January 2006.

concern include the infamous *Anarchist's Cookbook, The Al-Qaeda Manual, The Mujahideen Poisons Handbook, The Terrorists Handbook, Women in Jihad,* and *Essay Regarding the Basic Rule of the Blood, Wealth and Honour of the Disbelievers,*[38] possession of which could potentially lead to a possession charge under the Terrorism Act 2000 in the United Kingdom.[39]

More recently blasphemous cartoons of Prophet Muhammad were published in *Jyllands-Posten,* a Danish newspaper based in Aarhus on 30 September 2005, and were subsequently published in several European newspapers. The publication of the cartoons has caused outrage and violent protests among the Muslim community around the world. Electronic versions of these cartoons were also circulated on the Internet and they currently remain accessible over the Internet. This caused, for example, the Supreme Court of Pakistan to order the government to block Internet sites displaying the blasphemous cartoons, including the popular blogging service Blogger[40] in March 2006.[41]

Evolving nature of online hate and Web 2.0 technologies

In time, this type of content would be presented in more attractive high-quality formats including that of online racist videos,[42] cartoons, music,[43] radio, and audio-visual transmissions in a variety of languages. Furthermore, games such as the US National Socialist Movement's *ZOG's Nightmare,* the National Alliance's Ethnic Cleansing, in which ethnic cleansing is the main theme,[44] and the modified version of an old racist game KZ (German for Concentration Camp) Manager, which involve the Turkish minorities in Germany, are freely available to download from a number of websites on the Internet.

---

38. See generally the UK case of *R. v. Malik* [2008] All ER (D) 201 (Jun) at http://cyberlaw.org.uk.

39. Section 57 of the Terrorism Act 2000 has been recently used in the UK for a number of prosecutions. Note BBC News, "Boy in Court on terror charges", 5 October 2007; BBC News, "Bomb suspect 'not into politics'" 20 October 2008; BBC News, "Teenage bomb plot accused cleared", 23 October 2008.

40. See www.blogger.com.

41. See "Supreme Court directs strict steps for banning blasphemous web-sites", *The Pakistan Newswire* (2 March 2006); "Pakistan Blocks Anti-President, 'Blasphemous' Blogs", *BBC Monitoring International Newswire* (6 March 2006); "Web Sites Carrying Blasphemous Images Blocked, Supreme Court Told", *Pakistan Press International* (20 March 2006); and "SC orders case against cartoon publishers", *Daily [Pakistan] Times* (18 April 2006).

42. See, e.g., "Videos of hate flout curbs on Islamists", *The Sunday Times* (London) (16 July 2006). The story covers the hate videos published on the website of Ahlus Sunnah wal Jamaah (ASWJ), a splinter of al-Muhajiroun.

43. Note that more than 600 CDs containing racist music are available for purchase through the US National Socialist Movement's website http://nsm88records.com.

44. A considerable number of such games were documented in the Simon Wiesenthal Center report "Digital Terrorism & Hate 2006" which is available online at www.wiesenthal.com.

In May 2008, the Simon Wiesenthal Center's "Online Terror and Hate: The First Decade" report pointed out that "extremists are leveraging 2.0 technologies to dynamically target young people through digital games, Second Life scenarios, blogs, and even Youtube and Facebook style videos depicting racist violence and terrorism". [45] Web 2.0 is a recent term which refers to new technologies designed to be used on the World Wide Web with the intention of enhancing information sharing, and collaboration among users rather than simply retrieving information with interactivity taking centre stage. Well-known examples include the development and evolution of web-based communities and hosted services such as the popular social networking sites Facebook and MySpace, video-sharing application YouTube, photo-sharing application Flickr, extremely popular blogging sites and communities such as Wordpress and Blogger, and user-driven multilingual, web-based, free content encyclopaedia project Wikipedia, and tag and share web pages using social bookmarking services such as del.icio.us and Digg.

Following the extreme popularity of these free-to-use Web 2.0 technologies, racist organisations and individuals have started to use Web 2.0 technologies and applications such as YouTube and other on-demand video and photo sites to disseminate audio-visual content involving hatred, [46] and to "dynamically target young people". [47] For example, it was documented in Germany that YouTube hosted controversial videos such as *Jud Süß* (The Jew Süss), a 1940 anti-Semitic propaganda film, as well as content from banned German rock band Landser which depicts Nazi military operations in their music video clips. It was reported by the London *Sunday Times* that the Central Council of Jews in Germany was planning to bring criminal charges against YouTube with regard to the availability of this particular Nazi propaganda video on YouTube. [48] YouTube subsequently removed the video clips concerned but the council complained that there were several other Nazi propaganda clips that were not removed by YouTube and Google. Jugendschutz.net, the German Internet hotline which tackles the problem of online hate, documented about 700 videos with right-wing content on YouTube during the course of 2007. Jugendschutz.net reported in their 2007

---

45. The Simon Wiesenthal Center, iReport: "Online Terror and Hate: The First Decade", May 2008, at www.wiesenthal.com/ireport. Note further Agence France Presse, "Web 2.0 gives new tools to hate groups: experts", 18 November 2008.

46. *The International Herald Tribune*, "Putting a box around the tube; Governments see risk in Internet sharing sites," 23 April 2007; *The People*, "Mein Space; Exclusive Revealed. How Sick UK Nazis Target Your Kids on Cult", 23 September 2007, p. 31; *The Jerusalem Post*, "Neo-Nazi gang 'had been operating for 2 years'. One indicted member was electrician in PM's office", 12 September 2007; *The Voice*, "Myspace and YouTube prime targets for bigots", 12 September 2007, at www.voice-online.co.uk/, Wolf, C., "The Web fuels hate speech", *The International Herald Tribune*, 16 November 2007.

47. The Simon Wiesenthal Center, iReport: "Online Terror and Hate: The First Decade", May 2008, at www.wiesenthal.com/ireport.

48. *The Sunday Times*, "Nazi videos on YouTube spark legal challenge", 2 September 2007.

annual report that other video-sharing platforms based on YouTube with neo-Nazi themes have been developed during 2007. Similarly, Austria's Defence Ministry launched an investigation following media reports suggesting that a particular YouTube video clip showed Austrian soldiers making Hitler salutes in Austrian army barracks.[49]

In April 2008, a *New York Times* article revealed that "among the millions of clips on the video-sharing Web site YouTube are 11 racially offensive Warner Brothers cartoons that have not been shown in an authorised release since 1968".[50] According to the *New York Times*, the cartoons, known as the "Censored 11", have been unavailable to the public for forty years. Subsequently, the majority of these offensive videos were removed but some are still accessible through YouTube.

A French Jewish group, the National Bureau of Vigilance Against Anti-Semitism (BNVCA), announced in August 2008 that it would take legal action against YouTube and Dailymotion over a clip showing a host of Jewish public figures to the soundtrack of a pre-war anti-Semitic song.[51] The clip shows a slideshow of more than 150 French politicians, TV stars, journalists, writers, philosophers, actors, singers and comedians with the sound of a song recorded before the Second World War, called *Rebecca's wedding*, which describes the guests at a Jewish wedding as dirty, rude and dishonest. The French group decided to take legal action due to the anti-Semitic nature of the video clip.

Racist ideas and content are also disseminated through MySpace[52] and Facebook.[53] The presence of the racist British National Party (BNP) on Facebook prompted a major boycott of Facebook by high-profile companies including Vodafone, and Virgin Media, who pulled their advertisements from Facebook. An investigation by a campaign group, Unite Against Fascism, discovered that there were Facebook profile images of Ku Klux Klan members posing with a sword under the subtitle "Local BNP meeting, blacks welcome".[54] More recently, the National Education, Health and Allied Workers Union in South Africa condemned the racist content and comments posted by a group of University of North West students on a Facebook site.[55] There were also reports to suggest that white supremacist groups

---

49. Associated Press, "Austrian defence minister investigates video of soldiers in Nazi salutes", 4 September 2007.

50. *The New York Times*, "Cartoons of a Racist Past Lurk on YouTube", 28 April 2008.

51. See AFP, "French Jewish group to sue YouTube", 14 August 2008.

52. New Media Age, "MySpace gets tough to keep ads away from extreme pages", 16 August 2007.

53. *The Calgary Sun* (Alberta), "The new face of hate; The swaggering skinheads and marching jack-boots have all but vanished, but make no mistake: The poisonous ideology of white supremacy is alive and well in Canada", 23 September 2007.

54. *The Evening Standard* (London), "Facebook told: Outlaw racist BNP user groups", 17 August 2007; *Nottingham Evening Post*, "MP joins call for Facebook ban on BNP", 16 August 2007; Press Association, "Petition calls for Facebook ban on BNP", 15 August 2007.

55. "Call for action on Facebook racists", *The Mercury* (South Africa), 8 October 2008.

created the networking site Eurspace based on the popularity of social networking sites.

More recently, in November 2008, Facebook removed "several pages from its site used by Italian neo-Nazis to incite violence after European politicians accused the Internet social networking site of allowing a platform to racists".[56] The media reports suggested that seven different Facebook groups had been created with titles advocating violence against Romani people. Following complaints Facebook, which does not pre-screen content going on its system, stated that it would "remove any groups which are violent or threatening",[57] and which therefore violate its terms of use which bans users from posting anything which is hateful, or racially, ethnically or other-wise objectionable.[58] The existence of such groups was described as "repulsive" by Martin Schulz, Socialist leader in the European Parliament, who lodged a complaint with Facebook based in California. The Simon Wiesenthal Center, instead, asked Facebook to create technology to filter out hate speech and racist content.

Furthermore, it was reported that even Internet-based virtual gaming worlds such as Second Life[59] and World of Warcraft have been used by certain groups to disseminate racist content and to create presence on such virtual fantasy environments.

Close relationship between racist discourse and racist violence

The relationship between hate speech on the Internet and hate-motivated violence has not been investigated in a comprehensive manner, but numerous cases strengthen the assumption that there is a link under specific circumstances. [60]

According to a recent report of the Office for Democratic Institutions and Human Rights (ODIHR) of the Organization for Security and Co-operation in Europe (OSCE), "the intersection of racist discourse on the Internet and racist violence was a theme that received increasing attention in 2006, including the use of the Internet to identify particular individuals as targets for violence and to disseminate their personal information".[61] For example, according to the report, "explicit

---

56. Reuters, "Facebook Pulls Italian Neo-Nazi Pages After Outcry", 14 November 2008.
57. Ibid.
58. See Facebook's terms of use at www.facebook.com/home.php#/terms.php?ref=pf.
59. Washington Internet Daily, "Online Hate Speech Deserves More Attention, U.S. Helsinki Commission Hears", 16 May 2008.
60. ODIHR, Hate Crimes in the OSCE Region: Incidents and Responses, Annual Report for 2006, OSCE/ODIHR (2007), p. 83.
61. ODIHR, Hate Crimes in the OSCE Region: Incidents and Responses, Annual Report for 2006, OSCE/ODIHR (2007), p. 64.

instructions for racist attacks on particular individuals in Russia were found on the websites of skinhead groups".[62]

The ODIHR report also pointed out that "instructions for racist, anti-Semitic, and homophobic violence were found on a Redwatch website hosted in the United States that was maintained by a right-wing organisation in Poland".[63] Redwatch, originally produced by "Combat 18", started publishing the names and addresses of anti-racist campaigners in Britain in print format in 1993, almost ten years before they set up their website.[64] It now has branches in Germany and Poland and the Polish version, which was hosted in the United States, "posted the names, addresses, and telephone numbers of representatives of Jewish, anti-racism, and left-wing organisations and encouraged violence against them" according to the ODIHR report. In June 2006, the Polish police arrested two individuals for ties to the website and charged eight others with collaborating on the site. Polish authorities also asked the United States for help in closing down the website.[65] The ODIHR report claims that following the arrests and prosecutions, the Polish version was closed down, but despite various attempts the UK version is still up and running, and that since 2004, the "number of extremist websites posting hit lists has been on the rise".[66] The UK version shows photographs of anti-racist activists, many taken during protests against the British National Party, alongside the slogan: "Remember places, traitors' faces, they'll all pay for their crimes."

Similarly, it was reported by *Der Spiegel* in July 2008 that neo-Nazi groups in Germany are "trying to intimidate left-wing politicians and activists by publishing their names, photos and addresses on Web sites, often accompanied by increasingly blatant threats".[67] According to *Der Spiegel*, "calls for violence against left-wing activists, trade unionists and journalists are becoming increasingly blatant on the approximately 1 700 far-right Web sites in Germany".[68] Several examples of neo-Nazi websites revealing personal details and addresses and calling for violence were cited by *Der Spiegel* including the following:

- A Bavarian group of neo-Nazis set up an online dossier of almost 200 men and women living in and around Nuremberg. It published photos of them that it had secretly taken at demonstrations.

---

62. Ibid.
63. Ibid.
64. See "RACE magazines publish names and addresses of 'Red' Activists", *The Guardian*, 20 February 1993; and "Rapid increase in racial attacks 'Widely Ignored'", *The Guardian*, 20 February 1993.
65. BBC News, "Polish Police Make Four Arrests in Swoop for Fascist Group", 1 June 2006.
66. ODIHR, Hate Crimes in the OSCE Region: Incidents and Responses, Annual Report for 2006, OSCE/ODIHR (2007), p. 83.
67. *Der Spiegel*, "Neo-Nazis Using Web Sites to Threaten Opponents", 24 July 2008, at www.spiegel.de.
68. Ibid.

–   One website mocks the sister of an anti-Nazi activist for frequently spend-
    ing her holidays in Turkey.

–   A judge in the northern city of Kiel who had sentenced a member of the
    far-right National Democratic Party to pay a heavy fine was hit even harder.
    Neo-Nazis published his address on a website, revealed how many children
    he had and that "some of our readers would relish the opportunity to slay
    a judge or public prosecutor in the wild".

–   Neo-Nazis in the western state of Hesse published maps showing the loca-
    tions of left-wing politicians or members of anti-Nazi citizens' groups.

As in the case of the Redwatch UK website, the German efforts to remove some
of these websites proved to be hopeless. The majority of these websites are based
outside German jurisdiction and they are usually hosted in the United States.

Seeking solutions

The Internet has thus become the medium of choice for propaganda, disseminating hatred,[69] recruitment,[70] training,[71] fundraising,[72] and for communications[73]
by racist as well as terrorist organisations.

Obviously there is major concern about the availability of racist content, hate
speech and terrorist propaganda on the Internet, and many governments and
international and regional–international organisations, including the Council of
Europe, the European Union, the UN and the OSCE are in agreement that racism
and manifestations of racism through the Internet should not and will not be
tolerated. However, the major question that is being faced by international
organisations and state-level regulators is how to regulate the flow of racist content over the Internet. The question becomes even more complex by the fact
that different political, moral, cultural, historical and constitutional values exist
between different states. This undoubtedly complicates efforts to find an "appropriate balance between the rights to freedom of opinion and expression and to
receive and impart information and the prohibition on speech and/or activities

---

69. Note the study conducted by Glaser, J., Dixit, J., Green, D.P., "Studying Hate Crime with the Internet:
What Makes Racists Advocate Racial Violence?" (2002) *Journal of Social Issues* 58(1) spring, pp. 177-
193.
70. Hylton, H., "How Hizballah Hijacks the Internet," *Time Magazine*, 8 August 2006, at www.time.com/.
71. Publications such as *Mujahideen Explosive Handbook* and the *Encyclopaedia of the Afghan Jihad*
are some of the publications disseminated and distributed through the Internet. Note "Terror law
vague, accused to argue", *The Globe and Mail* (Canada), 30 August 2006 and "Abu Hamza trial: Islamic
cleric had terror handbook, court told", *The Guardian*, London, 12 January 2006.
72. Note the Communication from the European Commission to the European Parliament and the
Council concerning terrorist recruitment: addressing the factors contributing to violent radicalisation, Brussels, 21.9.2005, COM(2005) 313 final.
73. See "Foiled plots", *The Globe and Mail* (Canada), 11 August 2006.

promoting racist views and inciting violence".[74] That balance is yet to be attained at an international level, and "in today's multicultural context, striking the right balance is becoming increasingly important, but at the same time more difficult".[75]

It has become clear during the policy discussions of the last ten years that, in particular, the United States of America opposes any regulatory effort to combat racist publications on the Internet on freedom of expression grounds based upon the values attached to the First Amendment of the US Constitution. At the same time, there are other organisations or states which regard harmonised national legislation and international agreements as the way forward. For example, ECRI believes that "national legislation against racism and racial discrimination is necessary to combat these phenomena effectively".[76] This view, supported by many member states of the Council of Europe, led to the development of an Additional Protocol to the Convention on Cybercrime, concerning the criminalisation of acts of a racist and xenophobic nature committed through computer systems between 2001 and 2003. The US Government wholeheartedly supported the development of a cybercrime convention within the Council of Europe region and ratified the convention as an external supporter, but decided not to support or get involved with the development of the Additional Protocol to the Convention on Cybercrime. Hence, fundamental disagreements remain as to the most appropriate and effective strategy "for preventing dissemination of racist messages on the Internet, including the need to adopt regulatory measures to that end".[77]

Despite these fundamental differences, the growing problem of racist content on the Internet has naturally prompted vigorous responses from a variety of agents, including governments, supranational and international organisations as well as from the private sector. A detailed overview of these regulatory and non-regulatory initiatives will be provided in this book.

---

74. Report of the Intergovernmental Working Group on the effective implementation of the Durban Declaration and Programme of Action on its fourth session (Chairperson-Rapporteur: Juan Martabit (Chile)), E/CN.4/2006/18, 20 March 2006, at http://daccessdds.un.org/doc/.

75. ECRI, Expert Seminar: Combating racism while respecting freedom of expression, Conference Proceedings, Strasbourg, 16-17 November, 2006, p. 5.

76. Note within this context the ECRI General Policy Recommendation No. 7 on national legislation to combat racism and racial discrimination, CRI (2003) 8, adopted on 13 December 2002, at www.coe.int, para. 1 of the explanatory report.

77. The meeting on the relationship between racist, xenophobic and anti-Semitic propaganda on the Internet and hate crimes held by the OSCE in Paris on 16-17 June 2004.

2. Key issues: the global and decentralised nature of the Internet and its impact upon governance

Typically, the stance taken by governments is that what is illegal and punishable in an offline format must also be treated as illegal and punishable online. There are, however, several features of the Internet which fundamentally affect approaches to its governance. These features and the nature of the Internet will be broadly discussed in this chapter.

The new communications and information technologies have loosened the state's exclusiveness of control of its territory, reducing its capacities for cultural control and homogenisation. It is a commonplace that digitalised communications, satellites, fax machines, and computer networks have rendered the state licensing and control of information media all but impossible, not merely undermining ideological dictatorships but also all attempts to preserve cultural homogeneity by state force.[78]

Along with television, satellites, fax machines, and mobile phones, computers and modems played an important role in the globalisation of information systems "rendering national boundaries invisible".[79] The scandal of Chernobyl, the tragic events leading to the overthrow of Ceausescu in Romania[80] and the massive political upheavals in Russia following first the Gorbachev affair and then the attempted overthrow of Yeltsin's fledgling democracy could all be directly linked to the free flow of information and the power of modern communications media.[81] The impact of new technologies and especially the Internet on the nation states becomes evident since the mid 1990s. As Held states, "the very process of governance may escape the reach of the nation state",[82] and this is true for the

---

78. Hirst, P. and Thompson, G., "Globalization and the Future of the Nation State", (1995) *Economy and Society*, 24(3), 408-442, p. 419.

79. See Hudson, H. E., *Global Connections: International Telecommunications Infrastructure and Policy*, New York: Van Nostrand Reinhold, 1997, chapter 1.

80. See generally Federal Research Division of the Library of Congress, *Romania – A Country Study*, 1989, at http://memory.loc.gov/frd/cs/rotoc.html. See further Coup d'Etat of 1989 in Romania at www.timisoara.com.

81. Martin, W. J., *The Global Information Society*, Guildford: Aslib Gower, 1995, 9-10. See also Sparks, C., *Communism, Capitalism and the Mass Media*, London: Sage, 1997.

82. See Held, D., *Democracy and the Global Order*, Cambridge: Polity, 1995, p. 16.

governance of the Internet and new technologies where the typical character-istics of a nation state such as control of information lose their significance lead-ing into fragmentation of the nation state.[83]

Eastern European and also Burmese dissidents used and (continue to use in the case of Burma) the Internet to tell the world the human rights abuses in their countries.[84] As the new technologies such as the Internet do not recognise boundaries and resist individual state attempts to suppress or censor any kind of information, individual governments increasingly find it difficult to govern and control the flow of information inside and outside their nation states. According to Ithiel de Sola Pool, "a revolution in communications technology is taking place today, a revolution as profound as the invention of printing".[85] At the same time governments such as China, with a strong notion of nation states, will continue to try to control the free flow of information and new technologies. Therefore, it would be wrong to assume that the impact of new technologies on nation states will be a "dramatic" shift towards democratisation and openness.[86]

What is so different about the Internet?

The Internet is the largest communication network in the world. In fact, it is often referred to as the "network of networks". It is undoubtedly global, and based on a distributed and decentralised open and non-proprietary architecture system with invisible national boundaries. Nobody owns the Internet, and there is no single entity, no single government governing it.[87] The very design of the technology creates a potentially infinite and unbreakable communications com-

---

83. Control of information by means of nation-state regulation is still possible for printing press, radio, and television, and to some extent satellite communications. But note the EU Council Directive ("Television without Frontiers" Directive) 89/552/EEC of 3 October 1989 on the coordination of cer-tain provisions laid down by Law, Regulation or Administrative Action in Member States concerning the pursuit of television broadcasting activities, Official Journal L 298, 17/10/1989 p. 0023-0030 as amended by the Directive 97/36/EC of the European Parliament and of the Council of 30 June 1997, L 202 60 30.7.1997. See generally http://europa.eu.int on EU Audiovisual Policy. Note also the Commission initiative to set out rights to use a satellite dish in the Internal Market, July 2001, at http://europa.eu.int. Furthermore note also the impact of Article 10 of the European Convention on Human Rights on broadcasting: *Sacchi v. Italy*, Case No. 6452/74, Decision of 12 March 1976, D.R. 5; *Groppera Radio AG and others v. Switzerland*, Application No. 00010890/84, Series A No. 173, 28 March 1990; *Autronic AG v. Switzerland*, Series A No. 178, 22 May 1990.
84. See, for example, the Free Burma Coalition's website at http://freeburma.org for the Burmese pro-democracy movement from the University of Wisconsin at Madison USA. See further Cleaver, H., "The Zapatistas and the Electronic Fabric of Struggle", at www.utexas.edu.
85. See Pool, I. S., *Technologies without Boundaries*, Cambridge, MA: Harvard University Press, 1990.
86. See, for example, *Freedom of Expression and the Internet in China*, a Human Rights Watch Backgrounder, August 2001, at www.hrw.org/backgrounder/asia/china-bck-0701.htm.
87. Note, though, arguments in relation to the governance of domain names and the role played by ICANN, the Internet Corporation for Assigned Names and Numbers (www.icann.org).

plex which cannot be readily bounded by one national government or even several or many acting in concert:

> ... the Internet is too widespread to be easily dominated by any single government. By creating a seamless global-economic zone, borderless and unregulatable, the Internet calls into question the very idea of a nation state.[88]

The Internet is a complex, anarchic, multinational environment where old concepts of regulation, reliant as they are upon tangibility in time and space, may not be easily applicable or enforceable and that is why the wider concept of governance may be more suitable with responsibility for rule-making distributed to a variety of players at both public and private levels of governance. The decentralised nature of the Internet means there is no unique solution for effective regulation at the national level. At the same time, the Internet is not a "lawless place",[89] nor is it an unregulatable and uncontrollable environment. Rather the Internet "poses a fundamental challenge for effective leadership and governance".[90]

It would, therefore, be wrong to dismiss the role that may be played by the governments especially for the creation of laws and for maintaining the policing of the state and for co-ordinating and aligning national policy with initiatives and policies at both supranational and international levels of Internet governance. According to Hirst and Thompson, "nation states are now simply one class of powers and political agencies in a complex system of power from world to local levels but they have a centrality because of their relationship to territory and population."[91]

States try to regulate but ...

States around the globe usually try to resolve Internet-content-related problems by means of introducing new laws or amending existing laws as many governments believe that the Internet "is just another new device, from the governance perspective, no different to its predecessors"[92] such as the telegraph, the telephone, radio, or satellite systems. However, despite the introduction of new laws, or amendments to existing laws criminalising publication or distribution of certain types of content, in almost all instances extraterritoriality remains a major problem with regards to the availability of Internet content hosted or distributed from outside the jurisdiction in which it is deemed illegal. Therefore, the creation

---

88. Barlow, J. P., "Thinking Locally, Acting Globally", (1996) *Cyber-Rights Electronic List*, 15 January.

89. Reidenberg, J. R, "Governing Networks and Cyberspace Rule-Making" (1996) *Emory Law Journal* (45), p. 911.

90. Ibid.

91. Ibid.

92. Eduardo Gelbstein and Jovan Kurbalija, "Internet Governance: Issues, Actors, and Divide", DIPLO report, 2005, at www.diplomacy.edu/isl/ig/, p. 16.

23

of new laws, or amendment of old laws, pursuing the "new wine in old bottles"[93] theory is not necessarily effective to resolve Internet-related problems. As will be outlined in this book, laws are not necessarily harmonised at a global, or even on a pan-European level, and what is deemed illegal in one country may be perfectly legal in another country. The difficulties that are witnessed by individual states are therefore more evident in terms of "Internet content regulation" where different rules, laws, and regulations exist based upon different cultural, moral, political, and religious values.

On the other hand, many academics argue that the Internet is fundamentally different from other communication technologies with its decentralised and borderless nature which therefore require a different approach to its governance. Governance theorists also dismissed the idea of a "centralised governance model" as a complex communication network such as the Internet "cannot be put under a single governance umbrella, such as an international organisation"[94] dismissing possible UN or a similar international organisation's solitary control.

If the Internet is so different, and the new wine requires new bottles, who is then going to set up the standards for Internet governance? There is no straightforward answer for this fundamental question. However, there have been attempts at setting the standards at an international level through the establishment of the Working Group on Internet Governance and the related World Summit on the Information Society.

Emergence of Internet governance

> Clearly, there is need for governance, but that does not necessarily mean that it has to be done in the traditional way, for something that is so very different. (Kofi Annan, 2004)[95]

According to the Working Group on Internet Governance (WGIG),[96] which was set up by the Secretary-General of the United Nations in accordance with the mandate given to him by the first phase of the World Summit on the Information Society (WSIS), held in Geneva in December 2003, "governance is a part of many different processes related to the Internet, including the development of technical

---

93. Ibid., p. 15.
94. Ibid., p. 17.
95. Kofi Annan, Global Forum on Internet Governance, 24 March 2004 (*Internet Governance: A Grand Collaboration*, March 2004).
96. See generally www.wgig.org/.

standards and the management of core resources, as well as regulation of the misuse and abuse of the Internet".[97]

Internet governance as it is emerging may include different regulatory models at the national level including:

- government regulation (legislation);
- jurisprudence (court decisions);
- social norms (customs);
- self-regulation (ISPs / Internet industry);
- co-regulation;
- regulation through code (software and/or technical);
- education and awareness campaigns.

International conventions, agreements, and law developed at the supranational, regional–international, or international levels could also be part of this governance model. It is not always necessary to have all these levels within a particular Internet governance model and their inclusion or exclusion will depend upon the problem faced by the regulators or the subject matter of the policy issue to be governed. For example, while there may be more emphasis on self-regulation and self-regulatory tools, and education and awareness campaigns for the protection of children from accessing harmful content on the Internet, there would certainly be more emphasis on government regulation, the law, and policing with regards to combating illegal content such as child pornography or encountering criminal conduct such as hacking and denial of service attacks.

Furthermore, increasingly, there is more emphasis on involving all stakeholders (both public and private) and relevant intergovernmental and international organisations within the Internet governance models and debate. Undoubtedly, governments do have authority over public policy, while the private sector (Internet industry + the ISPs) have expertise with regards to technical issues and infrastructure. Societal, community, and human rights issues can be addressed by the civil society. Finally the intergovernmental and international organisations such as the Council of Europe, OECD, UN, and EU can co-ordinate and facilitate the development of standards together with their member states. This multi-stakeholder approach was recognised at the World Summit on the Information Society during its second-phase meetings in Tunis which provided a definition for Internet governance, and according to this working definition Internet governance is the

---

97. The WGIG Background Report, June 2005, at www.wgig.org/docs/BackgroundReport.doc, para. 31. See further the WGIG Report, June 2005, at www.wgig.org/docs/WGIGREPORT.doc, and Drake, W. J., ed., *Reforming Internet Governance: Perspectives from the Working Group on Internet Governance (WGIG)*, United Nations ICT Task Force, 2005, at www.wgig.org/docs/book/WGIG_book.pdf.

development and application by governments, the private sector and civil society, in their respective roles, of shared principles, norms, rules, decision-making procedures, and programmes that shape the evolution and use of the Internet.[98]

With this recognition, it is established that "effective" rule-making will not necessarily be confined to a single state or body due to the global nature of the medium itself. It would be true to say that the "nation states have become the local authorities of the global system"[99] in the fragmented post-modern states due to the impact of the new communication technologies. The WSIS Tunis Agenda for the Information Society recognised that:

– policy authority for Internet-related public policy issues is the sovereign right of states. They have rights and responsibilities for international Internet-related public policy issues;

– the private sector has had, and should continue to have, an important role in the development of the Internet, both in the technical and economic fields;

– civil society has also played an important role on Internet matters, especially at community level, and should continue to play such a role;

– intergovernmental organisations have had, and should continue to have, a facilitating role in the co-ordination of Internet-related public policy issues;

– international organisations have also had and should continue to have an important role in the development of Internet-related technical standards and relevant policies.[100]

The majority of WSIS initiatives are non-binding and in the form of soft law rather than prescriptive hard law. However, with regard to criminal activity on the Internet the WSIS Tunis document underlined the "importance of the prosecution of cybercrime, including cybercrime committed in one jurisdiction, but having effects in another".[101] The document also affirmed that measures undertaken to ensure Internet stability and security, to fight cybercrime, must protect and respect the provisions for privacy and freedom of expression as contained in the relevant parts of the Universal Declaration of Human Rights and other international documents and conventions such as the European Convention on Human Rights.[102]

---

98. Tunis Agenda for the Information Society, Second Phase of the WSIS (16-18 November 2005, Tunis), at www.itu.int, para. 34. The definition was originally developed and proposed by the WGIG Background Report, June 2005, at www.wgig.org, para. 43. See further the Tunis Commitment of November 2005 – Second Phase of the WSIS (16-18 November 2005, Tunis), at www.itu.int.
99. Hirst, P. and Thompson, G., "Globalization and the Future of the Nation State", (1995), p. 414.
100. Ibid.
101. Ibid., para. 40.
102. Ibid., para. 42.

Of course there will be challenges and difficulties in recognising the legitimate socio-cultural differences and approaches to the Internet and its regulation by nation states, and as previously mentioned these difficulties are more evident in the field of Internet content regulation especially with regards to the availability of racist content, hate speech, and terrorist propaganda on the Internet. Efforts to govern such content at national, supranational, regional–international and international levels will be assessed in the subsequent chapters.

3.   Governance of racist content on the Internet

This chapter will provide an overview of the elements of a possible pluralistic Internet governance approach highlighting the difficulties encountered by individual states in the fight against hate speech and racist content on the Internet, and difficulties encountered in their efforts to provide a harmonised response to hate and racism on the Internet at an international level.

Harmonisation efforts to combat illegal content, even for universally condemned content such as child pornography, have been protracted and are ongoing.[103] Efforts to harmonise laws to combat racist content on the Internet have proved to be even more problematic. While child pornography is often regarded as a clear-cut example of "illegal content", racist content has been much more difficult to categorise due to constitutional, legal, political, religious, moral, and historical differences between states.

While some forms of racist content or hate speech are regarded as illegal content in certain states, the same content may not be regarded as illegal in others. Although "hate speech" is "understood as covering all forms of expression which spread, incite, promote or justify racial hatred, xenophobia, anti-Semitism or other forms of hatred based on intolerance, including intolerance expressed by aggressive nationalism and ethnocentrism, discrimination and hostility against minorities, migrants and people of immigrant origin"[104] at the Council of Europe level, there is no universally accepted definition of it, especially within the laws of the individual member states of the Council of Europe, or even at the European Court of Human Rights level.[105] However, all Council of Europe member states with the exception of Andorra and San Marino provide for an offence of incitement to

---

103. Rights of the Child: Report submitted by Mr Juan Miguel Petit, Special Rapporteur on the sale of children, child prostitution and child pornography, E/CN.4/2005/78, 23 December 2004. Note also the Addendum to this report: E/CN.4/2005/78/Add.3, 8 March 2005. Note further Akdeniz, Y., *Internet Child Pornography and the Law: National and International Responses*, Ashgate, 2008.

104. Recommendation on Hate Speech, No. R (97) 20, adopted by the Committee of Ministers of the Council of Europe on 30 October 1997.

105. Note cases such as *Gündüz v. Turkey*, 4 December 2003, para. 40; *Erbakan v. Turkey*, 6 July 2006, para. 56, and *Sürek v. Turkey*, judgment of 8 July 1999. See generally Weber, A., "The case law of the European Court of Human Rights on Article 10 relevant for combating racism and intolerance", in ECRI, Expert Seminar: Combating Racism while Respecting Freedom of Expression, Proceedings, Strasbourg, 16-17 November 2006, published in July 2007.

hatred even though significant variations exist especially with regards to the nature of the offence and the maximum prison sentence incurred for such an offence (from one year to ten years) among member states at the Council of Europe level.[106]

Furthermore, different approaches towards negationism (historical revisionism), and Holocaust denial within different Council of Europe member states is a good example of evident contrasting policies in this field. While Germany, France, and Austria criminalise the denial of the Jewish Holocaust, not all the member states of the Council of Europe opted to criminalise such action. Similarly, there exist specific laws in certain European countries such as France and Germany in which the simple act of displaying Nazi objects or memorabilia, including exhibition of uniforms, insignia or emblems resembling those worn or displayed by the Nazis, is prohibited by criminal provisions. At the same time, in other European states such as the United Kingdom, it is perfectly legal to deny the existence of the Holocaust or display or wear Nazi objects without facing prosecution. For example, David Irving, a well-known British Holocaust denier, was sentenced to three years' imprisonment in Austria in February 2006[107] but he has committed no such crime in the UK. Similarly, in January 2005, Prince Harry apologised for wearing a swastika armband to a friend's fancy dress party in the UK, but he did not commit any criminal offence.[108] More recently, Fredrick Töben, a well-known Holocaust denier from Australia, was arrested at Heathrow airport in London because of a pending European arrest warrant issued by the German authorities. The warrant was issued because of Töben's writings on his website denying the existence of the Holocaust.[109] On 19 November 2008, Töben was released after the German Government gave up its legal battle to extradite him from Britain.[110] These examples show that certain acts may be regarded as morally wrong or considered to

---

106. European Commission for Democracy through Law (Venice Commission), Report on the relationship between freedom of expression and freedom of religion: the issue of regulation and prosecution of blasphemy, religious insult and incitement to religious hatred, adopted by the Venice Commission at its 76th Plenary Session (Venice, 17-18 October 2008), CDL-AD(2008)026, at www.venice.coe.int, paras. 33 and 40, pp. 9-10.
107. See "Irving jailed for 3 years after denying Holocaust", *The Daily Telegraph* (21 February 2006); "Irving jailed for denying Holocaust: Three years for British historian who described Auschwitz as a fairytale", *The Guardian* (21 February 2006); and "Irving gets three years' jail in Austria for Holocaust denial", *The Independent* (21 February 2006). Note that David Irving was also convicted in Germany in 1993 of insulting the memory of the dead, for describing the Auschwitz I gas chamber as an *Attrappe* ("fake") at a rally on 21 April 1990, in the *Löwenbräukeller* in Munich. See Long, A., "Forgetting the Fuhrer: The recent history of the Holocaust denial movement in Germany" (2002) 48(1) *Australian Journal of Politics & History* 72, at p. 83.
108. See BBC News, "Harry says sorry for Nazi costume", 13 January 2005, at http://news.bbc.co.uk/1/hi/uk/4170083.stm.
109. *The Daily Telegraph*, "Alleged Holocaust denier allowed bail", 29 October 2008; BBC News, "Holocaust key to extradition case", 3 October 2008, at http://news.bbc.co.uk/1/hi/uk/7648980.stm.
110. *The Times*, "Holocaust denier Fredrick Töben wins German extradition fight", 20 November 2008.

be offensive by many, but are nevertheless not criminalised by law within certain jurisdictions, and evidently differences exist between states even within the pan-European region.

Therefore, harm criteria remain distinct within different jurisdictions, albeit within the same European region, with individual states deciding what is legal and illegal. The Council of Europe member states have a certain margin of appreciation in assessing whether a "pressing social need" exists to introduce speech-based restrictions to their national laws based on Article 10 of the European Convention on Human Rights principles as laid down by the jurisprudence of the European Court of Human Rights. Undoubtedly differences do exist and content regarded as racist, harmful or offensive does not always fall within the boundaries of illegality in all states. In many states "freedom of expression extends not only to ideas and information generally regarded as inoffensive but even to those that might offend, shock, or disturb. Such are the demands of that pluralism, tolerance and broadmindedness without which there is no 'democratic society'."[111] However, if speech or content incite violence against an individual or a public official or a sector of the population, "the State authorities enjoy a wider margin of appreciation when examining the need for an interference with freedom of expression".[112] Nevertheless, the state action is subject to European supervision through the European Court of Human Rights, and the necessity of the content-based restrictions must be convincingly established by the contracting states.

Apart from the variations of the regulatory treatment of racist content and hate speech within the European region we also witness different legal responses to racist discourse in North America (especially in the United States). Therefore, achieving a proper balance between the desire to control racist content and to protect freedom of expression has inevitably proved challenging on the Internet.

Once within the strict boundaries and control of individual states, whether through paper-based publications (such as pamphlets, local papers, and even books), or audio-visual transmissions limited to a particular area (such as local radio), or public demonstrations and talks, currently with its digital transmission and availability through the Internet such content respects neither national rules nor boundaries. Typically the stance taken by governments is that what is illegal and punishable in an offline form must also be treated equally online. There are, however, several features of the Internet which fundamentally affect approaches to its governance, and while rules and boundaries still exist, enforcement of the existing rules to digital content becomes evidently problematic on the Internet. Racist content deemed illegal by, for example, state A is often made available or

---

111. *Handyside v. the United Kingdom* (1976), Application No. 5493/72, Series A vol. 24; *Castells v. Spain* (1992), Application No. 11798/85, Series A vol. 236. Note also *Lingens v. Austria*, judgment of 8 July 1986, Series A, No. 103.
112. *Sürek v. Turkey* (No. 4), judgment of 8 July 1999, Application No. 24762/94.

distributed from outside state A's physical borders and jurisdiction. It is also often the case that the content and conduct deemed to be illegal by state A is transmitted or made available from state B in which that particular content or conduct is not criminalised. Nevertheless, the problematic content in question remains visible and accessible in state A regardless of its territorial laws. It is often the case that states which, unlike state A, criminalise such content would not be willing to assist state A in its fight against such content and conduct. Moreover, the prosecution of such criminals or their extradition for prosecution become undoubtedly problematic. Even then, as witnessed in high-profile successful prosecutions such as the cases of Ernst Zündel and Fredrick Töben in Germany, and David Irving in Austria, their views, publications and websites continue to be hosted and made available from outside these particular jurisdictions in which they are criminalised. Therefore, although laws and rules exist, individual states struggle to effectively tackle the problem of racist content on the Internet, as will be explored further in this book.

As stated above, the decentralised nature of the Internet means that there is no unique solution for effective regulation at the national level. The legal and investigative possibilities at the national level are restricted by the global, distributed and decentralised architecture of the Internet. Problems witnessed at the national level inevitably force the states to seek regional or global solutions through the involvement and aid of international organisations.

A pluralistic Internet governance approach as it is currently emerging may include several layers including the national (and the local), supranational (for example, European Union) or regional (Council of Europe or OSCE), and international (United Nations). The effect of supranational/regional and international developments on nation-state governance cannot be underestimated, and the aligning of strategies and policies may be necessary to find common solutions for Internet-related problems. However, realistically, based upon the underlining regulatory differences between the states with regard to what should be regarded as criminal content, regulatory harmonisation may never be achieved. Despite these difficulties, there has been a serious attempt at regulatory harmonisation at the Council of Europe level with the development of an additional protocol to the Convention on Cybercrime on the criminalisation of acts of a racist or xenophobic nature committed through computer systems, and its impact as well as implementation will be discussed later in this book.

Furthermore, the third World Conference against Racism, Racial Discrimination, Xenophobia and Related Intolerance organised by the United Nations took place in Durban in 2001, and a review conference will be held in April 2009. The states participating in the United Nations World Conference adopted a Declaration and Programme of Action containing recommendations intended for the strengthening of the international human rights framework to combat racism, racial discrimination, xenophobia and related intolerance. The Durban Programme of Action, among other significant recommendations, urged states to "implement legal sanctions, in accordance with relevant international human rights law, in respect of incitement to racial hatred through new information and communications technologies, including the Internet, and further urges them to apply all relevant human rights instruments to which they are parties, in particular the International Convention on the Elimination of All Forms of Racial Discrimination, to racism on the Internet".[113]

However, not all states may sign and ratify the Council of Europe additional protocol or adopt legislation to criminalise such content, as will be shown later in this book. In the absence of regulatory harmonisation, Internet governance may comprise not only regulatory action by governments but also social norms, self-regulation (ISPs), co-regulation (hotlines), co-operation with the ISPs (notice and takedown provisions), regulation through code and technical means (such as rating and filtering tools), as well as education and awareness campaigns.

The forthcoming chapters of this book will provide a critical overview of key developments at national, regional international, and international levels of this emerging pluralistic Internet governance model.

---

113. Report of the World Conference against Racism, Racial Discrimination, Xenophobia and Related Intolerance, Durban, 31 August – 8 September 2001, A/CONF.189/12, GE.02-10005 (E) 100102, 25 January, 2002 at www.un.org/WCAR/aconf189_12.pdf, para. 145.

4. National approaches to Internet governance and its limitations

This chapter will provide an overview of methods and models for governing racist content on the Internet at the state level. Examples from the European region will be used to show how hate speech and racist content on the Internet are tackled at state level. The chapter will also show the limitations of the national approaches and cross-jurisdictional problems encountered at the state level. An assessment of Article 10 of the European Convention on Human Rights and the jurisprudence of the European Court of Human Rights with regard to the treatment of hate speech will also be provided.

Historically, states have been keen to apply their existing national laws to the Internet. Where there seemed to be gaps, or the effectiveness of existing laws was questioned, new laws have been developed to tackle online problems at the national level. It has become quickly apparent, however, that enforcement is problematic and the application of national laws to control the free flow of information on the global Internet can often prove ineffectual due to the multi-national and borderless nature of the Internet. Some of the significant developments at the national level within the Council of Europe region will be outlined in this chapter.

A number of court cases have targeted the creators of racist content, as well as those hosting or providing access to such content in a number of jurisdictions in the Council of Europe region, as well as in other jurisdictions such as Australia and Canada. The most significant of these cases will be highlighted in this chapter to illustrate the difficulties encountered at a national level while tackling racist Internet content and hate speech.

An overview of significant national regulatory initiatives within the Council of Europe region

This section will provide an overview of some of the regulatory initiatives at the member states level including legal measures adopted to address racist content within the Council of Europe region.

In terms of legislative measures aimed at combating racism on the Internet Austria has adopted a legal framework enabling security authorities and courts to effectively combat right-wing extremist, xenophobic, anti-Semitic and racist acts according to a progress report of the Office of the United Nations High

Commissioner for Human Rights (OHCHR).[114] The existing legal framework to combat racist acts, conduct, and publications is also applicable to the Internet and the Austrian Penal Code provides that whoever publicly agitates or incites someone in any manner which threatens the public order because of race, nationality, or ethnic background shall be sentenced. It was reported by the National Focal Point of the European Monitoring Centre on Racism and Xenophobia (EUMC) that in 2001 every third crime with an extreme right-wing background was committed by making use of the Internet.[115] Furthermore, P2P file-sharing software is regularly used to facilitate the exchange of so-called white power music and lyrics via the Internet. Right-wing groups in Austria increasingly use the Internet to co-ordinate their actions and according to the OHCHR report the Internet is under permanent surveillance by the Austrian Federal Agency for State Protection and Counter-Terrorism.

Azerbaijan also criminalises, through Article 10 of the Media Act of 7 December 1999, making use of the mass media including the Internet and other forms of dissemination for purposes of advocating violence and brutality, the fomenting of national, racial or social discord or intolerance or the commission of other unlawful acts.[116] Similarly, Croatia, which ratified the Council of Europe's Additional Protocol to the Convention on Cybercrime, concerning the criminalisation of acts of a racist and xenophobic nature committed through computer systems in March 2003, criminalises through its Penal Code (as amended in July 2004) the direct spreading of racist or xenophobic materials by using computer systems. The Croatian provisions include the distribution or otherwise making available content that denies, significantly diminishes, approves or justifies the criminal act of genocide or crimes against humanity, with the aim of spreading racial, religious, gender-based, national or ethnic hatred based on the colour of skin, sexual affiliation or other characteristics, or with the aim of slighting.[117]

---

114. Progress report of the Office of the United Nations High Commissioner for Human Rights (OHCHR Report 2006), Implementation of relevant recommendations of the third session of the Intergovernmental Working Group on the Effective Implementation of the Durban Declaration and Programme of Action, United Nations Economic and Social Council, E/CN.4/2006/15, 16 February 2006, para. 8.

115. Ludwig Boltzmann Institute of Human Rights Research Association (BIM-FV), in co-operation with the Department of Linguistics (University of Vienna), and the Institute of Conflict Research (IKF), *National Analytical Study on Racist Violence and Crime: RAXEN Focal Point for Austria* (2003), report compiled for the National Focal Point of the European Monitoring Centre on Racism and Xenophobia (EUMC), at www.eumc.at/. Note further Österreich, Bundesministerium für Inneres (2002) Verfassungsschutzbericht 2001 (Report on the Protection of the Constitution 2001), p. 30, www.bmi.gv.at/.

116. OHCHR Report 2006, para. 9. Note further Article 283 of the Criminal Code, which criminalises acts intended to arouse national, racial, social or religious hatred or enmity or belittle national dignity, and acts intended to restrict the rights of citizens, or to establish superiority among citizens on the basis of national, racial or social status or their attitude to religion.

117. OHCHR Report 2006, para. 12.

In Denmark, the criminal law provisions that specifically address racist statements and other crimes of a racist nature are also applicable to crimes committed through the use of the Internet. The Danish provisions cover the dissemination of statements or other information by which a group of people is threatened, insulted or degraded on account of race, colour, national or ethnic origin, religion or sexual orientation. Section 266(b) of the Danish Criminal Code prohibits the dissemination of racist statements and racist propaganda. According to a Venice Commission report, "the group of people that are protected include individuals defined according to their religious worship".[118] The report stated that between 1 January 2001 and 31 December 2003 the Danish courts considered 23 cases concerning violation of section 266(b) of the Danish Criminal Code, and 21 convictions were secured. During the same period, the Danish courts considered seven cases which involved statements published on the Internet[119] concerning violation of section 266(b). For example, in February 2003 the Eastern High Court found the editor of a website guilty of violating section 266(b)(1) and (2) of the Danish Criminal Code for publishing an article named "Behind Islam" which included several degrading statements about Muslims in December 1999. The court also regarded the publication of the article on the Internet as propaganda, making it also a violation of section 266(2)(b). The website editor was sentenced to 20 day-fines of DKK 300.[120]

In another judgment, in March 2003, the Eastern High Court found a spokesperson of the Danish branch of the organisation Hizb-ut-Tahrir guilty of the dissemination of a handbill containing degrading, insulting and threatening remarks about Jews. The remarks were also published on the website of the organisation Hizb-ut-Tahrir. He was sentenced for having published on the website (and on the leaflets that were handed out): "Kill them wherever you find them and drive them away from the place that they drove you away from. The Jews are a slanderous group of people, and they betray and violate obligations and pacts, and they invent lies …" and "coward Jews …" and other similar statements. He was sentenced to sixty days of imprisonment for violating sections 266(b)(2), 266(1), and 23 of the Danish Penal Code but his sentence was suspended.[121] Similarly,

---

118. European Commission for Democracy through Law (Venice Commission), Annex II: Analysis of the Domestic Law concerning Blasphemy, Religious Insult and Inciting Religious Hatred in Albania, Austria, Belgium, Denmark, France, Greece, Ireland, Netherlands, Poland, Romania, Turkey, United Kingdom on the basis of replies to a questionnaire, CDL-AD(2008)026add2, Study No. 406/2006, 22 October 2008, at www.venice.coe.int/, p. 27.

119. OHCHR Report 2006, para. 14.

120. Reported in the Danish *Weekly Law Journal* 2003, p. 751, U.2003.751/2Ø. Taken from Documentation and Advisory Centre on Racial Discrimination (DACoRD), *National Analytical Study on Racist Violence and Crime: RAXEN Focal Point for Denmark* (2003), compiled for the National Focal Point of the European Monitoring Centre on Racism and Xenophobia (EUMC), at www.eumc.at/.

121. Reported in the *Weekly Danish Law* Journal 2003, p. 1428, UfR .2003.1428Ø. Taken from the above EUMC study.

the Supreme Court in December 2003 sentenced a member of the Progressive Party to twenty days' suspended imprisonment for having made the following statement on a website:

> The solution is a three-stage plan: 1) Capture all Muslims in Denmark (for this purpose approximately 10 000 additional policemen are needed). 2) Gathering of the Muslims in concentration camps (one concentration camp in each county). 3) Deportation to a destination of choice (the living standard in the camps must be gradually reduced for each month that the deadline for leaving the country is overrun).

The Supreme Court of Denmark in agreement with the Eastern High Court characterised the statements as propaganda and confirmed the decision of the Eastern High Court which overruled an earlier decision of the City Court of Copenhagen.[122]

In France, the availability of racist content on the Internet is a major concern, and despite strong laws, racist organisations and individuals seem to transmit their views from outside the French jurisdiction. In its 2004 report on France ECRI noted with concern that "Internet sites aimed at the French population disseminate xenophobic, anti-Semitic and/or anti-Islamic ideas".[123] Under Article R645-1 of the French Criminal Code, it is an offence to wear or publicly display insignia, uniforms or emblems likely to remind the public of those characteristic of the perpetrators of crimes against humanity, carrying a maximum fine of €1 500.[124] Furthermore, the French law of 29 July 1881 defines a number of offences deriving from the verbal (oral or written) and non-verbal expression of various forms of racism, specifically racial defamation; racial insult; incitement to racial discrimination, hatred, or violence; denial of or apology for crimes against humanity.[125] According to a RAXEN Focal Point for France report "a law of 1 July 1972 modified the law of 29 July 1881 on press freedom by introducing aggravated penalties for racist speech or writing. Subsequent legislation has enhanced this framework by clarifying its terms and extending its scope to acts as well as verbal utterances."[126] According to this 2004 report:

> Racist offences are material facts from which racist intent may be imputed. Some have no identified victim but are judged to impugn humanity or some section of it (e.g. press offences), to violate the respect due to the dead (e.g. the profanation of graves and other memorials), or to deny the indignity of past atrocities (e.g. Holocaust

---

122. A summary of this judgment has been published in the Danish *Weekly Law Journal* 2004, p. 734, UfR.2004.734 H. Taken from the above-mentioned EUMC study.

123. ECRI, Third Report on France, CRI (2005) 3, adopted on 25 June 2004 and made public on 15 February 2005, at www.coe.int/, para. 106.

124. See ADRI, *National Analytical Study on Racist Violence and Crime: RAXEN Focal Point for France*, 2004, compiled for the National Focal Point of the European Monitoring Centre on Racism and Xenophobia (EUMC).

125. Ibid., para. 3.1.2.

126. Ibid., p. 11.

denial, usually called in French "*négationisme*", which was made a specific offence by a law of 1990).[127]

Several convictions were secured in France. For example, a person found guilty of incitement to hatred against Jews in various Internet forums was sentenced to eighteen months' imprisonment (suspended) and three further years of probation.[128] According to the Cour de cassation it is sufficient that the relevant text containing the "incitement" "should tend to provoke 'a feeling of hostility or rejection' against a certain group of people".[129] However, it was noted by ECRI that "while it has been possible to take action in respect of certain websites, the French authorities sometimes meet with legal obstacles to their action which are impossible to overcome, due especially to the extraterritorial origin of the transmissions".[130]

It should also be noted that according to the ECRI report[131] section 6.7 of Law No. 2004-575 of 21 June 2004 on confidence in the digital economy aims to prevent and penalise the dissemination of racist content on the Internet by obliging French ISPs and hosting companies to help combat incitement to racial hatred by implementing a notification procedure which makes it easy for Internet users to draw their attention to this sort of content. Once made aware of the existence of such content on their servers, the ISPs and the hosting companies must then report to the public authorities. The companies are also obliged to publicise the ways in which they endeavour to counter such phenomena on the Internet. One of the more significant court cases targeting the distribution of racist content on the Internet was the Yahoo! case in France, which will be discussed in detail below.

The availability of racist content on the Internet is a major concern in Germany, and there are several websites that carry such content, and "Right-wing extremists also use discussion forums, guest books and newsgroups, as well as anonymous emails to spread hate crime".[132] There has been an increase in so-called propaganda crimes in Germany in the last ten years or so, and this is often attributed to the use of the Internet in Germany according to various research and studies.[133] According to Jugendschutz.net, approximately 1 600 German right-wing websites are reported to exist, and there have been 1 000 or more such websites in existence

---

127. Ibid., para. 3.1., p. 10.

128. TGI Paris 26 March 2002, *Mrap et al. v. Taleb* No. 0028602422. See the above-mentioned RAXEN study.

129. Court of Criminal Appeal, 14 May 2002, *MRAP Isère v. Hugues*, Dr. Pénal October 2002, 15.

130. ECRI, Third Report on France, CRI (2005) 3, adopted on 25 June 2004 and made public on 15 February 2005, at www.coe.int/, para. 106.

131. Ibid.

132. UN Committee on the Elimination of Racial Discrimination (CERD), 18th Periodic Report submitted by Germany under Article 9 of the International Convention on the Elimination of All Forms of Racial Discrimination, submitted on 16 January 2007, CERD/C/DEU/18, 31 January, 2008, para. 260.

133. European Forum for Migration Studies (EFMS), Institute at the University of Bamberg, *National Analytical Study on Racist Violence and Crime: RAXEN Focal Point for Germany*, written by Rühl, S. and Will, G., 2004, compiled for the National Focal Point of the European Monitoring Centre on Racism and Xenophobia (EUMC).

since 2000. The German prosecutors have been successful in dealing with web-sites carrying racist propaganda when such sites are hosted in Germany or those who run the websites can be identified in Germany or elsewhere, and German law enforcement authorities are notorious for going after German-born indi-viduals like Ernst Zündel, who was extradited from Canada for prosecution in Germany for denying the Holocaust, and Fredrick Töben, an Australian citizen who is currently facing extradition from the United Kingdom to Germany for prosecution for Holocaust denial.[134] Furthermore, if the website deemed illegal according to German law is hosted abroad, and the removal of such content is not possible, the German ISPs can be required to block access to those sites as long as blocking is technically possible and feasible.[135]

German criminal law includes provisions on communication or propaganda offences. Section 86 of the German Penal Code regulates the distribution of propaganda material of unconstitutional organisations (or of a former National Socialist party). This provision criminalises the distribution of Nazi slogans, flyers, and other propaganda material including music and the provision covers mater-ial in data format and distribution through the Internet. The maximum sentence for a section 86 offence is three years' imprisonment. The mere possession of such propaganda material is not criminalised by this section. Similarly, section 86a of the Penal Code criminalises the use of certain symbols (such as swastikas, flags, military insignia, Hitler salutes, or other Nazi symbols) associated with unconstitutional organisations in public, in a meeting or in publications. As in the case of section 86 this particular offence also involves a maximum three years' imprisonment sentence. 68 429 propaganda crimes (including both sections 86 and 86a) were investigated in Germany between 1995 and 2000. While there were a total of 2 092 convictions involving section 86 between 2000 and 2004 in Germany,[136] there were a total of 2 986 convictions involving section 86a between 2000 and 2004.

Section 130(1) of the German Penal Code criminalises the Agitation of the People, and anyone who incites, advocates hatred against segments of the population including national, racial, religious groups or a group defined by national cus-toms and traditions (for example, non-Germans or Jewish people) or calls for violent or arbitrary measures against them, or assaults the human dignity of oth-ers by insulting, maliciously maligning, or defaming segments of the population can be sentenced to prison for between three months and five years. The provi-

---

134. *Daily Mail*, "Holocaust denier David Irving compares British justice to Nazi Germany in court outburst", 4 October 2008; *The Guardian*, "Holocaust denial accused intended no offence, extradition hearing told", 17 October 2008.

135. Az 1 StR 184/00, and Az 8 B 2567/02. See further the 2004 EFMS study mentioned above.

136. Covering the territory of the former Federal Republic of Germany, including the whole of Berlin as there are yet no statistics for the whole of the Federal Republic of Germany, including all five new *Länder*. See UN Committee on the Elimination of Racial Discrimination (CERD), 18th Periodic Report submitted by Germany under Article 9 of the International Convention on the Elimination of All Forms of Racial Discrimination, submitted on 16 January 2007, CERD/C/DEU/18, 31 January 2008, paras. 85-89.

sion, through section 130(2), extends to writings which incite hatred or call for violent or arbitrary measures against segments of the population or which assault the human dignity of others by insulting, maliciously maligning or defaming segments of the population. The production, dissemination, public display, or making accessible of such content through, for example, the Internet is therefore criminalised and punished with a maximum imprisonment term of three years. Furthermore, section 130(3) provides a maximum five-year imprisonment sentence for whoever approves of or denies or renders harmless an act committed under the rule of National Socialism of the type indicated in section 220a(1) of the Penal Code (Genocide) in a manner capable of disturbing the public peace. Holocaust denial crimes under section 130(3) can also be committed in writing. Section 131 criminalises the production, distribution, and public display of materials which glorify violence and illustrate cruel or otherwise inhuman violence against people of all kinds, and those who commit this offence could be imprisoned for up to one year. A total of 8 205 investigations took place with regard to sections 130 and 131 crimes in Germany between 1995 and 2000. There were a total of 1 388 convictions involving section 130(1), 307 involving section 130(2), and 110 involving section 130(3) between 2000 and 2004 in Germany.[137]

More than 80%of these propaganda crimes are reportedly committed anonymously, which makes them harder to police, and the majority of the perpetrators are located outside the German jurisdiction, primarily in the USA. According to official reports, the "right-wing scene exploits the laws applicable there, which generally permit the dissemination of such content".[138] However, some US hosting companies are co-operating with the German authorities and removing such content if notified by the German authorities. The federal government supports the work of Jugendschutz.net (Protection of Young People.net), a joint institution representing all the highest youth protection agencies of the *Länder*.[139] The German authorities through the Jugendschutz.net hotline monitor the extent of criminal Internet activity with regard to propaganda crimes.[140] Furthermore, in North Rhine-Westphalia, ISPs based in that *Land* have been made responsible for the illegal content they host. According to the ECRI third report on Germany, "while this measure is reported to have resulted, for the most part, in the spontaneous removal of such illegal content by the service providers, in some instances court cases are also reported to have been initiated".[141]

In Sweden, the white supremacist groups have used the Internet to produce and disseminate race hate propaganda since about 1993. The Swedish Penal Code

---

137. Ibid., para. 90.
138. Ibid., para. 262.
139. Ibid., para. 263.
140. Section 86, German Criminal Code.
141. ECRI Third Report on Germany, June 2004, CRI (2004) 23, para. 110.

states that (chapter 16, section 8) "a person who, in a disseminated statement or communication, threatens or expresses contempt for a national, ethnic or other such group of persons with allusion to race, colour, national or ethnic origin" has committed a crime. This particular provision also covers Internet publications and distribution.[142] More specifically, the 1998 Act on Responsibility for Electronic Bulletin Boards requires the suppliers of electronic bulletin boards to supervise their systems to an extent which is reasonable considering the extent and objective of the system on offer. An electronic bulletin board means a service for conveyance of electronic messages, basically Internet-based discussion forums. If a particular message posted to the forums contains racial agitation (section 8, Penal Code) or child pornography (section 10, Penal Code) among other types of illegal content, the 1998 Act then requires, through Article 5, the suppliers of the service to remove and delete such content. A fine or imprisonment is possible for those who intentionally or through gross negligence violate Article 5.

Spain also criminalises the dissemination of racist ideas, and its Criminal Code prohibitions extend to the Internet. Chapter 16, section 8 of the Spanish Criminal Code prohibits racial agitation, and this covers statements or communications which threaten or express contempt for a national, ethnic or other such group of persons with allusion to race, colour, national or ethnic affiliation or religious belief. The provisions also cover images or gestures, and the Spanish Supreme Court ruled in 1996 that "the bearing of symbols that can be associated with the Nazi persecution of the Jews and other persons can constitute racial agitation".[143]

As in the case of above-mentioned European states, the United Kingdom is also concerned about the availability and dissemination of racist content through the Internet. The racial hatred offences are regulated through Part III of the Public Order Act 1986 and Racial and Religious Hatred Act 2006. Section 17 of the 1986 Act defines "racial hatred" as hatred against a group[144] of persons defined by reference to colour, race, nationality (including citizenship) or ethnic or national origins.[145] Prior to the introduction of the Anti-terrorism, Crime and Security Act 2001 (ATCSA), Part III of the Public Order Act limited the incitement to racial hatred offences to racial groups "in Great Britain". Since the ATCSA came into force

142. OHCHR Report 2006, para. 24.
143. OSCE/ODIHR, Combating Hate Crimes in the OSCE Region: An Overview of Statistics, Legislation, and National Initiatives, OSCE, 2005, at www.osce.org/.
144. Racial group means any group of people who are defined by reference to their race, colour, nationality (including citizenship) or ethnic or national origin. This could include Gypsies and Travellers, refugees, or asylum seekers or others from less visible minorities. There has been a legal ruling that Jews and Sikhs are included in the definition of racial group. See Crown Prosecution Service Racist and Religious Crime Prosecution Policy, March 2008, at
www.cps.gov.uk/publications/prosecution/rrpbcrbook.html.
145. Amended by the Anti-Terrorism, Crime and Security Act 2001 ss 37, 125, Sch 8 Pt 4.

on 13 December 2001, it is now possible to incite hatred against a racial group abroad.

Furthermore, it is an offence to use threatening, abusive or insulting words or behaviour or to display (section 18, 1986 Act), publish or distribute any such written material with the intention of stirring up racial hatred, or as a result of which racial hatred is likely to be stirred up (section 19, 1986 Act).[146] It is also an offence to give a public performance of a play (section 20, 1986 Act), to distribute, show or play a recording (section 21, 1986 Act) or to broadcast a programme (section 22, 1986 Act) which has or is likely to have such an effect. The possession of racially inflammatory material (written material or a recording) with a view to displaying, publishing, distributing, showing, playing or broadcasting it for the purpose of stirring up racial hatred[147] is also an offence (section 23, 1986 Act).[148] Therefore, the "possession offence" is not an absolute one. It is not an offence to simply have material of this kind in possession nor, it would appear, to simply download the material. The possession becomes an offence if the material is possessed with a view to distributing it with intent to stir up racial hatred. In this way the law on incitement to racial hatred differs significantly from that relating to child pornography.

According to section 27(1), no proceedings for an offence under this Part may be instituted in England and Wales except by or with the consent of the Attorney General. A person guilty of an offence under this Part is liable (a) on conviction on indictment to imprisonment for a term not exceeding seven years or a fine or both; (b) on summary conviction to imprisonment for a term not exceeding six months or a fine not exceeding the statutory maximum or both.[149] Despite these strong provisions, not many people are prosecuted with regard to incitement to racial hatred offences. Between 1987 and 2004 in England and Wales 65 prosecutions resulted in 44 convictions and five acquittals, six cases were dropped by the prosecution and 10 other outcomes were obtained.

Furthermore, there were only 13 prosecutions in 2005 (six convictions), one prosecution in 2004, none in 2003, one in 2002, three in 2001, and five in 2000 in terms of the section 19 offence of publishing or distributing written material

---

146. Section 19(2) of the Public Order Act 1986 states that "in proceedings for an offence under this section it is a defence for an accused who is not shown to have intended to stir up racial hatred to prove that he was not aware of the content of the material and did not suspect, and had no reason to suspect, that it was threatening, abusive or insulting".

147. Or, having regard to all the circumstances, racial hatred is likely to be stirred up.

148. Section 19(3) of the Public Order Act 1986 states that "in proceedings for an offence under this section it is a defence for an accused who is not shown to have intended to stir up racial hatred to prove that he was not aware of the content of the written material or recording and did not suspect, and had no reason to suspect, that it was threatening, abusive or insulting".

149. Section 27(3), Public Order Act 1986.

intended or likely to stir up racial hatred.[150] The Attorney General decided on three occasions that it would not be in the public interest to consent to a prosecution for offences of incitement to racial hatred between 1987 and 2004.

The Racial and Religious Hatred Act 2006, which received the Royal Assent on 16 February 2006, came into force on 1 October 2007.[151] The measures contained in the 2006 Act are "widely considered to be a response to requests from the Muslim community to bring protection for Muslims and other faiths into line with that of Jews and Sikhs. The requests grew stronger in response to an increased threat of 'reprisal' attacks on Muslims after the terrorist attacks in New York and Washington DC in September 2001 and the activity of the British National Party."[152]

The Schedule to the 2006 Act entitled "Hatred against Persons on Religious Grounds" became Part 3A of the Public Order Act 1986, and the new provisions introduce offences involving stirring up hatred against persons on racial or religious grounds. Section 29A defines religious hatred as hatred against a group[153] of persons defined by reference to religious belief or lack of religious belief. Similar to the Part 3 offences under the 1986 Act section 29B criminalised the use of words or behaviour or display of written material, section 29C criminalised the publication or distribution of written material, section 29E criminalised the distribution, showing, or playing a recording, and section 29G criminalised the possession of inflammatory material. The penalties for these offences are the same as in the 1986 offences.

These offences need to be balanced with the right to freedom of expression, and therefore section 29J entitled "Protection of freedom of expression" states that "nothing in this Part shall be read or given effect in a way which prohibits or restricts discussion, criticism or expressions of antipathy, dislike, ridicule, insult or abuse of particular religions or the beliefs or practices of their adherents, or of any other belief system or the beliefs or practices of its adherents, or proselytising or urging adherents of a different religion or belief system to cease practising their religion or belief system".

As noted previously in this book there is no law criminalising the denial of the Holocaust in the UK. The British Government deplores attempts to deny the Holocaust, including those views expressed in a pseudo-intellectual manner, but

---

150. See House of Commons Hansard Written Answers (Racial Violence) for 28 March 2007 (pt 0032).
151. The Racial and Religious Hatred Act 2006 (Commencement No. 1) Order 2007, SI 2007 No. 2490 (C. 93). For the Explanatory Notes to the Racial and Religious Hatred Act 2006 see www.opsi.gov.uk/.
152. House of Commons, "The Racial and Religious Hatred Bill", Research Paper 05/48, 16 June 2005.
153. Religious group means any group of people defined by reference to their religious belief or lack of religious belief. For example, this includes Muslims, Hindus and Christians, and different denominations and branches within those religions. It would also include people with no religious belief at all. See the Crown Prosecution Service Racist and Religious Crime Prosecution Policy, March 2008, at www.cps.gov.uk/publications/prosecution/rrpbcrbook.html.

has no intention of criminalising this type of expression. The government believes that "criminalising Holocaust denial in the UK would represent an unnecessary infringement of freedom of expression".[154] It is, however, acknowledged by the government that "if Holocaust denial is expressed in a way that is threatening, abusive, or insulting and incites racial hatred, or is likely to do so, then that would be unlawful under the Public Order Act 1986".[155]

In terms of case law, five white supremacists, part of a group known as the Racial Volunteer Force, who formerly belonged to the violent Neo-Nazi group Combat 18, were involved in an extreme right-wing website and magazine and were sentenced to a total of fifteen years in November 2005 for conspiracy to stir up racial hatred. The judge said that the group had sprung up in early 2003 to "encourage readers to resort to violence against people with non-white backgrounds. The real danger is that it only needs to fall into the hands of one or two individuals who might be persuaded to take up the suggestions and cause a great deal of damage".[156] The material included details of how to make a nail bomb, with advice on dipping the nails in manure to cause additional infectious harm. Another article, entitled "Roast a Rabbi", had the recipe for an incendiary device and offered "100 team points" for the first person to torch a synagogue.

Another noteworthy case involved racist e-mails posted on the Anthony Walker memorial website. The online book of condolence was set up after Anthony Walker, a black teenager, was killed with an ice axe in Huyton, Merseyside during 2005. Neil Martin, 29, was charged with a racial hatred offence after he posted racist messages on the website. Martin was accused of racially aggravated harassment and stirring up racial hatred.[157] Martin was imprisoned for two years and eight months in October 2006 after he pleaded guilty to the charges.[158]

The limitations of the legal system are also evidenced in the United Kingdom in respect to a website hosted outside Britain that started publishing hit lists around 2003.[159] Redwatch, produced by "Combat 18", started publishing the names and

---

154. The Minister of State, Home Office (Baroness Scotland of Asthal), EU: Holocaust Denial, Lords Hansard text for 20 April 2007 (pt 0001).
155. Ibid.
156. *The Guardian*, "Five jailed for trying to stir up race hate violence", 5 November 2005; Press Association, "White supremacists jailed over race-hate magazine", 4 November 2005.
157. *The Sun* (England), "Net race hate rap", 3 May 2006; *Liverpool Daily Echo*, "Racist Insults on Anthony Website", 2 May 2006; *The Guardian*, "Man admits posting racist Anthony Walker messages", 6 July 2006.
158. BBC News, "Walker race hate messager jailed", 6 October 2006, at:
http://news.bbc.co.uk/1/hi/england/merseyside/5412558.stm.
159. See "Pictures of children on fascist site", *Evening Chronicle* (Newcastle), 17 January 2003; "Student is target on hate website", *UK Newsquest Regional Press – This is Lancashire*, 9 April 2003; "Extreme-right Website Targets Lecturer", *Times Educational Supplement*, 25 April 2003; "Race Hate Website Targeting Activists", *The [Sheffield] Star*, 23 October 2003; "Neo-Nazis target MEP", *UK Newsquest Regional Press – This is Lancashire*, 23 December 2003; "Anti-racism councillor caught in far right web", *The [Stoke] Sentinel* 4 January 2004; and "Web outing won't stop my battle to beat racism", *The [Stoke] Sentinel* 5 January 2004.

addresses of anti-racist campaigners in Britain in print format in 1993, almost ten years before they set up the website.[160] As the printed publication encouraged violence, several warnings were issued by the Special Branch to the targets named by Redwatch during the late 1990s.[161] In late 2003, the Home Office and the former Home Secretary, David Blunkett, were put under pressure to shut down the website.[162] There were further calls for action from the House of Lords in January 2004.[163] After Lord Greaves brought this issue to the attention of Parliament, his picture and details were also posted on the Redwatch website.[164] The Home Office launched an investigation in March 2004,[165] but this did not develop into anything. There were further calls for action within the British Parliament in June 2006 following an incident involving an attack on an anti-fascist campaigner whose details were listed on the website.[166] Angela Eagle, MP, stated that "what is certain is that both the incitement to violence and the attacks are continuing, despite the fact that the existence of this website was exposed and caused widespread concern several years ago".[167]

Obviously, concerns were raised about the US hosting of the website, and the government "initiated inquiries with the US Department of Justice to establish whether hosting such a website constitutes a breach of US law, regulations or industry good practice".[168] No action was taken in the US. Websites like Redwatch are designed to encourage violence, but freedom of speech should not include the freedom to conspire to attack people. As Hari rightly questions, what possible other purpose is there but to encourage attacks or, at the very least, intimidation?[169] Where or how do we draw the line with regard to freedom of expression, and what are its limits with regards to hate speech and racist content within the European context? The next section will try to answer these fundamental questions.

---

160. See "RACE magazines publish names and addresses of 'Red' Activists", *The Guardian*, 20 February 1993; and "Rapid increase in racial attacks 'Widely Ignored'", *The Guardian*, 20 February 1993.

161. See "Warning to VIPs on Nazi list of targets", *Evening Standard* (London), 23 February 1996; and "Yard alerts targets on Nazi hit list", *Mail on Sunday* (London), 2 April 1995.

162. See "Special report: Website linked to far right hit list: Home Secretary under pressure to clamp down on fascist", *The Guardian*, 17 December 2003.

163. See "Lords demand action to shut racist websites", *Yorkshire Evening Post*, 10 January 2004.

164. See "Call to close hard right website", *The Guardian*, 15 January 2004.

165. See "Home Office begins inquiry into far-right hate website", *Morning Star* (London), 16 March 2004.

166. See "MPs in move to close far-right website", *The Guardian*, 20 July 2006.

167. UK, HC *Parliamentary Debates*, vol. 447, col. 1436, p. 1437, 21 June 2006.

168. Ibid., at col. 1442.

169. Johann Hari, "Violence, Hatred and Freedom of Speech", *The Independent* (London), 5 December 2003.

Council of Europe member states' laws and compatibility with freedom of expression

Freedom of expression, guaranteed by Article 10 of the European Convention on Human Rights (the Convention) constitutes one of the essential foundations of a democratic society and the European Court of Human Rights has described it as "one of the basic conditions for the progress of democratic societies and for the development of each individual".[170] Subject to Article 10(2), "it is applicable not only to 'information' or 'ideas' that are favourably received or regarded as inoffensive or as a matter of indifference, but also to those that offend, shock or disturb. Such are the demands of that pluralism, tolerance or broadmindedness without which there is no democratic society."[171]

A strict three-part test to adhere to is required for any content-based restriction according to the European Court of Human Rights jurisprudence. First, any interference with freedom of expression must be prescribed by law, and it is required that not only must a law exist but also that it be accessible, reasonably precise, and not allow for the unfettered exercise of discretion. If the interference is in accordance with law, then secondly the aim of the restriction should be legitimate based on the Article 10(2) limitations in the interests of national security, public safety or the economic well-being of the country, for the prevention of disorder or crime, for the protection of health of morals, or for the protection of the rights and freedoms of others. Finally, the restrictions need to be necessary in a democratic society,[172] and the state interference should correspond to a "pressing social need".[173] The state response and the limitations provided by law should be "proportionate to the legitimate aim pursued".[174] The European Court of Human Rights requires the reasons given by the national authorities to be relevant and sufficient.[175]

Having said that, states enjoy a "certain but limited" margin of appreciation in assessing the need for an interference but this limited margin goes hand in hand with European supervision through the European Court of Human Rights whose extent will vary according to each case. The Court is therefore empowered to give the final ruling on whether a "restriction" is reconcilable with freedom of expression as protected by Article 10.[176] The Court's supervision will be strict

---

170. Handyside judgment of 7 December 1976, Series A No. 24, para. 49.

171. *Castells v. Spain* judgment of 23 April 1992, Series A No. 236.

172. See Sunday Times *v. the United Kingdom (No. 2)*, Series A No. 217, 26.11.1991, para. 50; *Okçuoğlu v. Turkey*, No. 24246/94, 8.7.1999, para. 43.

173. See *Sürek v. Turkey (No. 1)* (Application No. 26682/95), judgment of 8 July 1999, Reports 1999; Sürek (No. 3) judgment of 8 July 1999.

174. See Bladet Tromsø and Stensaas judgment of 20 May 1999, Reports 1999.

175. Başkaya and Okçuoğlu judgment of 8 July 1999, Reports 1999.

176. *Lingens v. Austria*, 8 July 1986, Series A No. 103, p. 26, para. 41.

because of the importance given to freedom of expression. While the measure taken need not be shown to be "indispensable", the necessity for restricting the right must be convincingly established.[177] According to the Council of Europe Committee of Experts for the Development of Human Rights (DH-DEV) "at the core of the examination of any interference in the exercise of freedom of opinion is therefore a balancing of interests, in which the Court takes account of the significance of freedom of opinion for democracy".[178]

According to the Court's jurisprudence there is, however, little scope for restrictions under Article 10(2) on political speech or on debate of matters of public interest.[179] However, criminalisation of speech which incites violence against an individual or a public official or a sector of the population is deemed to be compatible with Article 10.[180] In such cases the state authorities enjoy a wider margin of appreciation when examining the need for an interference with freedom of expression, and it does remain open for competent state authorities to adopt measures even of a criminal law nature intended to react appropriately to such remarks.[181] The joint concurring opinion of Judges Palm, Tulkens, Fischbach, Casadevall and Greve in *Sürek v. Turkey (No. 4)* stated that:

> it is only by a careful examination of the context in which the offending words appear that one can draw a meaningful distinction between language which is shocking and offensive – which is protected by Article 10 – and that which forfeits its right to tolerance in a democratic society.[182]

Furthermore, Judge Bonnello stated that "punishment by the national authorities of those encouraging violence would be justifiable in a democratic society only if the incitement were such as to create 'a clear and present danger'".[183] According to Judge Bonnello, "when the invitation to the use of force is intellectualised, abstract, and removed in time and space from the foci of actual or impending violence, then the fundamental right to freedom of expression should generally prevail".[184]

---

177. Autronic AG judgment of 22 May 1990, Series A No. 178, para. 61.
178. Council of Europe Steering Committee for Human Rights (CDDH), Committee of Experts for the Development of Human Rights (DH-DEV), Working Group A, Report on "hate speech", document GT-DH-DEV A(2006)008, Strasbourg, 9 February 2007, at www.coe.int/, para. 22. Note further the case of Handyside judgment of 7 December 1976, Series A No. 24, para. 49.
179. *Erdoğdu and İnce v. Turkey*, 8 July 1999, Application Nos. 25067/94 and 25068/94.
180. *Sener v. Turkey*, 18 July 2000, Application No. 26680/95.
181. *Sürek v. Turkey (No. 4)* (Application No. 24762/94), judgment of 8 July 1999.
182. Ibid.
183. Ibid.
184. Ibid.

The European Court also referred to "hate speech" in a number of its judgments. The Court in *Gündüz v. Turkey*[185] emphasised that tolerance and respect for the equal dignity of all human beings constitute the foundations of a democratic, pluralistic society. That being so, the Court stated that "as a matter of principle it may be considered necessary in certain democratic societies to sanction or even prevent all forms of expression which spread, incite, promote or justify hatred based on intolerance (including religious intolerance), provided that any 'formalities', 'conditions', 'restrictions' or 'penalties' imposed are proportionate to the legitimate aim pursued".[186] According to the Court, "only statements which promote a certain level of violence qualify as hate speech",[187] but "there can be no doubt that concrete expressions constituting 'hate speech', which may be insulting to particular individuals or groups, are not protected by Article 10 of the Convention".[188] In a recent report on hate speech, the Council of Europe Committee of Experts for the Development of Human Rights (DH-DEV) emphasised that[189] the Strasbourg Court has, however, not developed a precise definition of the notion of "hate speech". While in some cases, the Court held that expressions of racial hatred came within the meaning of Article 17 of the Convention,[190] such a conclusion has been carefully avoided in others.[191] The Court most notably established in *Jersild v. Denmark*[192] that there can be no doubt that concrete expressions constituting hate speech, which may be insulting to particular individuals or groups, are not protected by Article 10 of the Convention.[193]

Certain expressions such as hate speech are not protected by Article 10 through an exception provided by Article 17 of the Convention which states that "Nothing in this Convention may be interpreted as implying for any State, group or person any right to engage in any activity or perform any act aimed at the destruction of any of the rights and freedoms set forth herein or at their limitation to a greater extent than is provided for in the Convention".

---

185. *Gündüz v. Turkey,* Application No. 35071/97 judgment of 4 December 2003, para. 40. With regard to hate speech and the glorification of violence, see *Sürek v. Turkey (No. 1)* No. 26682/95, para. 62, ECHR 1999-IV.

186. Ibid.

187. Ibid.

188. Ibid., para. 41. See similarly *Jersild v. Denmark*, judgment of 23 September 1994 para. 35. Note further *Ergin v. Turkey*, judgment of 4 May 2006, para. 34; *Alinak and Others v. Turkey*, judgment of 4 May 2006, para. 35; *Han v. Turkey*, judgment of 13 September 2005, para. 32.

189. Council of Europe Steering Committee for Human Rights (CDDH), Committee of Experts for the Development of Human Rights (DH-DEV), Working Group A, Report on "hate speech", document GT-DH-DEV A(2006)008, Strasbourg, 9 February 2007, at www.coe.int, para. 6.

190. Note the case of *Norwood v. the United Kingdom*, decision of 16 November 2004.

191. Note the case of *Garaudy v. France*, decision of 24 June 2003; *Seurot v. France*, decision of 18 May 2004.

192. *Jersild v. Denmark*, judgment of 23 September 1994, Series A No. 298, p. 25, para. 35.

193. See *Gündüz v. Turkey,* Application No. 35071/97 judgment of 4 December 2003, para. 41.

The protection offered by Article 17 is broad and covers all the fundamental rights enshrined within the Convention. In *Lawless v. Ireland*,[194] the Court clearly established the relationship between Article 17 and the other articles of the Convention:

> Whereas in the opinion of the Court the purpose of Article 17, insofar as it refers to groups or to individuals, is to make it impossible for them to derive from the Convention a right to engage in any activity or perform any act aimed at destroying any of the rights and freedoms set forth in the Convention; whereas, therefore, no person may be able to take advantage of the provisions of the Convention to perform acts aimed at destroying the aforesaid rights and freedoms; whereas this provision which is negative in scope cannot be construed a contrario as depriving a physical person of the fundamental individual rights guaranteed by Articles 5 and 6 of the Convention.

According to a Committee of Experts for the Development of Human Rights (DH-DEV) report,

> a clear distinction is made between the exercise of those individual rights and freedoms guaranteed by the Convention, which may not give rise to a complaint under Article 17 and cannot be invalidated by this article under any circumstances, and an alleged right, not guaranteed by the Convention, to destroy rights and freedoms. This is not therefore an additional restriction on a particular right, for example the right to freedom of expression, but a general guarantee designed to provide lasting support for the system of democratic values underlying the Convention. The development of Article 17 has passed largely unnoticed and there have even been long periods in which it was applied only sporadically and sparingly without any analytical investigation of its content. However, recently it has had a new lease of life and is being applied in new spheres.[195]

The DH-DEV report further stated that from the 1990s onwards, the Court's and Commission's case law,[196] particularly in relation to anti-Semitism began dealing with a new criterion of incompatibility with the Convention on the basis of Article 17.[197] For example, the European Commission on Human Rights ruled that the applicant's publication in *Remer v. Germany*[198] attempted to incite hatred against

---

194. *Lawless v. Ireland*, judgment of 14 November 1960.

195. Council of Europe Steering Committee for Human Rights (CDDH), Committee of Experts for the Development of Human Rights (DH-DEV), Working Group A, Report on "hate speech", document GT-DH-DEV A(2006)008, Strasbourg, 9 February 2007 at www.coe.int., para. 55.

196. Note in particular *Honsik v. Austria*, No. 25062/94, decision of 18 October 1995, European Commission of Human Rights; *Remer v. Germany*, No. 25096/94, decision of 6 September 1995, European Commission of Human Rights; *Lehideux and Isorni v. France*, judgment of 23 September 1998; *W.P. v. Poland*, No. 42264/98, decision of 2 September 2004; *Witzsch v. Germany*, No. 7485/03, decision of 13 December 2005.

197. GT-DH-DEV report, para. 61.

198. *Remer v. Germany*, No. 25096/94, decision of 6 September 1995, European Commission of Human Rights.

Jews, and this ran counter to one of the basic ideas of the Convention, namely justice and peace, and further reflected racial and religious discrimination. While finding the application inadmissible, and therefore no violation of Article 10, the Commission stated that "the public interests in the prevention of crime and dis-order in the German population due to incitement to hatred against Jews, and the requirements of protecting their reputation and rights, outweigh, in a demo-cratic society, the applicant's freedom to impart publications denying the exist-ence of the gassing of Jews in the concentration camps under the Nazi regime, and the allegations of extortion".[199]

In a number of cases the Commission and the Court established that denying crimes against humanity is one of the most serious forms of racial defamation of Jews and of incitement to hatred of them. In *Walendy v. Germany*,[200] the Commission described the denial of historical facts as an insult to Jews as the applicant's pub-lication denied "historical facts about the mass murder committed by the totalitar-ian Nazi regime".[201] This was seen by the Commission as a form of "continuation of the former discrimination against the Jewish people". The Commission referred to Article 17 of the Convention and stated that "Article 17 covers essentially those rights which will facilitate the attempt to derive therefrom a right to engage per-sonally in activities aimed at the destruction of any of the rights and freedoms set forth in the Convention. In particular the Commission has repeatedly found that the freedom of expression as expressed in Article 10 of the Convention may not be invoked in a sense contrary to Article 17".[202] The DH-DEV report stated that "in this case, the issue was no longer the compliance with the Convention of an extreme-left-wing or extreme-right-wing totalitarian political system but an aggres-sive speech targeting a particular community, which was addressed from the angle of relations between individuals and communities".[203]

Similarly, in *Garaudy v. France*,[204] the application was inadmissible under Article 17 of the Convention as "the denial or rewriting of this type of historical fact undermines the values on which the fight against racism and anti-Semitism are based and constitutes a serious threat to public order. Such acts are incompat-

---

199. Ibid.
200. *Udo Walendy v. Germany*, No. 21128/92, decision of 11 January 1995, European Commission of Human Rights.
201. Ibid.
202. Ibid. Note further No. 12194/86, Dec. 12.5.88, *Kühnen v. the Federal Republic of Germany*, D.R. 56, p. 205 and No. 19459/92, Dec. of 29.3.93 unpublished.
203. GT-DH-DEV report, para. 64.
204. *Garaudy v. France*, decision of 24 June 2003. In this case the applicant was prosecuted in France with regard to his book *The Founding Myths of Israeli Politics*, which included the chapters entitled "The Myth of the Nuremberg Trials" and "The Myth of the Holocaust". These chapters were the subject of his prosecution. Relying on numerous quotations and references, the applicant questions the reality, extent and seriousness of these historical events that are not the subject of debate between historians, but – on the contrary – are clearly established.

ible with democracy and human rights because they infringe the rights of others. Its proponents indisputably have designs that fall into the category of aims prohibited by Article 17 of the Convention".[205] According to the Court, "there is no doubt that, like any other remark directed against the Convention's underlying values, the justification of a pro-Nazi policy could not be allowed to enjoy the protection afforded under Article 10"[206] and that there is "a category [of] clearly established historical facts – such as the Holocaust – whose negation or revision would be removed from the protection of Article 10 by Article 17".[207] The DH-DEV report argued that in this decision, the Court added two important elements that should be noted:

> Firstly, it associated the fight against racism and anti-Semitism with the fundamental values of the Convention, particularly with those set out in the preamble. In so doing, it incorporated a range of contemporary political activities, namely those designed to combat racism and anti-Semitism, into the body of values to be protected as a matter of priority.[208]

> Secondly, the speech complained of in the Garaudy decision was said to "infringe the rights of others". Here, as well, there is a substantial step forward in the description of the interest that has been infringed. It is not just a case of a vague insult but of an infringement of the rights of third parties.[209]

Garaudy can be contrasted with *Giniewski v. France*[210] in which a critical analysis of the Pope's position in an encyclical, "The Splendour of Truth", which sought to develop an argument about the scope of a particular doctrine and its possible links with the origins of the Holocaust, was interpreted by the Court not to violate Article 10. The Court ruled that while the published text, as the applicant himself acknowledged, contained conclusions and phrases which may offend, shock or disturb some people, the Court has reiterated on several occasions that such views do not in themselves preclude the enjoyment of freedom of expression.[211] According to the Court, the article in question was not "gratuitously offensive",[212] or insulting,[213] and does not incite disrespect or hatred, nor did it cast doubt in any way on clearly established historical facts like in Garaudy.[214] The Court emphasised that the applicant had made a contribution, which by definition was open to discussion, to a wide-ranging and ongoing ideological debate, without sparking off any controversy that was gratuitous or detached from the reality of contemporary thought.

---

205. Ibid.
206. Ibid.
207. See further *Lehideux and Isorni v. France*, judgment of 23 September 1998.
208. GT-DH-DEV report, para. 67.
209. GT-DH-DEV report, para. 68.
210. *Giniewski v. France*, Application No. 64016/00, judgment of 31 January 2006.
211. See, in particular, *De Haes and Gijsels v. Belgium*, 24 February 1997, para. 46, Reports 1997-I.
212. See *Otto-Preminger-Institut v. Austria*, 20 September 1994, Series A No. 295-A, para. 49.
213. Contrast İ.A. v. Turkey, No. 42571/98, para. 29, ECHR 2005-VIII.
214. Contrast *Garaudy v. France* (dec.), No. 65831/01, ECHR 2003-IX.

The applicant in *Witzsch v. Germany*[215] made the impugned statements in a private letter which was later handed to the police. It did not matter for the Court that the applicant's denial of Hitler's and the National Socialists' responsibility in the extermination of the Jews which showed the applicant's disdain towards the victims of the Holocaust were not published publicly before a larger audience. The Court observed that the general purpose of Article 17 is to make it impossible for individuals to take advantage of a right with the aim of promoting ideas contrary to the text and the spirit of the Convention.

The Court also relied on Article 17 of the Convention outside the sphere of historical revisionism and anti-Semitism related applications most notably in *Norwood v. the United Kingdom*.[216] The case involved a member of the British National Party (BNP: an extreme right-wing political party) displaying a poster supplied by the BNP on the window of his first-floor flat, with a photograph of the twin towers in flames, the words "Islam out of Britain – Protect the British People" and a symbol of a crescent and star in a prohibition sign. The Court noted that the words and images on the poster amounted to a public expression of attack on all Muslims in the United Kingdom. Such a general, vehement attack against a religious group, linking the group as a whole with a grave act of terrorism, is incompatible with the values proclaimed and guaranteed by the Convention, notably tolerance, social peace and non-discrimination. The applicant's display of the poster in his window constituted an act within the meaning of Article 17, which did not, therefore, enjoy the protection of Article 10.[217]

More recently in *Leroy v. France*,[218] the Strasbourg Court held that the publication of a drawing (cartoon) representing the attack on the twin towers of the World Trade Center, with a caption which parodied the advertising slogan of a famous brand: "We have all dreamt of it ... Hamas did it" provoked a certain public reaction, capable of stirring up violence and demonstrating a plausible impact on public order in a politically sensitive region, namely the Basque Country. The drawing was published in the Basque weekly newspaper Ekaitza on 13 September 2001, two days after the attacks of 11 September. The applicant complained that the French courts had denied his real intention, which was governed by political and activist expression, namely that of communicating his anti-Americanism through a satirical image and illustrating the decline of American imperialism. The European Court, however, considered that the drawing was not limited to criticism of American imperialism, but supported and glorified the latter's violent destruction. In this regard, the European Court based its finding on the caption which accompanied the drawing, and noted that the applicant had expressed his moral support for those whom he presumed to be the perpetrators of the

---

215. *Witzsch v. Germany*, No. 7485/03, decision of 13 December 2005.
216. *Norwood v. the United Kingdom*, No. 23131/03, decision of 15 November 2004.
217. Similarly note the case of *Seurot v. France*, No. 57383/00, decision of 18 May 2004.
218. *Leroy v. France*, Application No. 36109/03, Chamber judgment of 02.10.2008.

attacks of 11 September 2001. Through his choice of language, the applicant commented approvingly on the violence perpetrated against thousands of civilians and diminished the dignity of the victims. In the European Court's opinion, this factor – the date of publication – was such as to increase the applicant's responsibility in his account of, and even support for, a tragic event, whether considered from an artistic or a journalistic perspective. Therefore, no violation of Article 10 was found by the Court.[219]

As can be seen from the cases above, the European Court's jurisprudence is constantly evolving and the concept of the rights of others and of victims have been taken into account, and speech which interferes with such concepts has been excluded from the protection of Article 10 through Article 17 of the Convention in the fight against racism. However, as noted by the DH-DEV report, "all the case law concerning Article 17, and hence concerning the new forms of 'hate speech', places the emphasis on the identification of the threat to the Convention's absolute values, making no use of the criteria for the application of Article 10, such as the risk of provoking violence, the proportionality of the interference or the appropriateness thereof in view of the legitimate aim pursued. This is an important point, as the order of priorities is reversed under Article 17, its aim being to safeguard the democratic framework underlying all the rights and freedoms set out in the Convention."[220]

An overview of significant national regulatory initiatives outside the Council of Europe region

This section will provide an overview of the regulatory regimes in Australia, Canada and the United States of America.

In Australia, section 18C(1) of the Racial Discrimination Act 1975 (RDA), which states "that any public act that is reasonably likely, in all circumstances, to offend, insult, humiliate or intimidate people on the basis of their race, colour or national or ethnic origin, is unlawful unless it is done reasonably and in good faith in certain specific circumstance" could be applied to Internet-based publications and content. However, there are no "criminal sanctions" associated with this infringement, and only an administrative complaint mechanism has been integrated into the 1975 law. A complaint can be registered with the Human Rights and Equal Opportunity Commission (HREOC). The most common types of racial hatred complaints were so far about the media, neighbourhood disputes, employment,

---

219. Similarly, no violation of Article 10 was found by the Court in *Orban and others v. France* (Application No. 20985/05, Chamber judgment of 15.01.2009) on account of the applicants' conviction for publicly defending war crimes, following the publication of a book named *Services Spéciaux Algérie 1955-1957* ("Special Services Algeria 1955-1957"). According to the Court, penalising a publisher for having assisted in the dissemination of a witness account written by a third party concerning events which formed part of a country's history would seriously hamper contribution to the discussion of matters of public interest and should not be envisaged without particularly good reason.
220. GT-DH-DEV report, para. 76.

personal conflict and public debate. To date, there have been very few complaints about racial hatred on the Internet.[221]

The most important complaint with regard to the Internet is the case of *Jones v. Töben.*[222] This concerned the website of the Adelaide Institute, run by Fredrick Töben, which breached the provisions of the RDA 1975 by denying the Jewish Holocaust. The content of the website was found to be offensive to Jewish people and was ordered to be removed from the site. This case will be discussed in detail below.

Racist material on the Internet that is offensive, harassing or threatening may also be a criminal offence under Commonwealth as well as State and Territory law.[223] This will depend upon the nature of the material published but variations do exist and in some states only civil sanctions are provided.

At the federal level, it is an offence to use the Internet intentionally to disseminate material that results in a person being menaced or harassed under section 85ZE of the Crimes Act 1914 entitled "Improper use of carriage services". This provision, however, was repealed by Crimes Legislation Amendment (Telecommunications Offences and Other Measures) Act (No. 2) 2004,[224] and an updated offence was introduced through Part 10.6 of the Australian Criminal Code Act 1995. The newly introduced section 474.17 entitled "Using a carriage service to menace, harass or cause offence" provides that a person will be guilty of an offence if the person "uses a carriage service; and the person does so in a way (whether by the method of use or the content of a communication, or both) that reasonable persons would regard as being, in all the circumstances, menacing, harassing or offensive". Up to three years' imprisonment is provided for this offence.

As in other states, the availability and dissemination of hate speech and propaganda created significant problems in Canada. Under the Canadian Criminal Code,[225] and through section 13(1) of the Canadian Human Rights Act, hate speech is prohibited, and hate propaganda is not tolerated:[226]

---

221. See Australian Human Rights Commission, *Racial Vilification Law in Australia*, Race Discrimination Unit, HREOC, October 2002, at www.humanrights.gov.au.

222. *Jones v. Töben* [2002] FCA 1150 (17 September 2002) and *Töben v. Jones* [2003] FCAF 137 (27 June 2003).

223. Australian Human Rights Commission, *Cyber-Racism*, 2008, at www.humanrights.gov.au. Note further Australian Human Rights Commission, *An International Comparison of the Racial Discrimination Act 1975*, (2008), at www.humanrights.gov.au.

224. See generally http://law.ato.gov.au.

225. See section 318 (Advocating Genocide); section 319(1) (Public Incitement to Hatred); section 319(2) (Willful Promotion of Hatred). All of these offences require the consent of the Attorney General before a proceeding can be instituted. According to the B'Nai Brith Canada, *Hate on the Internet: 3rd International Symposium, Taking Action Against Hate on the Internet: A Legal Analysis* report, "no charges have ever been laid under section 318 or 319(1) of the *Criminal Code*" (2007, at www.hateontheinternet.com/PDF/legalanalysis.pdf, p. 8).

226. *Canada (Human Rights Commission) v. Taylor*, [1990] 3 S.C.R. 892.

It is a discriminatory practice for a person or a group of persons acting in concert to communicate telephonically or to cause to be so communicated, repeatedly, in whole or in part by means of the facilities of a telecommunication undertaking within the legislative authority of Parliament, any matter that is likely to expose a person or persons to hatred or contempt by reason of the fact that that person or those persons are identifiable on the basis of a prohibited ground of discrimination.

Although originally section 13 of the Canadian Human Rights Act prohibited the communication of hatred or contempt telephonically, an amendment was made in 2001 to ensure that the Act clearly applies to the Internet. In its amended version, section 13(2) states that:

For greater certainty, subsection (1) applies in respect of a matter that is communicated by means of a computer or a group of interconnected or related computers, including the Internet, or any similar means of communication, but does not apply in respect of a matter that is communicated in whole or in part by means of the facilities of a broadcasting undertaking.

However, as will be seen below, even prior to this amendment taking place it was well established by the Canadian Human Rights Tribunal in *Citron et al. v. Zündel*[227] that telephonic communications include the Internet. A further amendment by way of section 13(3) of the Canadian Human Rights Act was introduced in 2001 to provide protection to ISPs or web-hosting companies from liability for content involving hatred posted to their servers by third parties. Section 13(3) states that:

For the purposes of this section, no owner or operator of a telecommunication undertaking communicates or causes to be communicated any matter described in subsection (1) by reason only that the facilities of a telecommunication undertaking owned or operated by that person are used by other persons for the transmission of that matter.

According to the Canadian Human Rights Commission 2007 Annual Report,[228] the Canadian Human Rights Tribunal (CHRT) has issued more than 15 decisions in complaints against Canadians connected to hate websites or materials.

In all instances the Tribunal has ruled against the respondents and ordered them to close down their websites and pay damages – sending a powerful message of social solidarity to all those targeted by hatred and contempt. As effective as section 13 has been, the Commission recognises that complaints are only one tool of many that must be used to combat hatred in Canadian society. The Commission is continuing to work with civil society organisations and governments towards developing a comprehensive strategy to combat hatred in all its aspects.

---

227. *Citron and Toronto Mayor's Committee v. Zündel*, 2002 CanLII 23557.
228. Published in March 2008, and available at www.chrc-ccdp.ca/pdf/ar_2007_ra_en.pdf.

The CHRT in *Warman v. Kouba*[229] set out a non-exhaustive list of 11 hallmarks of hate messages, accompanied by an elaboration on each of the hallmarks. These hallmarks are:

1. **The Powerful Menace Hallmark**: the targeted group is portrayed as a powerful menace that is taking control of the major institutions in society and depriving others of their livelihoods, safety, freedom of speech and general well-being;

2. **The True Story Hallmark**: the messages use true stories, news reports, pictures and reference from purportedly reputable sources to make negative generalisations about the targeted group;

3. **The Predator Hallmark**: the targeted group is portrayed as preying upon children, the aged, the vulnerable, etc.;

4. **The Cause of Society's Problems Hallmark**: the targeted group is blamed for the current problems in society and the world;

5. **The Dangerous or Violent by Nature Hallmark**: the targeted group is portrayed as dangerous or violent by nature;

6. **The No Redeeming Qualities Hallmark**: the messages convey the idea that members of the targeted group are devoid of any redeeming qualities and are innately evil;

7. **The Banishment Hallmark**: the messages communicate the idea that nothing but the banishment, segregation or eradication of this group of people will save others from the harm being done by this group;

8. **The Sub-human Hallmark**: the targeted group is de-humanised through comparisons to and associations with animals, vermin, excrement, and other noxious substances;

9. **The Inflammatory Language Hallmark**: highly inflammatory and derogatory language is used in the messages to create a tone of extreme hatred and contempt;

10. **The Trivialising or Celebration of Past Tragedy Hallmark**: the messages trivialise or celebrate past persecution or tragedy involving members of the targeted group;

11. **The Call to Violent Action Hallmark**: calls to take violent action against the targeted group.

If more of these hallmarks are met by a section 13 complaint to the CHRT, it is more likely that a complaint will be successful. If successful, the CHRT may award damages and/or ask the infringing party to cease and desist the publication of

---

229. *Warman v. Kouba*, 2006 CHRT 50.

the impugned material on the Internet.[230] The Canadian Human Rights Tribunal investigation with regard to the complaint brought against Ernst Zündel and his website Zundelsite[231] will be discussed in detail below.

As in any other jurisdiction the constitutional protection offered for freedom of expression is not absolute in the United States of America. The First Amendment generally prevents government from proscribing speech, or even expressive conduct[232] because of disapproval of the ideas expressed, and the protection offered by the First Amendment to the US Constitution extends to content that includes hate speech or racist content. Based on the Supreme Court decisions and principles the US government can only regulate speech-based content in a few limited areas which are "of such slight social value as a step to truth that any benefit that may be derived from them is clearly outweighed by the social interest in order and morality".[233] Therefore, based on the limited categorical approach, obscenity,[234] child pornography,[235] defamation,[236] fighting words[237] and true threats[238] are excluded from the protection offered by the First Amendment.

In Chaplinsky, the Supreme Court described "fighting words" as words which "by their very utterance, inflict injury or tend to incite an immediate breach of the peace", and such words did not receive the same degree of constitutional protection as other speech since "such utterances are no essential part of any exposition of ideas, and are of such slight social value as a step to truth that any benefit that may be derived from them is clearly outweighed by the social interest in order and morality".[239] Fighting words which are "personally abusive epithets which, when addressed to the ordinary citizen, are, as a matter of common knowledge, inherently likely to provoke violent reaction" are generally proscribable under the First Amendment.[240] Furthermore, "the constitutional guarantees of free speech and free press do not permit a State to forbid or proscribe advocacy of the use of force or of law violation except where such advocacy is directed to

---

230. See sections 53 and 54 of the Canadian Human Rights Act. Note for a recent application *Warman v. Guille & Canadian Heritage Alliance*, 2008 CHRT 40, decided on 30 September 2008.

231. See www.zundelsite.org.

232. See, e.g., *Texas v. Johnson*, 491 U.S. 397, 406, 109 S.Ct. 2533, 2540, 105 L.Ed.2d 342 (1989).

233. See, e.g., *Chaplinsky v. New Hampshire*, 315 U.S. 568, 571-572.

234. See *Roth v. United States*, 354 U.S. 476, 77 S.Ct. 1304, 1 L.Ed.2d 1498 (1957), but note also *Miller v. California*, 413 U.S. 15, 93 S.Ct. 2607, 37 L.Ed.2d 419 (1973).

235. *New York v. Ferber* 458 U.S. 747 (1982). Note Schauer, F., "Codifying the First Amendment: *New York v. Ferber*" (1982) *Sup. Ct. Rev* 285, 317.

236. See *Beauharnais v. Illinois*, 343 U.S. 250, 72 S.Ct. 725, 96 L.Ed. 919 (1952), but note also *New York Times Co. v. Sullivan*, 376 U.S. 254, 84 S.Ct. 710, 11 L.Ed.2d 686 (1964); and *Gertz v. Robert Welch, Inc.*, 418 U.S. 323, 94 S.Ct. 2997, 41 L.Ed.2d 789 (1974).

237. *Chaplinsky v. New Hampshire*, 315 U.S. 568.

238. See, e.g., *Watts v. United States*, 394 U.S. 705.

239. *Chaplinsky v. New Hampshire* (1942) 315 U.S. 568 at 572.

240. Ibid., at 572. Note further *Cohen v. California*, 403 U.S. 15, 20 (1971).

inciting or producing imminent lawless action and is likely to incite or produce such action".[241]

Furthermore, in *R.A.V. v. City of St. Paul*,[242] the Supreme Court explained that a blanket ban on the use of "odious racial epithets" by "proponents of all views" constitutes mere content-based regulation, while a ban on the use of racial slurs by one group of speakers but not "those speakers' opponents" constitutes viewpoint discrimination. In this case, the Supreme Court held the Minnesota statute at issue,[243] which criminalised conduct such as placing a burning cross or Nazi swastika, which one knows to arouse anger, alarm, or resentment on the basis of race, religion, etc. to be unconstitutional because it prohibited only some fighting words based not on their being especially offensive, but only on the point of view that they are used to express.

However, in *Virginia v. Black*,[244] the Supreme Court held that a state, consistent with the First Amendment, may ban cross burning carried out with the intent to intimidate. The Court stated that the Ku Klux Klan has often used cross burnings as a tool of intimidation and a threat of impending violence, although such burnings have also remained potent symbols of shared group identity and ideology, serving as a central feature of Klan gatherings. According to the court, regardless of whether the message is a political one or is also meant to intimidate, the burning of a cross is a "symbol of hate". The Supreme Court ruled that a ban on cross burning carried out with the intent to intimidate is fully consistent with this court's holding in the R.A.V. case. According to Justice O'Connor, "while a burning cross does not inevitably convey a message of intimidation, often the cross burner intends that the recipients of the message fear for their lives. And when a cross burning is used to intimidate, few if any messages are more powerful."[245] Therefore, while certain limitations do exist, both Black and R.A.V. support the "premise that it is unconstitutional for the US Government to regulate speech on the basis of the opinion and ideology expressed". [246]

Additionally, the First Amendment permits a state to ban "true threats",[247] and "a prohibition on true threats protects individuals from the fear of violence and the

---

241. *Brandenburg v. Ohio*, 395 U.S. 444, 447 (1969).
242. *R.A.V. v. City of St. Paul*, 505 U.S. 377, at 392; 112 S.Ct. 2538, 120 L.Ed.2d 305 (1992).
243. The statute at issue stated: "Whoever places on public or private property a symbol, object, appellation, characterization or graffiti, including, but not limited to, a burning cross or Nazi swastika, which one knows or has reasonable grounds to know arouses anger, alarm or resentment in others on the basis of race, color, creed, religion or gender commits disorderly conduct and shall be guilty of a misdemeanor." See ibid.
244. *Virginia v Black et al.*, 538 U.S. 343 (2003).
245. Ibid.
246. Australian Human Rights Commission, "An International Comparison of the Racial Discrimination Act 1975, (2008)", at www.humanrights.gov.au.
247. See, e.g., *Watts v. United States*, 394 U.S. 705. Note further 18 U.S.C. para. 871, which criminalises threats of violence that are directed against the President of the United States.

disruption that fear engenders, as well as from the possibility that the threatened violence will occur".[248] A "true threat" means "a serious threat as distinguished from words as mere political argument, idle talk, or jest".[249] According to the Supreme Court in *Virginia v. Black*, "a prohibition on true threats protects individuals from the fear of violence and from the disruption that fear engenders, in addition to protecting people from the possibility that the threatened violence will occur".[250]

A number of Internet-related cases supported the "true threats" principle including the decision of the Ninth Circuit Court of Appeals in the Nuremberg Files case[251] in which anti-abortion activists published wanted posters that listed the names, home addresses and other personal information about abortion providers on their website. The information provided on the website which looked no more than a "hitlist" was considered to be a threat to the named doctors on the list and therefore was not considered to be protected speech by the Ninth Circuit Court of Appeals. According to a 6th Periodic Report submitted by the US Government under Article 9 of the International Convention on the Elimination of All Forms of Racial Discrimination to the UN Committee on the Elimination of Racial Discrimination, the Civil Rights Division of the Department of Justice has prosecuted several cases of Internet threats.[252]

Significant court cases targeting the distribution of racist content on the Internet

Following on from the overview of legislative response provided by a number of Council of Europe member states as well as observer states such as Canada

---

248. *R.A.V. v. City of St. Paul* (90-7675), 505 U.S. 377 (1992), at 388.

249. *United States v. Viefhaus*, 168 F.3d 392, 395 (10th Cir.1999) (quoting *United States v. Leaverton*, 835 F.2d 254, 257 (10th Cir.1987)).

250. *Virginia v. Black*, 538 U.S. 343, at 359-360, 123 S.Ct. 1536, 155 L.Ed.2d 535 (2003).

251. *Planned Parenthood of the Colombia/Willamette, Inc. v. American Coalition of Life Activists*, 290 F. 3d 1058 (9th Cir. 2002), cert denied, 539 U.S. 958 (2003).

252. See UN Committee on the Elimination of Racial Discrimination (CERD), 6th Periodic Report submitted by the USA under Article 9 of the International Convention on the Elimination of All Forms of Racial Discrimination, submitted on 24 April 2007, CERD/C/USA/6, 1 May 2007, para. 144. In *US v. Razani* (C.D. Cal.), the defendant sent threatening e-mails, including a death threat, to an Arab-American woman. The defendant pleaded guilty to violating 18 U.S.C. 874 (c) and was sentenced to six months' home detention and three years' probation on 3 April 2006. In *US v. Middleman* (D.C.), the defendant pleaded guilty to violating 18 U.S.C. 875 for sending threatening e-mails to the president of the Arab American Institute. This defendant was sentenced to ten months in prison on 14 October 2005. In *US v. Oakley* (D.C.), the defendant sent e-mails threatening to bomb the headquarters of the Council on American-Islamic Relations. This defendant pleaded guilty to violating 18 U.S.C. 844 (e), and was sentenced to three years' probation. In *US v. Bratisax* (E.D. Mich.), the defendant sent threatening e-mails to the Islamic Center of America. This defendant pleaded guilty to violating 18 U.S.C. 247 and was sentenced on 13 March 2006 to two years' probation. Note further Partners Against Hate, "Investigating Hate Crimes on the Internet", September 2003, at www.partnersagainsthate.org/.

and the United States of America, and the non-member-state Australia, this section will assess three significant court cases targeting the distribution of racist content on the Internet.

Yahoo! case (France/USA)

In May 2000, the League Against Racism and Anti-Semitism (la Ligue Internationale Contre le Racisme et l'Antisémitisme – LICRA) and the Union of French Jewish Students (UEJF) brought an action against Yahoo! Inc. and Yahoo! France. The French organisations alleged that Yahoo! Inc. hosted an auction website which contained for sale thousands of items of Nazi paraphernalia and that Yahoo! France provided a link and access to this content through the yahoo.com website. The French organisations alleged that the display and sale of such items are illegal in France.

In its defence, Yahoo! argued that its French subsidiary websites do not permit such postings. However, Yahoo! acknowledged that its main website (yahoo.com) based in the US does not impose any restrictions for such postings. Despite the limitations on its French subsidiary websites, users in France, or anywhere else in the world, were able to access the yahoo.com website based in the US. The legal dispute between the French organisations and Yahoo! started with a "cease and desist" letter sent to Yahoo!'s US headquarters in early April 2000 in which the French organisations stated that unless Yahoo! ceased presenting Nazi objects for sale within eight days, they would take legal action to enforce French law on Yahoo! As Yahoo! took no action, the French organisations filed civil law complaints against Yahoo! in the tribunal de grande instance de Paris for alleged violation of a French criminal statute, the Nazi Symbols Act, which criminalises the public display in France of Nazi-related "uniforms, insignia or emblems".[253]

The French Court in its initial judgment, on 22 May 2000,[254] held that access by French Internet users to the auction website containing Nazi objects constituted a contravention of French law, as an offence to the "collective memory" of the country. The court further held that the simple act of displaying such objects (e.g. exhibition of uniforms, insignia or emblems resembling those worn or displayed by the Nazis) in France constitutes a violation of the Penal Code and is therefore considered a threat to internal public order. On 22 May 2000 the tribunal de grande instance de Paris ordered Yahoo! Inc. to take all necessary measures to dissuade and render impossible any access via yahoo.com by Internet users in France to yahoo.com's auction service for Nazi memorabilia as well as to any other site or service that may be construed as an apology for Nazism or contesting the reality of Nazi crimes.

---

253. See le nouveau Code pénal, article R.645-2.
254. Trib. gr. inst. Paris, 20 November 2000, *League Against Racism and Anti-Semitism (LICRA), French Union of Jewish Students v. Yahoo! Inc. (USA), Yahoo! France* (Interim Court Order), at www.cdt.org/.

Yahoo! Inc. argued that the Court of Paris is not competent to make a ruling in this dispute and lacked jurisdiction over Yahoo! as its services are offered in the US. Despite any possible difficulties in executing its decision in the territory of the United States, this claim was rejected by the French court. Yahoo! Inc. also argued that there were no technical means capable of satisfying the terms of the order of 22 May 2000. Furthermore, Yahoo! Inc. on the assumption that such means existed, argued that their implementation would entail unduly high costs for the company, and might even place the company in jeopardy, and would, to a degree, compromise the existence of the Internet, being a space of liberty and scarcely receptive to attempts to control and restrict access.

Yahoo! Inc. argued throughout the trial that its services are directed essentially at surfers located in the territory of the United States of America, its servers are based in the USA, and that "a coercive measure instituted against it could have no application in the United States given that it would be in contravention of the First Amendment of the United States Constitution which guarantees freedom of opinion and expression to every citizen".

A panel of experts was appointed[255] by the French court following the May 2000 order to seek possible solutions which Yahoo! Inc. could implement to prevent French Internet users from accessing the offending web pages. According to the panel of experts, in order to satisfy the terms of the French court order requiring it to prevent access to auction services for Nazi objects, Yahoo! Inc. has to:

1. know the geographical origin and nationality of surfers wishing to access its auctions site,

2. prevent French surfers or surfers connecting from French territory from perusing the description of Nazi objects posted for auction, and even more importantly to prevent them from bidding.

The panel estimated that 70% of the IP addresses assigned to French surfers can be matched with certainty to a service provider located in France, and therefore can be filtered. But this finding was not without numerous exceptions as a large number of these, in the order of 20%, stem from the multinational character of the access provider or from the fact that they use the services of an international ISP or a private communications network. America Online (AOL) was the significant example to the exceptions as the dynamic IP addresses assigned by AOL to its users including those in France appear as being located in Virginia, USA. In this situation, according to the experts, the workstations of users residing in French territory appear on the Internet as if they are not located in French territory. This could also happen to French users who hide their real address on the Internet by using anonymising technologies (see, for example, www.anonymizer.com and www.safeweb.com).[256]

---

255. "Experts testify in French Yahoo! case over Nazi memorabilia", Associated Press, 6 November 2000.
256. See generally Akdeniz, Y., "Anonymous Now", *Index on Censorship*, The Privacy Issue, 2000 (3), June, pp. 57-62.

Two of the consultants, Laurie[257] and Wallon, considered that in addition to the geographical identification already practised by Yahoo! Inc. to target its advertising, it would also be desirable to ask surfers whose IP address is ambiguous to make a declaration of nationality. According to the experts:

> This declaration, given on honour, would only be required of surfers whose IP address cannot be identified as belonging to a French ISP ... At the discretion of Yahoo, this declaration could be made on the home page of the auctions site, or only in the context of a search for Nazi objects if the word "Nazi" is included in the user's request, immediately before the search engine processes the request.

In these circumstances, the consultants considered that it cannot be reasonably claimed that this would have a negative impact on the performance and response time of the server hosting the Yahoo! auctions service. Therefore, according to the two experts, the combination of two procedures, namely geographical identification of the IP address and declaration of nationality, would be likely to achieve a filtering success rate approaching 90%. However, according to Vinton Cerf, the third expert, there were several potential problems with the identification approach:

> For one thing, users can choose to lie about their locations. For another, every user of the website would have to be asked to identify his or her geographic location since the web server would have no way to determine a priori whether the user is French or is using the Internet from a French location.

Furthermore, according to Cerf, there may also be privacy concerns with this approach. For these and many other reasons, "it does not appear to be very feasible to rely on discovering the geographic location of users for purposes of imposing filtering of the kind described in the Court Order". Cerf approved the final report of the other two experts.

The French court in its November 2000 decision, by taking into account the experts' report, stated that it should be borne in mind that Yahoo! Inc. already carries out geographical identification of French surfers or surfers operating out of French territory and visiting its auctions site. This is evidenced by the fact that Yahoo! Inc. routinely displays French advertising banners in the French language targeted at the French Internet users. Moreover, the Court pointed out that Yahoo! Inc. is currently refusing to accept through its auctions service the sale of human organs, drugs, works or objects connected with paedophilia, cigarettes or live animals. In the views of the French court, it would "most certainly cost the company very little to extend its ban to symbols of Nazism, and such an initiative would also have the merit of satisfying an ethical and moral imperative shared by all democratic societies".

Therefore, according to the French court, Yahoo! Inc. had the opportunity of satisfying the injunctions contained in the order of 22 May 2000 in respect of the filtering of access to the auctions service for Nazi objects and any other site or

---

257. See further Laurie, B., "An Expert's Apology", 21 November 2000, at www.apache-ssl.org/.

service constituting an apology for Nazism (sites distributing *Mein Kampf* were mentioned). According to the court, Yahoo! had the technical measures at its disposal and it should have acted in the name of simple public morality. Based on this view, the Paris court rejected the plea of incompetence reiterated by Yahoo! Inc., and reaffirmed its May 2000 decision and ordered Yahoo! Inc. to comply with the injunctions contained in its order of 22 May 2000.[258] The court directed Yahoo! to:

> 1. re-engineer its content servers in the United States and elsewhere to enable them to recognise French Internet Protocol addresses and block access to Nazi material by end-users assigned such IP addresses;
>
> 2. require end-users with "ambiguous" IP addresses to provide Yahoo! with a declaration of nationality when they arrive at Yahoo!'s home page or when they initiate any search using the word "Nazi"; and
>
> 3. comply with the May 2000 Order within three months or face a penalty of 100 000 francs (approximately USD 13 300) for each day of non-compliance.

The French court has not imposed any penalty on Yahoo! for violations of the 22 May or 20 November orders. Subsequently, Yahoo! Inc. announced in January 2001 that it would no longer allow Nazi and Ku Klux Klan memorabilia to be displayed on its Yahoo! France website and that it would take a proactive approach to the problem by implementing a monitoring or filtering system. The new policy, which also included a ban on other forms of hate material, took effect on 10 January 2001.

Just before announcing its new policy, on 21 December 2000, Yahoo! Inc. asked the US District Court in San Jose to declare the French ruling in violation of the First Amendment[259] and to rule that the French court did not have jurisdiction over content produced by a US company. This was followed by LICRA filing a motion with the San Jose Court to dismiss Yahoo! Inc.'s case. Interestingly, the district court conducted its own research on yahoo.com, and found that even after Yahoo! changed its policy in January 2001, it appeared that the website did not fully comply with the French court orders with respect to its auction site. For example, the district court found that Yahoo! continued to allow the sale of items such as a copy of *Mein Kampf* and stamps and coins from the Nazi period on which the swastika is depicted.[260]

However, LICRA's motion was denied by the US District Court for the Northern District of California in San Jose and a motion for summary judgment was granted, with the court stating:

---

258. Ibid. See further Akdeniz, Y., "Case Analysis of League Against Racism and Anti-Semitism *(LICRA), French Union of Jewish Students v. Yahoo! Inc. (USA), Yahoo! France*" (2001) 1(3) *Electronic Business Law Reports* 110.

259. US Constitution amend. I.

260. See 169 F. Supp. 2d at 1185.

this case is not about the moral acceptability of promoting the symbols or propaganda of Nazism. Most would agree that such acts are profoundly offensive. By any reasonable standard of morality, the Nazis were responsible for one of the worst displays of inhumanity in recorded history. This court is acutely mindful of the emotional pain reminders of the Nazi era cause to Holocaust survivors and deeply respectful of the motivations of the French Republic in enacting the underlying statutes and of the defendant organizations in seeking relief under those statutes. Vigilance is the key to preventing atrocities such as the Holocaust from occurring again.[261]

The court also questioned "whether it is consistent with the Constitution and laws of the United States for another nation to regulate speech by a United States resident within the United States on the basis that such speech can be accessed by Internet users in that nation".[262] This was a crucial point in granting summary judgment in favour of Yahoo!.

However, LICRA's subsequent appeal to the US Court of Appeals for the Ninth Circuit that the district court did not properly exercise personal jurisdiction over the French organisations was successful, and the US Court of Appeals for the Ninth Circuit held that Yahoo! had made no allegation which could lead a court to conclude that the conduct of LICRA and UEJF was wrongful.[263] Although the Ninth Circuit Court of Appeals granted a petition from Yahoo! for the court to reconsider its decision,[264] before a decision was reached, an appeals court in Paris upheld a decision absolving Yahoo! from legal responsibility for the sale of Nazi paraphernalia auctioned through its website.[265] According to the French Appeals Court, Yahoo! did not seek to "justify war crimes and crimes against humanity" by allowing such sales on its US website.[266]

Ultimately, in January 2006, a 6-5 majority of the US Court of Appeals for the Ninth Circuit dismissed Yahoo!'s case,[267] reversing a lower court ruling that had

---

261. *Yahoo! Inc. v. La Ligue Contre Le Racisme et L'antisemitisme*, 169 F.Supp.2d 1181 (N.D. Cal. 2001).
262. Ibid. at 1186.
263. *Yahoo! Inc. v. La Ligue Contre Le Racisme et L'antisemitisme*, 379 F.3d 1120 (9th Cir. 2004).
264. *Yahoo! Inc. v. La Ligue Contre Le Racisme et L'Antisemitisme*, 399 F.3d 1010 (9th Cir. 2005). See further: "Yahoo! Sees Small Victory in Nazi Dispute", *Bizreport*, 11 February 2005, at www.bizreport.com/news/; and "Yahoo! Lawyers Ask Court for Protection", Associated Press Financial Wire, 28 March 2005.
265. Note that Yahoo! was acquitted by a Paris criminal court in February 2003, but the Association of Auschwitz Survivors and the French Movement Against Racism (MRAP) pursued a civil action against Yahoo! as the public prosecutor declined to appeal the court's decision on the criminal charges. See generally: "Auschwitz survivors continue challenge of internet sale of Nazi memorabilia", Agence France Presse, 19 January 2005; "Appeals court says former Yahoo exec not liable", Associated Press, 6 April 2005; "French Court Says Yahoo! Not Responsible For Nazi Sales", *National Journal's Technology Daily [Washington]*, 7 April 2005; and "Can the Internet Have Borders?", *The Washington Post*, 7 April 2005.
266. "Appeals court says former Yahoo exec not liable", Associated Press, 6 April 2005.
267. *Yahoo! Inc. v. La Ligue Contre Le Racisme et L'antisémitisme*, 433 F.3d 1199 (9th Cir. 2006). See also "Court rules against Yahoo in Nazi speech case", Reuters, 12 January 2006.

rejected the French organisations' attempts to enforce French laws against US companies in US courts.

The US Appeals Court concluded that "First Amendment issues arising out of international Internet use are new, important and difficult [and they] should not rush to decide such issues based on an inadequate, incomplete or unclear record".[268] The court argued that without knowing "whether further restrictions on access by French, and possibly American users are required, [it] cannot decide whether or to what degree the First Amendment might be violated by enforcement of the French court's orders".[269] The court also argued that it was extremely unlikely that any penalty, if assessed, could ever be enforced against Yahoo! in the United States. It was also the view of the court that "First Amendment harm may not exist at all, given the possibility that Yahoo! has now 'in large measure' complied with the French court's orders through its voluntary actions, unrelated to the orders".

The dissenting judgment recognised the "horrors of the Holocaust and the scourge of anti-Semitism, and France's understandable interest in protecting its citizens from those who would defend or glorify either",[270] but did not question the validity of the French orders on French soil. However, in strong words, the dissenting judgment stated that the majority, after properly opening the door to the federal courthouse by upholding personal jurisdiction, nonetheless turns a blind eye to the constitutional free speech interests of Yahoo!, throwing the case out of court because those interests are "not ripe for adjudication".[271] According to the dissenting judgment:

> [the majority's decision] leaves in place a foreign country's vague and overbroad judgment mandating a US company to bar access to prohibited content by Internet users from that country. This astonishing result is itself the strongest argument for finding Yahoo!'s claims ripe for adjudication.[272]

The dissenting members of the court further questioned whether it should be assumed that "US-based Internet service providers are now the policing agencies for whatever content another country wants to keep from those within its territorial borders – such as, for example, controversial views on democracy, religion or the status of women?"[273] The dissent concluded by stating that US courts "should not allow a foreign court order to be used as leverage to quash consti-

---

268. Yahoo!, ibid. at 1223.
269. Ibid. at 1224.
270. Ibid. at 1234. See also EUMC working paper, *Antisemitism: Summary overview of the situation in the European Union 2001-2005* (May 2006), online EUMC http://eumc.europa.eu/.
271. Ibid. at p. 1252.
272. Ibid.
273. Ibid.

tutionally protected speech by denying the United States-based target an adjudication of its constitutional rights in federal court".[274]

In May 2006, the US Supreme Court decided not to consider the Yahoo! case following an appeal by the two French associations arguing that the ruling leaves the door open for Yahoo! to try to use US courts to avoid judgments from courts in other countries. [275]

The Yahoo! case is an example of nation states' desire to enforce and apply national laws to a global and multinational medium. With the advancement of new technologies such as the Internet, cultural, moral, religious, historical and legal differences become more pronounced. While such differences are legitimate and acceptable, enforcement of such local and national standards to a company based in another country remains inherently problematic as was witnessed by the long saga of the Yahoo! legal dispute across two continents over a period of six years.

Zündel case (Canada/Germany)

Ernst Zündel, a German citizen who lived in Canada until his deportation in February 2005, is one of the "world's most prominent distributors of revisionist neo-Nazi propaganda through the use of facsimiles, courier, telephone, mail, media, shortwave radio transmissions, satellite videos and the Internet, through his website the Zundelsite".[276] In 1997, the Canadian Human Rights Tribunal[277] heard a complaint brought against Zündel and his website Zundelsite,[278] which was located on a server in the United States at the time.

Among the principal issues that the tribunal was called upon to decide was whether the website, in denying the Holocaust,[279] promoted hatred, and whether Zündel could be said to control the site given that it was physically located outside of Canada. It was alleged that by posting material to the Zundelsite, Zündel caused repeated telephonic communication that was likely to expose Jews to hatred or contempt. The tribunal was asked to determine whether it was a discriminatory practice to post material on a website if the material was likely to expose a person to hatred or contempt. Further, the tribunal was asked to consider

---

274. Ibid.

275. *Yahoo! Inc. v. La Ligue Contre Le Racisme et L'antisemitisme*, 433 F.3d 1199 (9th Cir. 2006), certiorari denied, 126 S. Ct. 2332 (2006); see also "Supreme Court won't consider Yahoo! case", Associated Press, 12 May 2006.

276. *Re Zündel* (2005), 251 D.L.R. (4th) 511 at para. 23, 2005 FC 295 (T.D.).

277. See www.chrc-ccdp.ca/default-en.asp. With regard to the activities of the Canadian Human Rights Commission, note the report entitled *Hate on the Net* (Ottawa: Association for Canadian Studies, Spring 2006) at www.chrc-ccdp.ca/pdf/hateoninternet_bil.pdf.

278. See www.zundelsite.org.

279. See generally Robert A. Kahn, *Holocaust Denial and the Law: A Comparative Study* (New York: Palgrave Macmillan, 2004). See also *R. v. Zündel* [1992] 2 S.C.R. 731; and Robert A. Kahn, "Rebuttal versus Unmasking: Legal Strategy in *R. v. Zündel*" (2000) 34(3) Institute for Jewish Policy Research 3.

what limits, if any, were to be applied to repeated communication of hate messages via the Internet. Finally, if these limits applied to the Internet, whether this would be a permissible restriction on freedom of speech under the Canadian Charter of Rights and Freedoms.[280] The original complaints were made in 1996 but the case proceeded very slowly and it took almost six years for the tribunal to bring this case to an end. A decision was finally published in January 2002.[281]

The tribunal referred to a number of previous cases and studies which found that hate propaganda poses a "serious threat to society".[282] The tribunal ordered that Zündel, and any other individuals who act in his name or in concert with him, cease to communicate telephonically content of the type contained on the Zundelsite, contrary to section 13(1) of the Canadian Human Rights Act.[283] In the view of the tribunal, the use of section 13(1) of the Act to deal with hateful telephonic messages on the Internet remains a restriction on the respondent's freedom of speech which is reasonable and justified in a free and democratic society.[284] In terms of the effect of the Internet to disseminate hatred, the tribunal stated that it was difficult "to see why the Internet, with its pervasive influence and accessibility, should be available to spread messages that are likely to expose persons to hatred or contempt. One can conceive that this new medium of the Internet is a much more effective and well-suited vehicle for the dissemination of hate propaganda".[285] The tribunal sent a clear message that hate could not be tolerated on the Internet or elsewhere. However, the Zundelsite continued to transmit through a server in the United States and continues to do so today.

---

280. Canadian Charter of Rights and Freedoms, Part I of the Constitution Act, 1982, being Schedule B to the Canada Act 1982 (UK), 1982, c. 11.

281. *Citron v. Zündel* (18 January 2002), T.D. 1/02, Canadian Human Rights Tribunal, at www.chrt-tcdp. gc.ca. See also: *Citron v. Zündel* (2000), 189 D.L.R. (4th) 131 (F.C.A.); and 195 D.L.R. (4th) 399 (F.C.A.); both involved administrative appeals during the course of the tribunal's consideration of the case. Similarly note also *Zündel v. Canada (Attorney General)* (T.D.), [1999] 4 F.C. 289 (T.D.).

282. See, e.g., *Canada (Human Rights Commission) v. Taylor*, [1990] 3 S.C.R. 892; see also *Report to the Minister of Justice of the Special Committee on Hate Propaganda in Canada* (Ottawa: Queen's Printer, 1966); see generally Philip Rosen, *Hate Propaganda in Current Issue Review 85-6E* (Ottawa: Canadian Parliamentary Research Branch, 2000), at www.parl.gc.ca/information/library /PRBpubs/856-e.pdf.

283. *Canadian Human Rights Act*, R.S.C. 1985, c. H-6, s. 13(1):
It is a discriminatory practice for a person or a group of persons acting in concert to communicate telephonically or to cause to be so communicated, repeatedly, in whole or in part by means of the facilities of a telecommunication undertaking within the legislative authority of Parliament, any matter that is likely to expose a person or persons to hatred or contempt by reason of the fact that that person or those persons are identifiable on the basis of a prohibited ground of discrimination.

284. See further Monette Maillet, "Hate Message Complaints and Human Rights Tribunal Hearings" in *Hate on the Net* (Ottawa: Association for Canadian Studies, Spring 2006) 78, at www.chrc-ccdp.ca/pdf/hateoninternet_bil.pdf.

285. See also: *Schnell v. Machiavelli and Associates Emprize Inc.* (20 August 2002) T.D. 11/02 (CHRT) [Schnell]; *Warman v. Kyburz* (9 May 2003) 2003 CHRT 18; and *Warman v. Warman* (23 September 2005) 2005 CHRT 36.

In the later case of *Warman v. Kyburz*, the Canadian Human Rights Tribunal rightly assessed that "the unique nature of Internet technology, including the jurisdictional challenges arising from the borderless world of cyberspace, as well as the 'moving targets' created by the use of mirror sites, raise real concerns as to the efficacy of cease and desist orders in relation to hate messages disseminated on the Internet".[286] Despite these difficulties and technical challenges, a "cease and desist order can have both a practical and symbolic effect".[287] Such a decision prevents (albeit not always successfully) the individuals or organisations concerned from continuing to publish material of a racist nature. Apart from trying to prevent and eliminate discriminatory practices, such a decision also has a significant symbolic value in the public denunciation of such actions, as well as enabling the open discussion of the principles enunciated therein.

As for Ernst Zündel, he moved to the United States in 2000, but was deported back to Canada in 2003 for alleged immigration violations. He was declared a national security threat by a Canadian Federal Court and was deported to Germany in February 2005.[288] Zündel was charged with inciting racial hatred, libel and disparaging the dead before the State Court in the south-western city of Mannheim,[289] and was sentenced to a five-year prison term in February 2007.[290] In a parallel development, David Irving, a well-known British Holocaust denier who also publishes his thoughts on this subject, was arrested in November 2005 in Austria on a warrant issued in 1989 under Austrian laws that make it a crime to deny the Holocaust.[291] Irving was sentenced to three years' imprisonment in February 2006.[292]

---

286. Kyburz, ibid. at para. 81. For Canadian Human Rights Tribunal decisions in Internet-related cases see further: *Warman v. Harrison* (15 August 2006) 2006 CHRT 30; *Warman v. Kulbashian* (10 March 2006) 2006 CHRT 11; *Warman v. Winnicki* (13 April 2006) 2006 CHRT 20; *Schnell*, ibid.; and *Warman*, ibid.

287. Harrison, ibid. at paras. 71-72.

288. Zündel made an unsuccessful complaint under Article 14 of the International Covenant on Civil and Political Rights (right to a fair trial) to the UN Human Rights Committee with regard to his deportation from Canada: *Zündel v Canada*, Admissibility, UN Doc CCPR/C/89/D/1341/2005; IHRL 2614 (UNHRC 2007); (2007) 10 IHRR 921, 20 March 2007.

289. Anthony Long, "Forgetting the Fuhrer: The recent history of the Holocaust denial movement in Germany" (2002) 48(1) *Australian Journal of Politics & History* 72.

290. See "5-year prison term urged for Holocaust denier", Associated Press, 26 January 2007.

291. See "Irving faces week in Austria cell", *BBC News*, 18 November 2005; and "Austria Arrests David Irving, Writer Known as a Holocaust Denier", *The New York Times*, 18 November 2005.

292. See "Irving jailed for 3 years after denying Holocaust", *The Daily Telegraph*, 21 February 2006; "Irving jailed for denying Holocaust: Three years for British historian who described Auschwitz as a fairytale", *The Guardian*, 21 February 2006; and "Irving gets three years' jail in Austria for Holocaust denial", *The Independent*, 21 February 2006. Note that David Irving was also convicted in Germany in 1993 of insulting the memory of the dead, for describing the Auschwitz I gas chamber as an *Attrappe* ("fake") at a rally on 21 April 1990, in the *Löwenbräukeller* in Munich. See Anthony Long, "Forgetting the Fuhrer: The recent history of the Holocaust denial movement in Germany" (2002) 48(1) *Australian Journal of Politics & History* 72, at 83. Note further *International Herald Tribune*, "Germany continues to prosecute individuals who deny the Holocaust", 8 October 2008.

Töben case (Australia/Germany)

Dr Fredrick Töben, a German-born Australian Holocaust revisionist who denies the existence of the Holocaust,[293] maintains the Adelaide Institute website[294] in Australia. A complaint lodged by the Executive Council of Australian Jewry (ECAJ) about the Adelaide Institute's website was heard by the Australian Human Rights and Equal Opportunity Commission (HREOC) in November 1998.[295] The material on the Adelaide Institute website was deemed to be in breach of section 18(c) of the Australian Racial Discrimination Act 1975[296] by the HREOC in October 2000 because its content denied the existence of the Holocaust and vilified Jewish people.[297]

The material posted on the Adelaide Institute website by Töben cast doubt on the Holocaust, and "suggested that homicidal gas chambers at Auschwitz were unlikely and that some Jewish people, for improper purposes including financial gain, had exaggerated the number of Jews killed during World War II".[298] The Commission's decision was never enforced, but in 2002, an Australian Federal Court agreed with that decision and ordered Töben to remove the content in question from his website.[299] The court was satisfied that Töben had published material on the World Wide Web which was reasonably likely, in all the circumstances, to offend, insult, humiliate and intimidate Jewish Australians or a group of Jewish Australians. As Branson J stated, it was "more probable than not that the material would engender in Jewish Australians a sense of being treated contemptuously, disrespectfully and offensively".[300] The court deliberated for some fourteen months before making this ruling, and Töben did not file any defence.

The Federal Court made orders requiring Töben to remove the offending material, as well as any other material substantially similar to the offending material, from all websites controlled by him or the Adelaide Institute, and not to publish or republish such material again. Töben appealed and in June 2003 the Full Court of the Federal Court of Australia held that Part IIA of the Racial Discrimination Act 1975 which deals with prohibiting offensive behaviour based on racial hatred was constitutionally valid as an exercise of the external affairs power:

---

293. For a detailed history of the Holocaust denial movement see Kenneth S. Stern, *Holocaust Denial* (1993), at American Jewish Committee www.ajc.org.

294. See www.adelaideinstitute.org.

295. "Jewish group seeking apology over website material", *AAP Newsfeed*, 2 November 1998.

296. Racial Discrimination Act 1975 (Cth.).

297. *Jones v. Töben*, 5 October 2000, Australian Human Rights and Equal Opportunity Commission, Case No. H97/120.

298. See Australian Race Discrimination Commissioner, *Racism and the Internet: Review of the operation of Schedule 5, Broadcasting Services Act 1992*, November 2002, online Australian Department of Communications, Information Technology and the Arts, at www.dcita.gov.au/.

299. *Jones v. Töben* [2002] FCA 1150, at www.austlii.edu.au/au/cases/cth/federal_ct/2002/1150.html.

300. Ibid. at para. 93.

In my opinion it is clearly consistent with the provisions of the [International Convention on the Elimination of all forms of Racial Discrimination] and the ICCPR that a State party should legislate to "nip in the bud" the doing of offensive, insulting, humiliating or intimidating public acts which are done because of race, colour or national or ethnic origin before such acts can go into incitement or promotion of racial hatred or discrimination. The authorities show that, subject to the requisite connection [with the external affairs power], it is for the legislature to choose the means by which it carries into or gives effect to a treaty. [301]

It is worth noting that Töben was previously prosecuted and imprisoned in Germany in December 2000 by the German Bundesgerichtshof (Federal High Court) for publishing the same material on the Adelaide Institute website.[302] To accomplish this, the German Federal High Court had to reverse a lower court decision which held that Töben could not be convicted under the law against inciting racial hatred because the inciting material existed on a foreign website. Töben was arrested in Germany[303] while attending a conference, and neither his Australian citizenship nor the fact that his web server was located in Australia served as a defence. The Bundesgerichtshof concluded that German laws banning the Nazi party and any glorification of it could be applied to Internet content originating outside German borders but accessed from within Germany, and in particular to the content on Töben's website.[304] Töben commented that Germany was "trying to rule the world again by saying that the people who access the Internet have no choice. If someone is offended by the material, they can switch off."[305] Töben was sentenced to ten months' imprisonment "for the offences of criminal defamation, several counts of disparaging the memory of the dead and of inciting the populace".[306]

---

301. *Töben v. Jones* [2003] FCAFC 137, at www.austlii.edu.au/au/cases/cth/FCAFC/2003/137.html. See further Australian Human Rights and Equal Opportunity Commission, *Change and Continuity: Review of the Federal Unlawful Discrimination Jurisdiction: Supplement September 2002 - August 2003* (Sydney, 2003), Carr J. at p. 2.

302. See Steve Gold, "German Landmark Nazi Ruling", *Newsbytes News Network* (12 December 2000). Note also that in another similar case American neo-Nazi Gary Lauck was jailed for four years in Hamburg after a court convicted him in 1996 of inciting racial hatred for sending anti-Semitic literature to Germany for many years; see "History's rewriter faces German jail", *The Australian*, 8 July 1999.

303. An English copy of the arrest warrant for Dr Fredrick Töben is available at www.ihr.org/. See further "Australian historian arrested in Germany for disputing Holocaust", Agence France Presse, 9 April 1999.

304. See Review of Reports, Studies and Other Documentation for the Preparatory Committee and the World Conference: Report of the High Commissioner for Human Rights on the use of the Internet for purposes of incitement to racial hatred, racist propaganda and xenophobia, and on ways of promoting international cooperation in this area, UN GAOR, UN Doc. A/CONF.189/PC.2/12 (2001).

305. See "Neo-Nazis Sheltering Web Sites In the US; German Courts Begin International Pursuit", *The Washington Post*, 21 December 2000.

306. See Greg Taylor, "Casting the Net Too Widely: Racial Hatred on the Internet" (2001) *Criminal Law Journal* 262. See further German Criminal Code, StGB, ss. 130(1),(3). For the German decision see Bundesgerichtshof, Urteil 12 December 2000 – 1 StR 184/00.

On 1 October 2008, Töben was arrested at Heathrow airport in London as he travelled from America to Dubai because of a pending European arrest warrant issued by the German authorities. The warrant was issued because of Töben's writings on his website denying the existence of the Holocaust.[307] German prosecutors were forced to appeal to the High Court of Justice after the District Judge at the City of Westminster Court ruled that the warrant was not valid as it was vague and imprecise, and did not say where and when Töben was alleged to have committed the offence of Holocaust denial. The arrest warrant simply referred to "worldwide Internet publications" and alleged that "the offender is committing the acts in Australia, Germany and in other countries".[308] District Judge Daphne Wickham said that Töben "would be released on bail if he could lodge £100 000 as 'security' with the court".[309] Töben's arrest in London attracted criticism as denial of the Holocaust is not criminalised in the UK. According to the London *Times*, "attempts to extradite him were seen by many as an assault on free speech".[310] Töben's lawyer argued that "the offence is not made out in the UK. If Dr Töben had been extradited back to Germany for Holocaust denial, which does not exist as an offence in this country, then we would have found ourselves in a situation where hypothetically, the Iranian Government could have asked for all the gay Iranian asylum seekers to be extradited back to Iran."[311] On 19 November 2008, Töben was released after the German Government gave up its legal battle to extradite him from Britain, and the appeal was withdrawn.[312]

Conclusion: limitations of national legal systems are evident

These examples reflect the complex nature of the Internet as well as the limitations of the application of existing laws to the Internet. New communication technologies challenge the territoriality notion of nation states[313] as the Internet does not respect boundaries[314] to the effect that no single nation state can effectively dominate or control the Internet by means of unilateral state regulation.[315]

---

307. *The Daily Telegraph*, "Alleged Holocaust denier allowed bail", 29 October 2008; BBC News, "Holocaust key to extradition case", 3 October 2008, at http://news.bbc.co.uk/1/hi/uk/7648980.stm.
308. Rozenberg, J., "Alleged Holocaust denier released", *The Daily Telegraph*, 21 November 2008.
309. Ibid.
310. *The Times*, "Holocaust denier Fredrick Töben wins German extradition fight", 20 November 2008.
311. Ibid.
312. See *District Court of Mannheim Germany v. Töben* (2008), Latham LJ, Blair J, Case No. CO/8582/2008, date: 24/11/2008.
313. See generally Christo Pierson, *The Modern State* (London: Routledge, 1996) at 5-35; Francis Harry Hinsley, *Sovereignty*, 2nd edn (Cambridge: Cambridge University Press, 1986) pp. 1-26; Max Weber, "Politics as vocation" in Hans Heinrich Gerth and Charles Wright Mills, eds., *From Max Weber* (London: Routledge, 1970) at p. 78; and David Held, *Democracy and the Global Order* (Cambridge: Polity, 1995) at p. 66.
314. See generally Brian Kahin and Charles Nesson, eds, *Borders in Cyberspace: Information Policy and Global Information Infrastructure* (Cambridge, Mass.: MIT Press, 1997).
315. See Goldsmith, J., "Unilateral Regulation of the Internet: A Modest Defence" (2000) 11 *EJIL* 135.

According to Castells, nation states are losing their capacity to govern due to the "globalisation of core economic activities, globalisation of media and electronic communication, and globalisation of crime".[316] This is also true for the governance of the Internet by individual nation states.

As outlined in this chapter, the effectiveness and application of state laws have been problematic in terms of encountering hate speech and racist content on the Internet. Court cases involving the prosecution of individuals who disseminate and publish racist content reflect the complex nature of the Internet as well as the limitations of the application of existing laws to the Internet. Internet and new communications technologies challenge the notion of nation state as the Internet does not respect territories, and has no boundaries to the effect that no single nation state can effectively dominate or control the Internet by means of unilateral state regulation.[317] It should be noted that the "Zündel saga" took nearly five years to be finalised in Canada.[318] Zündel was charged in Germany in relation to his website after he was extradited from Canada and was sentenced to a five-year prison term in February 2007.[319] Despite a Canadian order to stop the dissemination of such views through his website, and despite his imprisonment in Germany, Zündel's website is still up and running from Texas, USA, and is regularly updated with Zündel's "letters from prison". The Töben case[320] involving Holocaust denial was a similarly drawn-out affair in Australia and Töben's carefully drafted website is still active and regularly updated. On the same note, various cases related to Yahoo! in France and the US were initiated in 2000, and only came to a conclusion in May 2006 after almost six years.[321] Similarly, today Redwatch, which came to the attention of the British Home Office in 2003, still

---

316. See Manuel Castells, *The Power of Identity* (Vol. II of *The Information Age: Economy, Society and Culture*) (Oxford: Blackwell Publishers, 1997) pp. 244-62.

317. See Goldsmith, J., "Unilateral Regulation of the Internet: A Modest Defence", *European Journal of International Law* 11 (2000), 135-148.

318. *Sabina Citron Toronto Mayor's Committee on Community and Race Relations and Canadian Human Rights Commission v. Ernst Zündel*, Canadian Human Rights Tribunal, T.D. ½ 18/01/2002, at www.chrt-tcdp.gc.ca/.

319. Associated Press, "5-year prison term urged for Holocaust denier", 26 January 2007.

320. *Jones v. Töben*, Federal Court of Australia, [2002] FCA 1150. The decision can be accessed at www.austlii.edu.au/au/cases/cth/federal_ct/2002/1150.html; *Töben v. Jones* [2003] FCAFC 137 (27 June 2003). Töben was also prosecuted and imprisoned in Germany in relation to his website. In relation to Töben's Germany prosecution see Gold, S., "German Landmark Nazi Ruling," *Newsbytes*, 12 December 2000. See further Agence France Presse, "Australian historian arrested in Germany for disputing Holocaust", 9 April 1999. For the German decision see Bundesgerichtshof, Urteil 12 December 2000 - 1 StR 184/00.

321. Trib. gr. inst. Paris, 20 November 2000, *League Against Racism and Anti-Semitism (LICRA), French Union of Jewish Students v. Yahoo! Inc. (USA), Yahoo! France* (Interim Court Order), at www.cdt.org/. For the US cases see *Yahoo! Inc. v. La Ligue Contre Le Racisme et L'antisémitisme*, 169 F.Supp.2d 1181 (N.D. Cal. 2001); *Yahoo! Inc. v. La Ligue Contre Le Racisme et L'antisémitisme*, 379 F.3d 1120 (9th Cir. 2004); *Yahoo! Inc. v. La Ligue Contre Le Racisme et L'Antisémitisme*, 399 F.3d 1010 (9th Cir. 2005); *Yahoo! Inc. v. La Ligue Contre Le Racisme et L'antisémitisme*, 433 F.3d 1199 (9th Cir. 2006).

publishes lists and personal information about individuals who attend anti-fascist public demonstrations.

The legal system which is more adapted to deal with one-off traditional publications (such as newspapers and magazines) has been extremely slow in dealing with web-based publications and ubiquitous Internet content. While the circulation of one-off publications such as books, newspapers, and magazines can be controlled by confiscation and gagging orders or by general bans which prohibit the delivery or entry of such material, the same results cannot be achieved with web-based publications. Basically, websites cannot be torched or confiscated, or taken down, especially if the servers that contain them are physically located in another jurisdiction. The above-mentioned cases illustrate that the emergence of Internet governance entails a more diverse and fragmented regulatory network with no presumption that these will be anchored primarily in nation states.

A shift from unilateral state regulation into various forms and models of governance will almost inevitably be witnessed in the future and this will encompass alternatives to state regulation or additional forms of regulation such as self-regulation, co-regulation, or a mixture of these within future policies of states and international organisations. Such an approach is supported at the international level as was previously established in this book.[322] Increasingly, effective rule-making will not be confined to a single nation state due to the influence and impact of supranational and international developments and agreements and also due to the global and decentralised nature of the medium itself. This reality is reflected in attempts by supranational organisations such as the European Union, regional international organisations including the Council of Europe, and OSCE, as well as global international organisations including the United Nations, to develop harmonised policies. These supranational and international efforts to address the problem of racist Internet content and hate speech will be discussed in the next chapter of this book.

---

322. World Information Society Report 2007 at www.itu.int/. Note "Implementing the WSIS Outcomes" chapter at www.itu.int/. Note further WSIS Outcome Documents 2003-2005 at www.itu.int/. See further UN ICT Task Force Series 5 – Internet Governance: A Grand Collaboration, September 2004, available through www.unicttf.org. Note also the website of the United Nations Information and Communication Technologies Task Force at www.unicttf.org/ as well as the WSIS (World Summit on the Information Society) pages at www.itu.int/wsis/.

5.   Pan-European initiatives

This chapter will provide an overview of policy developments and initiatives across the pan-European region.

Developments at the Council of Europe, the European Union and the Organization for Security and Co-operation in Europe levels with regards to combating racist Internet content will be assessed in this chapter. As will be seen below, policy initiatives include regulatory as well as non-regulatory solutions aimed at addressing the problem of racist content and hate speech on the Internet.

Developments at the Council of Europe level

The Council of Europe[323] was the first international organisation to be founded in Europe after the Second World War and its main role is to strengthen democracy, human rights and the rule of law throughout its member states.

In 1996, ECRI called on the Council of Europe member states to ensure that national criminal, civil and administrative law expressly and specifically counters racism, xenophobia, anti-Semitism and intolerance.[324] In particular, ECRI asked for such law to cover oral, written, audio-visual expressions and other forms of expression, including the electronic media, and to criminalise incitement to hatred, discrimination or violence against racial, ethnic, national or religious groups or against their members on the grounds that they belong to such a group. The offences, according to ECRI, should also cover the production and distribution of such material.

In October 1997 the Committee of Ministers of the Council of Europe adopted a recommendation on "hate speech".[325] The recommendation originated in the Council of Europe's desire to take action against racism and intolerance, and the Committee of Ministers recommended that the member states' governments be guided by certain principles in their action to combat hate speech. In December 2002 ECRI adopted a recommendation on key components which should feature in the national legislation of member states of the Council of Europe in order for

---

323. See www.coe.int.
324. ECRI General Policy Recommendation No. 1: Combating racism, xenophobia, antisemitism and intolerance, adopted by ECRI on 4 October 1996, CRI (96) 43 rev.
325. Recommendation No. R (97) 20 on "hate speech".

racism and racial discrimination to be combated effectively.[326] ECRI recommended that the laws of the member states should penalise the intentional commitment of public incitement to violence, hatred or discrimination, public insults and defamation, or threats against a person or a grouping of persons on the grounds of their race, colour, language, religion, nationality, or national or ethnic origin.

In addition to the broader recommendations, deeply concerned with the growing problem of racist content and hate speech on the Internet, ECRI issued a general policy recommendation on combating the dissemination of racist, xenophobic and antisemitic material via the Internet in December 2000.[327] ECRI recommended that the member states of the Council of Europe ensure that relevant national legislation also applies to racist, xenophobic and anti-Semitic offences committed via the Internet and prosecute those responsible for these kinds of offence. Within this context, ECRI also recommended the clarification of the responsibility of content host and content provider and site publishers as a result of the dissemination of racist, xenophobic and anti-Semitic content over the Internet. ECRI also recommended the support of the self-regulatory measures taken by the Internet industry to combat racism, xenophobia and anti-Semitism on the Internet, such as anti-racist hotlines, codes of conduct and filtering software, and encouraged further research in this area.

However, these important recommendations were not necessarily followed by all member states of the Council of Europe, and the different approaches adopted at the state level to encounter racist content and hate speech led the Council of Europe to develop a harmonised policy to address these differences through of an Additional Protocol to the 2001 Convention on Cybercrime concerning the criminalisation of acts of a racist and xenophobic nature committed through computer systems.[328] The Convention on Cybercrime as well as the additional protocol will be discussed below.

Council of Europe Convention on Cybercrime

The Convention on Cybercrime (ETS No. 185) is the first international treaty to address criminal law and procedural aspects of various types of offending behaviour directed against computer systems, networks or data in addition to

---

326. ECRI General Policy Recommendation No. 7: National legislation to combat racism and racial discrimination, CRI(2003)8, adopted by ECRI on 13 December 2002.

327. ECRI General Policy Recommendation No. 6: Combating the dissemination of racist, xenophobic and antisemitic material via the Internet, CRI (2001) 1, adopted by ECRI on 15 December 2000.

328. See ETS No. 189 at http://conventions.coe.int. Note also Akdeniz, Y., *An Advocacy Handbook for the Non Governmental Organisations: The Council of Europe's Cyber-Crime Convention 2001 and the additional protocol on the criminalisation of acts of a racist or xenophobic nature committed through computer systems*, Cyber-Rights & Cyber-Liberties, December 2003 (revised and updated in February 2007), at www.cyber-rights.org/cybercrime/coe_handbook_crcl.pdf.

content-related crimes. It was finalised by the Council of Europe, and opened for accession by its member states in November 2001. A Committee of Experts on Crime in Cyberspace (PC-CY) was established within the Council of Europe aiming to draw up the Convention on Cybercrime to fight, *inter alia*, substantive offences committed through the use of the Internet in 1997.[329] Initially, the Council of Europe released the draft version of the Convention on Cybercrime[330] for public discussion in order to enhance the consultation process with interested parties in April 2000.[331] A number of non-member states such as the US, Canada, Japan, and South Africa also contributed to the development of the convention[332] through the PC-CY Committee.

In general, the convention aims to harmonise national legislation in this field, facilitate investigations and allow efficient levels of co-operation between the authorities of different member states of the Council of Europe and other third party states who would be signing the convention. It builds upon the previous work of the Council of Europe in relation to computer-related crimes,[333] but also expands upon it and would be binding on signing states when the ratification process is completed at the national level.

The substantive criminal law measures of the Convention on Cybercrime include offences[334] involving intentional illegal access of computer systems,[335] intentional illegal interception of non-public transmissions of computer data,[336] any intentional interference with computer data including deletion or alteration,[337] any intentional interference with a computer system,[338] misuse of certain devices designed or adapted primarily for the purpose of committing any of the offences established

---

329. European Commission, Interim report on Initiatives in EU Member States with respect to Combating Illegal and Harmful Content on the Internet, Version 7 (4 June 1997).

330. The text of the convention can be found at: http://conventions.coe.int.

331. Press release, Strasbourg, 27 April 2000.

332. The United States was invited to participate as an "observer" in both the 1989 and 1995 recommendations, as well as in the development of the Convention on Cybercrime. See Computer Crime and Intellectual Property Section (CCIPS) of the Criminal Division of the US Department of Justice, Frequently Asked Questions and Answers About the Council of Europe Convention on Cybercrime (Final Draft, released 29 June 2001), at: www.cybercrime.gov/.

333. Council of Europe Committee of Ministers, Recommendation No. R(89)9 of the Committee of Ministers to Member States on Computer-Related Crime (adopted by the Committee of Ministers on 13 September 1989 at the 428th meeting of the Ministers' Deputies), at www.coe.int/t/cm; Council of Europe Committee of Ministers, Recommendation No. R(95)13 of the Committee of Ministers to Member States Concerning Problems of Criminal Procedural Law Connected with Information Technology (adopted by the Committee of Ministers on 11 September 1995 at the 543rd meeting of the Ministers' Deputies), at www.coe.int/t/cm.

334. Attempt and aiding or abetting of the offences within Articles 2–10 are covered within Article 11.

335. Article 2, Convention on Cybercrime.

336. Article 3.

337. Article 4.

338. Article 5.

in accordance with Articles 2-5 of the convention,[339] and the possession of such devices with an intent to committing of such offences.[340] Moreover, the convention includes computer-related crimes such as forgery,[341] fraud,[342] and content-related offences such as child pornography.[343] Offences related to infringements of copyright and related rights are also included within the convention.[344]

The procedural law measures of the convention include conditions and safeguards,[345] expedited preservation of stored computer data,[346] expedited preservation and partial disclosure of traffic data,[347] production orders for law enforcement agencies for accessing data,[348] the search and seizure of stored computer data,[349] real-time collection of traffic data,[350] interception of content data,[351] extradition,[352] principles relating to mutual assistance,[353] and the creation of a 24/7 network of law enforcement points of contact.[354]

Following the first five ratifications, the Convention on Cybercrime came into force on 1 July 2004. The signing and ratification process for the Convention on Cybercrime has so far resulted in 42 member states (plus the external supporters the United States, Canada, South Africa, Japan and Montenegro) signing and 26 countries (Albania, Armenia, Bosnia and Herzegovina, Bulgaria, Croatia, Cyprus, Denmark, Estonia, Finland, France, Germany, Hungary, Iceland, Italy, Latvia, Lithuania, Moldova, the Netherlands, Norway, Romania, Serbia, Slovakia, Slovenia, Ukraine, the United States of America,[355] and "the former Yugoslav Republic of Macedonia") ratifying the convention as of June 2009 out of the potential 50 countries (47 Council of Europe member states plus the above-mentioned external supporters).[356] Andorra,

---

339. Article 6.
340. Article 6(1)(b).
341. Article 7.
342. Article 8.
343. Article 9.
344. Article 10.
345. Article 15.
346. Article 16.
347. Article 17.
348. Article 18.
349. Article 19.
350. Article 20.
351. Article 21.
352. Article 24.
353. Articles 25–34.
354. Article 35.
355. The US Senate approved the ratification of the Convention on Cybercrime on 3 August 2006. See CNet News, 5 August 2006, at http://news.com.com/.
356. See generally Akdeniz, Y., *An Advocacy Handbook for the Non Governmental Organisations: The Council of Europe's Cyber-Crime Convention 2001 and the additional protocol on the criminalisation of acts of a racist or xenophobic nature committed through computer systems*, Cyber-Rights & Cyber-Liberties, December 2003 (updated May 2008), at www.cyber-rights.org.

Liechtenstein, Monaco, Russia, San Marino and Turkey are the member states which have yet to sign the convention, and 18 Council of Europe member states who signed the convention have yet to ratify.

Additional Protocol concerning the criminalisation of acts of a racist and xenophobic nature committed through computer systems

In 1997, a recommendation of the Committee of Ministers of the Council of Europe on hate speech called upon member states "to take appropriate steps to combat hate speech by ensuring that such steps form part of a comprehensive approach to the phenomenon which also targets its social, economic, political, cultural, and other root causes".[357] Parallel to this political call, the committee drafting the Convention on Cybercrime discussed the possibility of including content-related offences other than child pornography within the convention such as the distribution of racist propaganda through computer systems. As there was no consensus on the inclusion of provisions involving the criminalisation of acts of a racist and xenophobic nature committed through computer systems, these were left out of the Convention on Cybercrime 2001. While European states such as France and Germany strongly supported inclusion, the United States of America, which has been influential in the development of the main Convention on Cybercrime, opposed the inclusion of speech-related provisions apart from child pornography.

Noting the complexity of the issue, the committee drafting the Convention on Cybercrime decided that the committee would refer to the European Committee on Crime Problems the issue of drafting an additional protocol to the convention.[358] The Parliamentary Assembly, in its Opinion 226 (2001) concerning the convention, recommended the immediate development of an additional protocol to the convention under the title "Broadening the scope of the convention to include new forms of offence", with the purpose of defining and criminalising, *inter alia*, the dissemination of racist propaganda.[359] In its Recommendation 1543 (2001)[360] on Racism and Xenophobia in Cyberspace, the Parliamentary Assembly considered racism "not as an opinion but as a crime". The Parliamentary Assembly noted that such a protocol will "have no effect unless every state hosting racist sites or messages is a party to it".[361]

---

357. Recommendation on Hate Speech, No. R (97)20, adopted by the Committee of Ministers of the Council of Europe on 30 October 1997.

358. Explanatory Report of the Additional Protocol to the Convention on Cybercrime, concerning the criminalisation of acts of a racist and xenophobic nature committed through computer systems, as adopted by the Committee of Ministers on 7 November 2002, at http://conventions.coe.int/, para. 4.

359. Ibid., para. 5.

360. Text adopted by the Standing Committee, acting on behalf of the Assembly, on 8 November 2001.

361. Para. 4 of Recommendation 1543 (2001).

While formulating the additional protocol, the committee took into account several other legal instruments and policy initiatives at the international level including the International Convention on the Elimination of All Forms of Racial Discrimination (CERD), Protocol No. 12 (ETS No. 177) to the Convention for the Protection of Human Rights and Fundamental Freedoms, the Joint Action of 15 July 1996 of the European Union adopted by the Council of the European Union on the basis of Article K.3 of the Treaty on European Union concerning action to combat racism and xenophobia, the work of the UN in relation to the World Conference against Racism, Racial Discrimination, Xenophobia and Related Intolerance (Durban, 31 August to 8 September 2001), the conclusions of the European Conference against racism (Strasbourg, 13 October 2000), the comprehensive study published in August 2000 by ECRI,[362] and the 2001 EU draft Council Framework Decision on combating racism and xenophobia.[363]

Provisions of the additional protocol

The additional protocol concerning the criminalisation of acts of a racist and xenophobic nature committed through computer systems aims to harmonise substantive criminal law in the fight against racism and xenophobia on the Internet and to improve international co-operation in this area. The Council of Europe believes that a harmonised approach in domestic laws may prevent misuse of computer systems for a racist purpose. The explanatory memorandum to the additional protocol states that "this kind of harmonisation alleviates the fight against such crimes on the national and on the international level",[364] and that "corresponding offences in domestic laws may prevent misuse of computer systems for a racist purpose by Parties whose laws in this area are less well defined".[365] The additional protocol entails an extension of the Convention on Cybercrime's scope, "including its substantive, procedural and international co-operation provisions, so as to cover also offences of racist and xenophobic propaganda".[366] Thus, apart from harmonising the substantive law elements of such behaviour, the protocol aims at "improving the ability of the Parties to make use of the procedural provisions of the Convention on Cybercrime including international co-operation and mutual legal assistance".[367]

---

362. CRI(2000)27.
363. This draft Framework Decision was never agreed upon. See the amended version which is currently being discussed at the EU level: Draft Framework Decision: Council of the European Union, Proposal for a Council Framework Decision on combating certain forms and expressions of racism and xenophobia by means of criminal law, Document No. 11522/07, 19 July 2007.
364. Ibid., para. 3.
365. Ibid.
366. Ibid., para. 7.
367. Ibid.

The definition of "racist and xenophobic material" contained in Article 2(1) of the additional protocol intends to "build upon existing national and international (UN, EU) definitions and documents as far as possible"[368] and refers to written material (for example, texts, books, magazines, statements, messages, etc.), images (for example, pictures, photos, drawings, etc.) or any other representation of ideas or theories which advocates, promotes or incites hatred, discrimination or violence, against any individual or group of individuals, based on race, colour, descent or national or ethnic origin, as well as religion if used as a pretext for any of these factors in such a format that it can be stored, processed and transmitted by means of a computer system.[369] According to the explanatory report of the Additional Protocol the definition contained in Article 2 "refers to certain conduct to which the content of the material may lead, rather than to the expression of feelings/belief/aversion as contained in the material concerned".[370] The explanatory report also clarifies the meaning of the word "advocates" and states that it "refers to a plea in favour of hatred, discrimination or violence".[371] The word "promotes" "refers to an encouragement to or advancing hatred, discrimination or violence",[372] and the word "incites" "refers to urging others to hatred, discrimination or violence".[373] According to the report the term "violence" refers to the unlawful use of force, while the term "hatred" refers to intense dislike or enmity.[374]

Measures to be taken at national level are explained in Chapter II of the additional protocol. As in the Convention on Cybercrime, all the offences contained in the additional protocol must be committed "intentionally" for criminal liability to apply.

Article 3 – Dissemination of racist and xenophobic material through computer systems

Article 3, entitled "Dissemination of racist and xenophobic material through computer systems", requires parties to adopt such legislative and other measures as may be necessary to establish as criminal offences under domestic law the distribution or otherwise making available of racist and xenophobic material to the public[375] through a computer system. An active dissemination of racist and xenophobic material, for example, through publicly accessible chat rooms, news-groups, discussion groups, or Web 2.0 applications such as YouTube and Facebook

---

368. Para. 13 of the explanatory report.
369. Para. 12 of the explanatory report.
370. Para. 13 of the explanatory report.
371. Para. 14 of the explanatory report.
372. Ibid.
373. Ibid.
374. Para. 15 of the explanatory report.
375. According to Para. 29 of the explanatory report the term "to the public" used in Article 3 makes it clear that private communications or expressions communicated or transmitted through a computer system fall outside the scope of this provision.

is required for a distribution offence to take place and "making available" refers to the "placing on line of racist and xenophobic material for the use of others".[376] According to the explanatory report, making available offence would also cover the "creation or compilation of hyperlinks in order to facilitate access to such material".[377] Therefore, if a website or a blog provides links to websites which contain material of a racist and xenophobic nature as defined in the additional protocol, the author of that particular blog or owner of the website may also be committing an Article 3 offence. In any case, criminal conduct defined in Article 3 needs to be committed intentionally and without right. The "intention" requirement would limit the liability of a website owner or blogger if they did not knowingly provide links to websites that carry racist and xenophobic content. It is possible that at the time the links were provided the linked websites did not contain such content, but subsequently started carrying content which could be deemed illegal under Article 3. Furthermore, the "intention" requirement of Article 3 would also limit the liability of ISPs provided they act as a conduit but this would not, for example, exclude "notice-based liability" as introduced by the EU Directive on Electronic Commerce.[378]

Article 3(2) states that parties to the additional protocol may reserve the right not to attach criminal liability to conduct defined in Article 3, where the racist and xenophobic material advocates, promotes or incites discrimination that is not associated with hatred or violence, provided that other effective civil or administrative remedies are available. According to the explanatory report, where a party cannot, due to established principles of its legal system concerning freedom of expression, provide for such remedies,[379] it may reserve the right not to implement the obligation under Article 3(1), provided that it concerns only the advocating, promoting or inciting to discrimination, which is not associated to hatred or violence.[380]

Article 4 – Racist and xenophobic motivated threat

Article 4 requires parties to criminalise racist and xenophobic motivated threats through a computer system and, as in Article 3, such conduct needs to be committed intentionally and without right. In many states within the Council of Europe

---

376. Para. 28 of the explanatory report.

377. Ibid.

378. Directive 2000/31/EC of the European Parliament and of the Council of 8 June 2000 on certain legal aspects of information society services, in particular electronic commerce, in the Internal Market (Directive on Electronic Commerce), [2000] OJ L 178/1. EU Member States had until January 2002 to implement the Directive into national law. See generally EC Commission, First Report on the application of Directive 2000/31/EC of the European Parliament and of the Council of 8 June 2000 on certain legal aspects of information society services, in particular electronic commerce, in the Internal Market (Directive on Electronic Commerce), COM(2003) 702 final.

379. See Article 3(3) of the additional protocol.

380. Para. 32 of the explanatory report.

region threats are already criminalised but according to the explanatory memorandum the drafters wanted to stress that threats for racist and xenophobic motives should be criminalised.[381] In terms of guidance it was explained in the explanatory memorandum that the notion of "threat" may refer to "a menace which creates fear in the persons to whom the menace is directed, that they will suffer the commission of a serious criminal offence".[382] Parties to the additional protocol will decide what should constitute a serious criminal offence but examples given included offences affecting the life, personal security or integrity, serious damage to properties of the victim or their relatives. Article 4 requires that the racist and xenophobic motivated threats have to be addressed either to (i) a person for the reason that he or she belongs to a group, distinguished by race, colour, descent or national or ethnic origin, as well as religion, if used as a pretext for any of these factors, or to (ii) a group of persons which is distinguished by any of these characteristics. Unlike the previous section, there is no requirement that the threats are made in a public forum, and the Article 4 offence extends to threats by private communications such as through electronic mail.

Article 5 – Racist and xenophobic motivated insult

Article 5 requires parties to criminalise racist and xenophobic motivated insults made in public through computer systems. As in Article 4 the insult should be addressed to a person or a group of persons because they belong or are thought to belong to a group distinguished by specific characteristics. According to the explanatory memorandum, the notion of "insult" refers to "any offensive, contemptuous or invective expression which prejudices the honour or the dignity of a person".[383] Unlike Article 4, insults made in private communications are not covered by Article 5. Furthermore, with regard to racist and xenophobic motivated insults, Article 5(2)(i) allows parties to require that the conduct must also have the effect that the person or group of persons, not only potentially, but are also actually exposed to hatred, contempt or ridicule. Parties may enter reservations with regard to this particular offence including the right not to apply in whole or in part the offence of racist and xenophobic motivated insults.

Article 6 – Denial, gross minimisation, approval or justification of genocide or crimes against humanity

Article 6 requires the criminalisation of expressions which deny, grossly minimise, approve or justify acts constituting genocide or crimes against humanity as defined by international law and recognised as such by final and binding decisions of the International Military Tribunal, established by the London Agreement

---

381. Para. 33 of the explanatory report.
382. Para. 34 of the explanatory report.
383. Para. 36 of the explanatory report.

of 8 April 1945. The Council of Europe through the explanatory memorandum provided three reasons for criminalising this type of content, namely, these behaviours have inspired or stimulated and encouraged racist and xenophobic groups in their action, including through computer systems.[384] Furthermore, the expression of such ideas insults (the memory of) those persons who have been victims of such evil, as well as their relatives.[385] Finally, it threatens the dignity of the human community.[386]

The scope of Article 6 is not limited to the crimes committed by the Nazi regime during the Second World War and established as such by the Nuremberg Tribunal, but also to genocides and crimes against humanity established by other international courts set up since 1945 by relevant international legal instruments (such as United Nations Security Council resolutions, multilateral treaties, etc.). Such courts may be, for instance, the International Criminal Tribunals for the former Yugoslavia, for Rwanda, and also the Permanent International Criminal Court. The provision intends to make it clear that "facts of which the historical correctness has been established may not be denied, grossly minimised, approved or justified in order to support these detestable theories and ideas".[387]

This provision is supported by the European Court of Human Rights, which made it clear in its judgment in Lehideux and Isorni[388] that the denial or revision of "clearly established historical facts – such as the Holocaust (whose negation or revision) would be removed from the protection of Article 10 by Article 17" of the European Convention on Human Rights. The Court stated that "there is no doubt that, like any other remark directed against the Convention's underlying values,[389] the justification of a pro-Nazi policy could not be allowed to enjoy the protection afforded by Article 10".[390] The Court, and previously, the European Commission of Human Rights, have found in a number of cases that the freedom of expression guaranteed under Article 10 of the Convention may not be invoked

---

384. Para. 39 of the explanatory report.

385. Ibid.

386. Ibid.

387. Para. 41 of the explanatory report.

388. Judgment of 23 September 1998. Note within this context also *Garaudy v. France*, 24 June 2003, inadmissible, Application No. 65831/01.

389. See, *mutatis mutandis*, the *Jersild v. Denmark* judgment of 23 September 1994, Series A No. 298, p. 25, para. 35.

390. Note also that the United Nations Resolution rejected any denial of the Holocaust as an historical event, either in full or part, in October 2005. See UN General Assembly Resolution on Holocaust Remembrance, A/60/L.12, 26 October 2005. Additionally, on 26 January 2007, the UN General Assembly adopted Resolution No. A/RES/61/255 (GA/10569) condemning any denial of Holocaust (www.un.org).

in conflict with Article 17, in particular in cases concerning Holocaust denial and related issues.[391]

A party under Article 6(2) may either (a) require that the denial or the gross minimisation referred to in Article 6(1) is committed with the intent to incite hatred, discrimination or violence against any individual or group of individuals, based on race, colour, descent or national or ethnic origin, as well as religion if used as a pretext for any of these factors, or otherwise, or (b) reserve the right not to apply, in whole or in part, the Article 6 offence.

Article 7 – Aiding and abetting

The purpose of Article 7 is to criminalise aiding or abetting the commission of any of the offences under Articles 3-6. Aiding and abetting offences have to be committed intentionally. The provision would not cover the ISPs and they are not required to monitor content or actions of their customers to avoid criminal liability.

Signature and ratification process

The additional protocol was opened for signature in Strasbourg on 28 January 2003. Since then 34 member states have signed it (including the external supporters Canada and South Africa). Following the initial five ratifications the additional protocol came into force on 1 March 2006. However, only 14 member states (Albania, Armenia, Bosnia and Herzegovina, Croatia, Cyprus, Denmark, France,[392] Latvia, Lithuania, Norway, Serbia, Slovenia, Ukraine, and "the former Yugoslav Republic of Macedonia") have ratified the additional protocol as of June 2009, and the national laws implementing the additional protocol came into force during the last two years within these member states.

Furthermore, the Council of Europe Convention on the Prevention of Terrorism (CETS No. 196), which came into force in June 2007, provides for a harmonised

---

391. Note the cases of *Glimmerveen and J. Hagenbeek v. the Netherlands*, Nos. 8348/78 and 8406/78, Commission decision of 11 October 1979, Decisions and Reports (DR) 18, p. 187; *Kühnen v. Germany*, No. 12194/86, Commission decision of 12 May 1988, DR 56, p. 205; *B.H., M.W., H.P. and G.K. v. Austria*, No. 12774/87, Commission decision of 12 October 1989, DR 62, p. 216; *Ochsenberger v. Austria*, No. 21318/93, Commission decision of 2 September 1994; *Walendy v. Germany*, No. 21128/92, Commission decision of 11 January 1995, DR 80, p. 94; *Remer v. Germany*, No. 25096/94, Commission decision of 6 September 1995, DR 82, p. 117; *Honsik v. Austria*, No. 25062/94, Commission decision of 18 October 1995, DR 83-A, p. 77; *Nationaldemokratische Partei Deutschlands, Bezirksverband München-Oberbayern v. Germany*, No. 25992/94, Commission decision of 29 November 1995, DR 84, p. 149; *Rebhandel v. Austria*, No. 24398/94, Commission decision of 16 January 1996; *Nachtmann v. Austria*, No. 36773/97, Commission decision of 9 September 1998; *Witzsch v. Germany* (dec.), No. 41448/98, 20 April 1999; *Schimanek v. Austria* (dec.), No. 32307/96, 1 February 2000; *Garaudy v. France* (dec.), No. 65831/01, ECHR 2003-IX; *Norwood v. the United Kingdom* (dec.), 23131/03, 16 November 2004.

392. France ratified the additional protocol on 10 January 2006, which came into force on 1 May 2006.

legal basis to fight the use of the Internet as a means for public provocation to commit terrorist offences,[393] recruitment for terrorism,[394] and training for terrorism[395] including through the Internet. Therefore, if signed and ratified by the member states, the distribution and publication of certain types of content deemed to be related to terrorist activity could be criminalised. While 43 member states signed the convention, 20 of them ratified it as of June 2009.

Developments at the European Union level

The European Union has been committed to combat any form of racism, anti-Semitism and xenophobia, and believes that racism and xenophobia are direct violations of the principles of liberty, democracy, respect for human rights and fundamental freedoms and the rule of law, principles upon which the European Union is founded and which are common to the member states.[396] The European Parliament has recently expressed concern about the rise of extremism in Europe,[397] in particular with regard to extremist movements and paramilitary groups and parties, some of which even have governmental responsibilities, which base their ideology, political discourse, practices and conduct on discrimination, including racism, intolerance, incitement to religious hatred, exclusion, xenophobia, anti-Semitism, anti-Gypsyism, homophobia, misogyny and ultranationalism. Furthermore, the EU's concerns extend to Islamic fundamentalist recruitment and violent propaganda campaigns based on the hatred of European values and anti-Semitism. The European Parliament urged the European Commission and the Council of the European Union to lead the search for appropriate political and legal responses in a resolution adopted in December 2007.[398]

It has been the intention of the EU since 1996[399] to address these concerns by introducing legislative action for harmonising laws and regulations of the member states and for "overcoming obstacles for efficient judicial cooperation which are mainly based on the divergence of legal approaches in the Member States".[400]

---

393. Article 5 of the Council of Europe Convention on the Prevention of Terrorism (CETS No. 196).
394. Article 6 of the Council of Europe Convention on the Prevention of Terrorism (CETS No. 196).
395. Article 7 of the Council of Europe Convention on the Prevention of Terrorism (CETS No. 196).
396. EU Council Framework Decision on combating certain forms and expressions of racism and xenophobia by means of criminal law, 2001/0270 (CNS), 16771/07, DROIPEN 127, Brussels, 26 February 2008, para. 1.
397. European Parliament Resolution of 13 December 2007 on combating the rise of extremism in Europe, P6_TA(2007)0623.
398. Ibid.
399. See Council Joint Action 96/443/JHA of 15 July 1996 concerning action to combat racism and xenophobia.
400. EU Council Framework Decision on combating certain forms and expressions of racism and xenophobia by means of criminal law, 2001/0270 (CNS), 16771/07, DROIPEN 127, Brussels, 26 February 2008, para. 3.

Although there have been significant initiatives to reach the aims and objectives set out by the EU in 1996, difficulties have been encountered in reaching consensus for a harmonised judicial response at the EU level. A draft framework decision on combating racism and xenophobia designed to ensure that racism and xenophobia are punishable in all member states by effective, proportionate and dissuasive criminal penalties was proposed in November 2001. However, no agreement has been reached on this initiative largely due to different approaches to limitations in the exercise of freedom of expression within the member states of the EU. Similar drawbacks were witnessed during discussions involving the draft Television Without Frontiers Directive[401] which, in its original version, included non-derogatory provisions to make "non-linear media services" and "linear media services" subject to the same minimum requirements in relation to the prohibition of incitement to hatred. With the draft directive, the European Commission wanted to ensure compliance with policy objectives relating to the protection of minors against harmful audiovisual content and the protection of human dignity including a ban on incitement to racial hatred. However, these provisions were dropped from the new Audiovisual Media Services Directive 2007 which replaced the Television Without Frontiers Directive.[402]

Council Framework Decision on combating certain forms and expressions of racism and xenophobia by means of criminal law

In 2005, during the German Presidency of the European Union, a new document drafted by Germany[403] included an EU-wide proposal to criminalise Holocaust denial and other forms of racist content. This was another attempt at harmonising criminal laws within the EU member states "in order to ensure the effective implementation of comprehensive and clear legislation to combat racism and xenophobia".[404]

It was thought that this initiative would also face similar obstacles based upon different approaches to limitations in the exercise of freedom of expression within the member states.[405] However, political agreement was reached at the Council

---

401. Proposal for a Directive of the European Parliament and of the Council amending Council Directive 89/552/EEC on the coordination of certain provisions laid down by law, regulation or administrative action in Member States concerning the pursuit of television broadcasting activities (Television without frontiers), COM(2005) 646 final.

402. Audiovisual Media Services Directive 2007/65/EC has been published in the Official Journal No. L 332 of 18 December 2007 and entered into force on 19 December 2007. EU Member States shall transpose it into national law by 19 December 2009.

403. See EU Annual Report on Human Rights – 2005, 12416/05, Brussels, 28 September 2005.

404. EU Council Framework Decision on combating certain forms and expressions of racism and xenophobia by means of criminal law, 2001/0270 (CNS), 16771/07, DROIPEN 127, Brussels, 26 February 2008, para. 4.

405. German Presidency Press Release, "Outlawing racism and xenophobia throughout Europe", 29 January 2007, at www.eu2007.de/en/.

of the European Union level in April 2007 on a compromised version of the original draft framework decision on the fight against racism and xenophobia.[406] Subsequently, after almost seven years of discussions, on 28 November 2008 the Framework Decision on combating racism and xenophobia was adopted by the Council of the European Union.[407] The European Union Agency for Fundamental Rights (FRA) welcomed the Council's adoption and sees the adoption of the framework decision as an important tool for the EU-wide condemnation of racist and xenophobic crime.[408]

The preamble to the framework decision on combating certain forms and expressions of racism and xenophobia by means of criminal law acknowledges that a stand-alone legislative response is not enough to combat racism and xenophobia, and a broader comprehensive framework which includes various measures including non-regulatory solutions is necessary. The preamble to the framework decision also emphasises that full harmonisation of criminal law provisions to combat racism and xenophobia may never be possible based on different historical, cultural, constitutional, and legal differences within the member states of the EU. That is why the framework decision is "limited to combating particularly serious forms of racism and xenophobia by means of criminal law".[409]

The framework decision includes such crimes as publicly inciting to violence or hatred[410] directed against a group of persons or a member of such a group defined by reference to race, colour, religion,[411] descent[412] or national or ethnic origin;[413] and the commission of these crimes by public dissemination or distribution of

---

406. Council of the European Union, Document 5118/07 DROIPEN 1.

407. Framework Decision 2008/913/JHA on combating certain forms and expressions of racism and xenophobia by means of criminal law of 28 November 2008, Official Journal of the European Union L 328/55, 6 December 2008.

408. See FRA welcomes new EU Framework Decision on combating racism and xenophobia, 28 November 2008, at www.ue2008.fr/.

409. EU Council Framework Decision on combating certain forms and expressions of racism and xenophobia by means of criminal law, 2001/0270 (CNS), 16771/07, DROIPEN 127, Brussels, 26 February 2008, para. 6.

410. "Hatred" should be understood as referring to hatred based on race, colour, religion, descent or national or ethnic origin. See Preamble to the Draft Framework Decision, para. 9.

411. "Religion" should be understood as broadly referring to persons defined by reference to their religious convictions or beliefs. See Preamble to the Draft Framework Decision, para. 8.

412. "Descent" should be understood as referring mainly to persons or groups of persons who descend from persons who could be identified by certain characteristics (such as race or colour), but not necessarily all of these characteristics still exist. In spite of that, because of their descent, such persons or groups of persons may be subject to hatred or violence. See preamble to the draft framework decision, para. 7.

413. See Article 1(a) entitled "Offences concerning racism and xenophobia" of the draft framework decision: Council of the European Union, Proposal for a Council Framework Decision on combating certain forms and expressions of racism and xenophobia by means of criminal law, Document No. 11522/07, 19 July 2007.

tracts, pictures or other material.[414] Furthermore, Article 1(c) of the framework decision criminalises publicly condoning, denying or grossly trivialising crimes of genocide, crimes against humanity and war crimes as defined in Articles 6, 7 and 8 of the Statute of the International Criminal Court.[415] The crime needs to be directed against a group of persons or a member of such a group defined by reference to race, colour, religion, descent or national or ethnic origin, and the criminal conduct needs to be carried out in a manner likely to incite to violence or hatred against such a group or a member of such a group.

Similarly, Article 1(d) criminalises publicly condoning, denying or grossly trivialising the crimes defined in Article 6 of the Charter of the International Military Tribunal appended to the London Agreement of 8 August 1945. As in the previous provisions the crime needs to be directed against a group of persons or a member of such a group defined by reference to race, colour, religion, descent or national or ethnic origin, and the criminal conduct needs to be carried out in a manner likely to incite to violence or hatred against such a group or a member of such a group.

In November 2008, when the Council of the European Union finally adopted the framework decision, Poland issued a statement and declared that the framework decision "does not encompass condoning, denying or trivialising crimes committed in central and eastern Europe by communist regimes, which could not be tried before international criminal courts for political reasons. However, such acts also constitute a grave infringement of fundamental values that are common to all Member States and are therefore deplorable to the same degree."[416] Latvia also made a similar statement,[417] and stated that the scope of application of the framework decision is limited only to the crimes committed by the Nazi regime, but does not cover the crimes committed by the Totalitarian Communist regime, although, while having particular social groups as the main target, these crimes were also committed on the grounds of ethnic and national origin, which constitutes an integral part of the content of racism as defined by the UN Convention on the Elimination of All Forms of Racial Discrimination adopted in 1966. Therefore Latvia considered it necessary that the EU apply similar criteria to the crimes committed by both totalitarian regimes and provide for an equal treatment regarding the public condoning, denying or gross trivialising of these crimes. According to Latvia,

---

414. See Article 1(b).

415. See Article 1(c).

416. See Council of the European Union, Proposal for a Council Framework Decision on combating certain forms and expressions of racism and xenophobia by means of criminal law, 14904/01 DROIPEN 105 COM(2001) 664 final, 15699/1/08, REV 1, Brussels, 25 November 2008.

417. Council of the European Union, Proposal for a Council Framework Decision on combating certain forms and expressions of racism and xenophobia by means of criminal law, 14904/01 DROIPEN 105 COM(2001) 664 final, 16351/1/08, REV 1, Brussels, 26 November 2008.

Preservation of historic memory, assessment of the crimes of totalitarian regimes and their ideologies as well as respect for the victims and freedom fighters is very important for historical justice and for the prevention of the crimes against humanity in the future. Accordingly a similar approach has to be made and all necessary actions have to be done at EU level in order to prevent the revival of any of totalitarian regimes, including Totalitarian Communist regime.[418]

In terms of limitations Article 1(2) states that member states may choose to punish only conduct which is either carried out in a manner likely to disturb public order or which is threatening, abusive or insulting.

The reference to religion in Article 1 crimes is intended to cover, at least, conduct which is a pretext for directing acts against a group of persons or a member of such a group defined by reference to race, colour, descent, or national or ethnic origin.[419]

Furthermore, Article 2(2) criminalises aiding and abetting in the commission of the conduct referred to in Article 1, and Article 2(1) requires the member states to ensure that instigating the conduct referred to in Article 1(1)(c) and (d) is punishable.

According to Article 4, for offences other than those referred to in Articles 1 and 2, member states should take the necessary measures to ensure that racist and xenophobic motivation is considered an aggravating circumstance, or, alternatively, that such motivation may be taken into consideration by the courts in the determination of the related penalties.

EU member states will be required to take the necessary steps to ensure that the above-mentioned criminal conduct is punishable by effective, proportionate and dissuasive criminal penalties of one to three years' imprisonment.[420] Although there is no reference to Internet-related publications, the framework decision refers to the commission of the above-mentioned crimes by public dissemination or distribution of tracts, pictures or other material which would broadly encompass any such distribution over the Internet.[421]

Furthermore, Article 5 provides liability for legal persons under certain circumstances, and Article 1 and 2 crimes can be committed by legal persons if the offences are committed for their benefit by any person, acting either individually or as part of an organ of the legal person, who has a leading position within the legal person.[422] In terms of penalties, Article 6 requires member states to introduce effective, proportionate and dissuasive penalties, which shall include criminal or

---

418. Ibid.
419. See Article 1(3).
420. See Article 3.
421. See Article 1(b).
422. See Article 5(1). According to Article 5(4) "Legal person" means any entity having such status under the applicable national law, with the exception of states or other public bodies in the exercise of state authority and public international organisations.

non-criminal fines, and by way of example refers to the exclusion from entitle-ment to public benefits or aid, temporary or permanent disqualification from the practice of commercial activities, placing under judicial supervision, and a judicial winding-up order.

Article 7 refers to the constitutional rules and fundamental principles and states that the provisions of the framework decision "shall not have the effect of mod-ifying the obligation to respect fundamental rights and fundamental legal prin-ciples, including freedom of expression and association, as enshrined in article 6 of the Treaty on European Union".[423] Similarly the provisions of the framework decision shall not "have the effect of requiring Member States to take measures in contradiction to fundamental principles relating to freedom of association and freedom of expression, in particular freedom of the press and the freedom of expression in other media as they result from constitutional traditions or rules governing the rights and responsibilities of, and the procedural guarantees for, the press or other media where these rules relate to the determination or limita-tion of liability".[424]

In terms of jurisdictional issues, Article 9(2) states that each member state should take the necessary measures to ensure that its jurisdiction extends to cases where the conduct is committed through an information system including the Internet and the measures should cover the following situations:

> (a) the offender commits the conduct when physically present in its territory, whether or not the conduct involves material hosted on an information system in its territory;

> (b) the conduct involves material hosted on an information system in its territory, whether or not the offender commits the conduct when physically present in its territory.

Despite this significant attempt at harmonising EU-wide policy, it remains to be seen how the framework decision will be implemented by the EU member states. According to Article 10, the framework decision needs to be implemented by member states by 28 November 2010. The Council of the European Union will then assess the extent to which member states have complied with the provi-sions of this framework decision by 28 November 2013.

The Netherlands expressed in November 2008 that it already complies with the obligation of criminalisation pursuant to Articles 1 and 2 of the framework deci-sion. Articles 137c, 137d and 137e of the Dutch Criminal Code give a broad criminalisation of inciting to hatred or violence, of insulting or discriminating because of, amongst others, race and religion. The term "race" also includes the characteristics of skin colour, origin and national or ethnic descent. Under the scope of these articles also fall condoning, denying or grossly trivialising the

---

423. See Article 7(1).
424. See Article 7(2).

international crimes referred to in Article 1 sub-paragraphs c and d, as far as such a conduct incites to hatred or violence, insults or discriminates because of race or religion.[425]

The EU Policy on harmful Internet content

With regard to harmful Internet content, the EU Action Plan on safer use of the Internet encourages self-regulatory initiatives to deal with illegal and harmful Internet content including the creation of a European network of hotlines for Internet users to report illegal content such as child pornography; the development of self-regulatory and content-monitoring schemes by access and content providers; and the development of internationally compatible and interoperable rating and filtering schemes to protect users. Furthermore, the EU Action Plan advocates measures to increase awareness among parents, teachers, children and other consumers of available options to help these groups use the networks safely by choosing the right control tools.

Although originally established as a three-year Action Plan, in 2002[426] the European Commission prolonged the work in this field for another two years, expanding the Action Plan-related work and projects to cover the EU candidate countries.[427] One of the main reasons for this expansion was the fact that illegal and harmful content on the Internet remained as a continuing concern for law-makers, the private sector, and parents. The coverage of the Action Plan was extended to new online technologies including mobile and broadband content, online games, peer-to-peer file transfer, and all forms of real-time communications such as chat rooms and instant messages. Action will be taken to ensure that a broader range of areas of illegal and harmful content and conduct of concern are covered, including racism and violence.[428]

In May 2005, the EU extended the Action Plan work for the period 2005-2008 to continue to promote safer use of the Internet and new online technologies, by strengthening the fight against illegal content such as child pornography and racist material, content that is potentially harmful to children and content unwanted by the end user. It is suggested by the extended Safer Internet Plus Action Plan that practical measures are still needed to encourage reporting of

---

425. Council of the European Union, Proposal for a Council Framework Decision on combating certain forms and expressions of racism and xenophobia by means of criminal law, 14904/01 DROIPEN 105 COM(2001) 664 final, 15699/1/08, REV 1, Brussels, 25 November 2008.
426. See EC, Follow-up to the Multiannual Community Action Plan on promoting safer use of the Internet by combating illegal and harmful content on global networks: Proposal for a decision of the European Parliament and of the Council amending Decision No. 276/1999/EC adopting a Multiannual Community Action Plan on promoting safer use of the Internet by combating illegal and harmful content on global networks, COM (2002) 152, Brussels.
427. Ibid. at para. 3.1.2. (Interface to candidate countries.)
428. See Safer Internet Action Plan: Work Programme 2003-2004 at 3, at http://ec.europa.eu.

illegal content to those in a position to deal with it, to encourage assessment of the performance of filter technologies and the benchmarking of those technologies, to spread best practice for codes of conduct embodying generally agreed canons of behaviour, and to inform and educate parents and children on the best way to benefit from the potential of new online technologies in a safe way.[429]

The four-year programme has a budget of €45 million and it focuses more closely on end users, namely parents, educators and children. The indicated budget breakdown suggests that almost half of the available budget will be spent on raising awareness (47-51%). Fighting against illegal content will receive 25-30%, tackling unwanted and harmful content 10-17%, and promoting a safer environment 8-12% of the budget.[430] In October 2008, the European Commission's Safer Internet programme was extended for the 2009-2013 period with an aim to improve safety for children surfing the Internet, promote public awareness, and create national centres for reporting illegal online content with a €55 million budget.[431] The Council of the European Union adopted the extended programme in December 2008.[432]

Despite these significant policy initiatives with regard to harmful Internet content, developing common approaches remains problematic in the face of cultural, moral and legal diversity at the EU level, which has been shaped by historical, political and social experiences of wartime conflict. The advisory role of the EU through the Safer Use of the Internet programme with regard to non-regulatory solutions is therefore significantly important.

Developments at the OSCE level

During the past few years there have been increasing demands within the OSCE to enhance its work in the area of action against racism, xenophobia, discrimination,

---

429. EC Decision No. 854/2005/EC of the European Parliament and of the Council establishing a Multiannual Community Programme on promoting safer use of the Internet and new online technologies, [2005] OJ L 149/1 at para. 7, at http://ec.europa.eu.
430. See also in this context the EU Proposal for a Recommendation of the European Parliament and of the Council on the protection of minors and human dignity and the right of reply in relation to the competitiveness of the European audiovisual and information services industry, currently under consideration by the European Parliament.
431. European Parliament legislative resolution of 22 October 2008 on the proposal for a decision of the European Parliament and of the Council establishing a multiannual Community programme on protecting children using the Internet and other communication technologies (COM(2008)0106 – C6-0092/2008 – 2008/0047(COD)).
432. See the EU press release, "EU adopts new Safer Internet Programme: €55 million to make the Internet a safer place for children", IP/08/1899, 09/12/2008 at http://europa.eu/rapid/.

and anti-Semitism.[433] The 11th Ministerial Council meeting in December 2003 in Maastricht encouraged the participating states to collect and keep records and statistics on hate crimes, including forms of violent manifestations of racism, xenophobia, discrimination and anti-Semitism. The Ministerial Council also gave concrete responsibilities to the OSCE institutions, including the Office for Democratic Institutions and Human Rights, which was tasked with serving as a collection point for information and statistics collected by participating states in full co-operation with, *inter alia*, the CERD, the ECRI, and the European Monitoring Centre on Racism and Xenophobia (EUMC),[434] as well as relevant non-governmental organisations (NGOs).

Since then the OSCE has organised a number of high-level conferences and meetings in recent years to address the problems of racism, xenophobia, discrimination, and anti-Semitism.[435] The need to combat hate crimes, which can be fuelled by racist, xenophobic and anti-Semitic propaganda on the Internet, was explicitly recognised by a decision during the 2003 Maastricht Ministerial Council.[436] This was reinforced by the OSCE Permanent Council Decision on Combating Anti-Semitism (PC.DEC/607)[437] and its Decision on Tolerance and the Fight against Racism, Xenophobia and Discrimination (PC.DEC/621)[438] in 2004. In November 2004, the OSCE also published a Permanent Council Decision on Promoting Tolerance and Media Freedom on the Internet (PC.DEC/633).[439]

The November 2004 Council Decision stated that participating states should investigate and, where applicable, fully prosecute violence as well as criminal threats of violence motivated by racist, xenophobic, anti-Semitic or other related

---

433. See generally OSCE Office for Democratic Institutions and Human Rights (ODIHR), *International Action Against Racism, Xenophobia, Anti-Semitism and Tolerance in the OSCE Region: A Comparative Study* (September 2004), at www.osce.org. See also: ODIHR, *Combating Hate Crimes in the OSCE Region: An Overview of statistics, legislation, and national initiatives* (June 2005), at www.osce.org; and ODIHR, *Challenges and Responses to Hate-Motivated Incidents in the OSCE Region* (October 2006), at www.osce.org.

434. Now taken over by the European Union Agency for Fundamental Rights (FRA). See http://fra.europa.eu/.

435. Conference on Anti-Semitism, Vienna (19 June 2003); Conference on Racism, Xenophobia and Discrimination, Vienna (4 September 2003); Conference on Anti-Semitism, Berlin (28 April 2004); Meeting on the Relationship between Racist, Xenophobic and Anti-Semitic Propaganda on the Internet and Hate Crimes, Paris (16 June 2004); Conference on Tolerance and the Fight Against Racism, Xenophobia and Discrimination, Brussels (13 September 2004); and Conference on Anti-Semitism, and other forms of Intolerance, Cordoba (8 June 2005).

436. See Maastricht Ministerial Council, *Decision No. 4/03 on Tolerance and Non-Discrimination* (2003) at para. 8.

437. See www.osce.org.

438. See www.osce.org.

439. See www.osce.org. Note also the Ministerial Council Decision No. 12/04 on Tolerance and Non-Discrimination, December 2004, at www.osce.org, as well as the Cordoba Declaration, CIO.GAL/76/05/Rev.2, 9 June 2005, at www.osce.org.

bias on the Internet.[440] Alongside the decision, the OSCE Representative on Freedom of the Media was given the task of actively promoting both freedom of expression and access to the Internet, and will continue to observe relevant developments in all participating states. This will involve monitoring and issuing early warnings when laws or other measures prohibiting speech motivated by racist or other related bias are enforced in a discriminatory or selective manner for political purposes which can lead to impeding of the expression of alternative opinions and views.[441] The Council also decided that participating states should study the effectiveness of laws and other measures regulating Internet content, specifically with regard to their effect on the rate of racist crimes,[442] as well as encourage and support analytically rigorous studies on the possible relationship between racist speech on the Internet and the commission of crimes motivated by such speech.[443]

---

440. See Maastricht Ministerial Council, *Decision No. 633: Promoting Tolerance and Media Freedom on the Internet* (2004), at decision No. 2, at www.osce.org.

441. Ibid. at decision No. 4.

442. Ibid. at decision No. 5.

443. Ibid. at decision No. 6.

6. International initiatives through the United Nations

This chapter will provide an overview of policy initiatives at the United Nations level.

The problem of the availability of racist content on the Internet is undoubtedly a global concern which is not limited or specific to the European region. States also attempted to reach consensus on how to combat the problem of racist content at the United Nations level. The broader, non-medium-specific initiative at the UN level involves the International Convention on the Elimination of All Forms of Racial Discrimination as well as more specific recommendations on raising awareness campaigns and the development of self-regulatory solutions by the Internet industry.

The International Convention on the Elimination of All Forms of Racial Discrimination

States Parties to the International Convention on the Elimination of All Forms of Racial Discrimination (ICERD), through Article 4,

> condemn all propaganda and all organisations which are based on ideas or theories of superiority of one race or group of persons of one colour or ethnic origin, or which attempt to justify or promote racial hatred and discrimination in any form.

Article 4 of ICERD clearly sets out the obligations of signing and ratifying states by stating that states parties undertake to adopt immediate and positive measures designed to eradicate all incitement to, or acts of, such discrimination and, to this end, with due regard to the principles embodied in the Universal Declaration of Human Rights and the rights expressly set forth in Article 5 of this convention, *inter alia*:

> (a) Shall declare an offence punishable by law all dissemination of ideas based on racial superiority or hatred, incitement to racial discrimination, as well as all acts of violence or incitement to such acts against any race or group of persons of another colour or ethnic origin, and also the provision of any assistance to racist activities, including the financing thereof;

> (b) Shall declare illegal and prohibit organizations, and also organized and all other propaganda activities, which promote and incite racial discrimination, and shall recognize participation in such organizations or activities as an offence punishable by law;

(c) Shall not permit public authorities or public institutions, national or local, to promote or incite racial discrimination.

Currently, with 173 ratifications by member states as of December 2008,[444] the ICERD provisions remain the most important normative basis upon which international efforts to eliminate racial discrimination could be built.[445] The CERD in its General Recommendations VII[446] and XV[447] explained that the provisions of Article 4 are of a mandatory character. According to CERD, to satisfy these obligations, states parties need to enact appropriate legislation as well as ensure that such legislation is effectively enforced. Nonetheless, harmonisation has not been established and there remain different interpretations and applications of Article 4. To date, 19 states have entered reservations and/or interpretative declarations in respect of Article 4. Most notably, the US Government declared that the United States "does not accept any obligation under this Convention, in particular under articles 4 and 7, to restrict those rights, through the adoption of legislation or any other measures, to the extent that they are protected by the Constitution and laws of the United States". As the Special Rapporteur on the promotion and protection of the right to freedom of opinion and expression noted in his 1998 report, "the ambivalence surrounding points related to the principle of the need to balance rights and protections is evident in the positions taken by Governments through the declarations and reservations they have entered to article 4".[448]

While there is an urgent need to review the functioning of ICERD and consider whether it should be updated, "great care must be taken to achieve an appropriate balance between the rights to freedom of opinion and expression and to receive and impart information and the prohibition on speech and/or activities promoting racist views and inciting violence"[449] as noted by the Special Rapporteur on the promotion and protection of the right to freedom of opinion and expression noted in his 1998 report. That balance is yet to be reached.

A study into the possible development of complementary international standards[450] in this field was commissioned following a request made by the

---

444. See Note by the Secretariat, Efforts by the Office of the United Nations High Commissioner for Human Rights for universal ratification of the International Convention on the Elimination of All Forms of Racial Discrimination, E/CN.4/2006/13, 15 February 2006.

445. See Report of the Committee on the Elimination of Racial Discrimination, Sixty-fourth session (23 February to 12 March 2004) Sixty-fifth session (2-20 August 2004), No. A/59/18, 1 October 2004.

446. General Recommendation No. 7: Legislation to eradicate racial discrimination (Article 4), 23/08/85.

447. General Recommendation No. 15: Organised violence based on ethnic origin (Article 4), 23/03/93.

448. Promotion and protection of the right to freedom of opinion and expression, Report of the Special Rapporteur, Mr Abid Hussain, E/CN.4/1998/40, 28 January 1998, para. 7.

449. Ibid., para. 8.

450. See UN General Assembly, Complementary International Standards: Report on the study by the five experts on the content and scope of substantive gaps in the existing international instruments to combat racism, racial discrimination, xenophobia and related intolerance, A/HRC/4/WG.3/6, 27 August 2007, at www.ohchr.org.

Intergovernmental Working Group on the effective implementation of the Durban Declaration and Programme of Action at its fourth session (Geneva 16-20 January 2006). This study focused on normative gaps as well as more recent phenomena such as incitement to racial hatred and dissemination of hate speech and xenophobic and caricatural pictures through traditional mass media and information technology, including the Internet. In addressing the underlying question as to whether there is a gap in international human rights law pertaining to combating incitement to racial and religious hatred and the dissemination of hate speech, the experts "discern a gap in application and consider that while there are provisions from various treaties addressing the issue, further guidance from treaty bodies as to the interpretative scope of these provisions and their threshold of application would be most useful".[451]

UN policy work with regard to combating racist Internet content

A call for a study of the use of new technologies (including video games and computer networks) for the propagation of racial hatred and the urgent proposal of a set of internal and international measures to end such abuses was issued following the first European meeting of National Institutions for the Promotion and Protection of Human Rights in November 1994.[452] Further calls for research to consider whether international measures should be taken to control information transmitted over the Internet were made during 1996[453] with the recognition that "no national legislation has any power over this worldwide network".[454]

The availability of racist and xenophobic propaganda through electronic networks and the responsive measures to be taken at the national and international levels were considered during a UN seminar to assess the implementation of the ICERD in Geneva during September 1996.[455] In the course of the seminar, Rabbi Abraham Cooper stated that "online discussion or chat groups provided an opportunity to denigrate minorities, promote xenophobia and identify potential

---

451. Ibid., para. 152.

452. See Maurice Glélé-Ahanhanzo, Implementation of the Programme of Action for the Second Decade to Combat Racism and Racial Discrimination – Report of the UN Special Rapporteur on contemporary forms of racism, racial discrimination, xenophobia and related intolerance, CHR Res. 1994/64, UN ESCOR, 51st Sess., UN Doc. E/CN.4/1995/78 (1995).

453. Secretary-General, Elimination of Racism and Racial Discrimination: Measures to combat contemporary forms of racism, racial discrimination, xenophobia and related intolerance, UN GA, 51st Sess., UN Doc. A/51/301 (1996).

454. Ibid. at para. 46.

455. Implementation of the Programme of Action for the Third Decade to Combat Racism and Racial Discrimination, Report of the United Nations seminar to assess the implementation of the International Convention on the Elimination of All Forms of Racial Discrimination with particular reference to Articles 4 and 6, Commission on Human Rights, 53rd Sess., UN Doc. E/CN.4/1997/68/Add.1 (1996).

recruits for the racist groups".[456] The seminar participants felt that the UN is responsible for ensuring that modern communications technologies are not used to spread racism. The consensus was that an international approach would help overcome the problem created by legislative differences making it possible for racist material produced in countries with no legal sanctions against incitement of racial hatred to be made available in countries where those legal restrictions exist by means of the Internet. Co-operation with the Internet industry, especially with ISPs, was also encouraged. In addition, the participants recalled that Article 4, paragraphs (a) and (b) of the ICERD contains the provisions on the basis of which states parties can take legal measures to ban organisations involved in spreading racist propaganda over the Internet. The recommendations adopted by the seminar called on the UN, in particular its Legal Office, and other international and regional organisations to undertake a systematic review of existing international instruments with the view to assessing their applicability and adaptability to parallel forms of communication on the Internet.

The Special Rapporteur on contemporary forms of racism, racial discrimination, xenophobia and related intolerance noted in his 1997 report that "emphasis should be placed on the use of modern communications technology, including the Internet, as a vehicle for incitement to racial hatred and xenophobia".[457] The Special Rapporteur recommended joint action, research, and studies at an international level on the use of the Internet as a vehicle for racist propaganda.[458] The Special Rapporteur also welcomed the initiative taken by the General Assembly in its resolution 51/81,[459] whereby the assembly recommended that a seminar be organised by the UN Centre for Human Rights (now the UN Office of the High Commissioner for Human Rights), in co-operation with the CERD, the UN Educational, Scientific and Cultural Organization (UNESCO), the International Telecommunication Union (ITU) and other relevant UN bodies, NGOs and ISPs, with a view to assessing the role of the Internet in light of the provisions of the ICERD.[460]

The Office of the High Commissioner for Human Rights organised a seminar on "the role of the Internet in the light of the provisions of the International Convention on the Elimination of All Forms of Racial Discrimination" in Geneva,

---

456. Ibid. at para. 60.
457. Maurice Glélé-Ahanhanzo, Racism, racial discrimination, xenophobia and related intolerance: Report of the UN Special Rapporteur on contemporary forms of racism, racial discrimination, xenophobia and related intolerance, CHR Res. 1997/73, Commission on Human Rights, 54th Sess., UN Doc. E/CN.4/1998/79 (1998), at para. 8.
458. Ibid. at para. 132.
459. Third Decade to Combat Racism and Racial Discrimination, GA Res. 51/81, UN GAOR, 51st Sess., UN Doc. A/RES/51/81 (1997), at para. 10.
460. See generally Secretary-General, Elimination of Racism and Racial Discrimination: Measures to combat contemporary forms of racism, racial discrimination, xenophobia and related intolerance, UN GA, 52nd Sess., UN Doc. A/52/471 (1997).

in November 1997.[461] The seminar concluded by strongly condemning the use of the Internet by some groups and persons to promote racism and hate speech in violation of international law.[462] The seminar further recommended that the Internet be used as an educative tool to combat racist propaganda, prevent the spread of racist doctrines and practices, and promote mutual understanding. The seminar also recommended that UN member states continue their co-operation and establish international juridical measures in compliance with the ICERD to prohibit racism on the Internet while respecting individual rights, especially freedom of expression.

In his 1998 report, the Special Rapporteur noted that "although the States have now become aware of the dangers these acts represent, very few efforts have been made to combat the phenomenon",[463] and that "only globally concerted action will be effective enough to halt the tendency to use the Internet for racist and xenophobic purposes, in view of the global, cross-frontier nature of that type of activity".[464] The Special Rapporteur questioned whether it would be possible to adopt appropriate legislation, on a country-by-country basis, against incitement to hatred and racial discrimination, which would conform with Articles 4 and 5 of the ICERD. In addition to taking possible legislative action, he also called upon the international community to undertake positive action to combat the abusive exploitation of the Internet on its own ground; that is, "by using the Internet itself to broadcast anti-racist and anti-xenophobic messages, and even to spread human rights education against racism".[465] In this respect, the Council of Europe's efforts were displayed in the launch of the ECRI website. In that same report, the Special Rapporteur once again recommended a consideration of possible action at the international level by immediately beginning studies, research and consultations on the use of the Internet for purposes of incitement of hatred, racist propaganda and xenophobia, as well as the creation of a programme of human rights education and exchanges over the Internet on experiences in the struggle against racism, xenophobia and anti-Semitism.

---

461. Maurice Glélé-Ahanhanzo, Racism, racial discrimination, xenophobia and related intolerance: Report of the UN Special Rapporteur on contemporary forms of racism, racial discrimination, xenophobia and related intolerance, CHR Res. 1997/73, Commission on Human Rights, 54th Sess., UN Doc. E/CN.4/1998/79 (1998), at para. 23.

462. Racism, Racial Discrimination, Xenophobia and Related Intolerance: Report of the expert seminar on the role of the Internet in the light of the provisions of the International Convention on the Elimination of All Forms of Racial Discrimination, Commission on Human Rights, 54th Sess., UN Doc. E/CN.4/1998/77/Add.2 (1998).

463. Maurice Glélé-Ahanhanzo, Racism, racial discrimination, xenophobia and related intolerance: Report of the UN Special Rapporteur on contemporary forms of racism, racial discrimination, xenophobia and related intolerance, CHR Res. 1997/73, Commission on Human Rights, 54th Sess., UN Doc. E/CN.4/1998/79 (1998), at para. 50.

464. Ibid.

465. Ibid. at para. 51.

In 1999, the Commission on Human Rights, noting with concern the increase in the use of new communication technologies (in particular the Internet) to disseminate racist ideas and incite racial hatred, stated that the use of Internet technologies could contribute to combating racial discrimination and related intolerance through initiatives such as websites used to disseminate anti-racist and anti-xenophobic messages.[466] The Special Rapporteur suggested that the issue of Internet use in the dissemination of racism and xenophobia should be included in the agenda of the World Conference on Racism and Racial Discrimination, Xenophobia and Related Intolerance. In his 2000 report, the Special Rapporteur strongly recommended the holding of further consultations at the international level with a view to regulating the use of the Internet and harmonising criminal legislation on use of the Internet for racist purposes.[467]

The work conducted by the UN High Commissioner for Human Rights led to the UN General Assembly, at the request of the UN Commission on Human Rights, to convene the third World Conference against Racism, Racial Discrimination, Xenophobia and Related Intolerance, which took place in Durban in 2001. The states participating in the World Conference adopted a Declaration and Programme of Action (Durban Declaration) containing recommendations intended to strengthen the international human rights framework for combating racism and related intolerance.

The Durban Declaration[468] recognised "the positive contribution that the exercise of the right to freedom of expression, particularly by the media and new technologies, including the Internet, and full respect for the freedom to seek, receive and impart information can make to the fight against racism, racial discrimination, xenophobia and related intolerance".[469] However, the document also expressed deep concern with the use of new information technologies "for purposes contrary to respect for human values, equality, non-discrimination, respect for others and tolerance, including to propagate racism, racial hatred, xenophobia, racial discrimination and related intolerance, and that, in particular, children and youth having access to this material could be negatively influenced by it".[470] The declaration explicitly recognised "the need to promote the use of new information and communication technologies, including the Internet, to contribute to the fight against racism, racial discrimination, xenophobia and related

---

466. See Secretary-General, Measures to combat contemporary forms of racism, racial discrimination, xenophobia and related intolerance, UN GA, 54th Sess., UN Doc. A/54/347 (1999).

467. See Secretary-General, Report of the Special Rapporteur of the Commission on Human Rights on contemporary forms of racism, racial discrimination, xenophobia and related intolerance, UN GA, 55th Sess., UN Doc. A/55/304 (2000).

468. See generally Report of the World Conference against Racism, Racial Discrimination, Xenophobia and Related Intolerance, Durban, 31 August to 8 September 2001, UN Doc. A/CONF.189/12 (2002), at www.un.org/WCAR/aconf189_12.pdf [Durban Declaration].

469. Ibid. at para. 90.

470. Ibid. at para. 91.

intolerance"[471] and declared that "new technologies can assist the promotion of tolerance and respect for human dignity, and the principles of equality and non-discrimination".[472] Among other significant recommendations, the Durban Declaration urged states to:

> implement legal sanctions, in accordance with relevant international human rights law, in respect of incitement to racial hatred through new information and communications technologies, including the Internet, and further urge[d] them to apply all relevant human rights instruments to which they are parties, in particular the International Convention on the Elimination of All Forms of Racial Discrimination, to racism on the Internet.[473]

The Durban Declaration also called upon the states to consider the following, while taking all necessary measures to guarantee the right to freedom of opinion and expression:

> (a) Encouraging Internet service providers to establish and disseminate specific voluntary codes of conduct and self-regulatory measures against the dissemination of racist messages and those that result in racial discrimination, xenophobia or any form of intolerance and discrimination; to that end, Internet providers are encouraged to set up mediating bodies at national and international levels, involving relevant civil society institutions;

> (b) Adopting and applying, to the extent possible, appropriate legislation for prosecuting those responsible for incitement to racial hatred or violence through the new information and communications technologies, including the Internet;

> (c) Addressing the problem of dissemination of racist material through the new information and communications technologies, including the Internet, *inter alia* by imparting training to law enforcement authorities;

> (d) Denouncing and actively discouraging the transmission of racist and xenophobic messages through all communications media, including new information and communications technologies, such as the Internet;

> (e) Considering a prompt and co-ordinated international response to the rapidly evolving phenomenon of the dissemination of hate speech and racist material through the new information and communications technologies, including the Internet; and in this context strengthening international co-operation.

> (f) Encouraging access and use by all people of the Internet as an international and equal forum, aware that there are disparities in use of and access to the Internet;

> (g) Examining ways in which the positive contribution made by the new information and communications technologies, such as the Internet, can be enhanced through replication of good practices in combating racism, racial discrimination, xenophobia and related intolerance;

---

471. Ibid. at para. 92.
472. Ibid.
473. Ibid. at para. 145.

(h) Encouraging the reflection of the diversity of societies among the personnel of media organizations and the new information and communications technologies, such as the Internet, by promoting adequate representation of different segments within societies at all levels of their organizational structure.[474]

In his 2002 report,[475] the Special Rapporteur expressed his hope that the concerned states and the international community will succeed in developing measures to nip this increasingly alarming phenomenon in the bud pursuant to the provisions of the Durban Declaration.[476]

In 2003 the UN General Assembly continued its condemnation of the misuse of print, audiovisual, electronic media, and the new communication technologies, to incite violence motivated by racial hatred, with a call for states to take all necessary measures to combat this form of racism in accordance with their commitments under the Durban Declaration,[477] in accordance with existing international and regional standards of freedom of expression and taking all necessary measures to guarantee the right to freedom of opinion and expression.

In his 2003 report, the Special Rapporteur[478] commended the November 2002 Council of Europe Council of Ministers on its adoption of the Additional Protocol to the Convention on Cybercrime concerning the Criminalisation of Acts of a Racist or Xenophobic Nature Committed Through Computer Systems.[479] The Special Rapporteur expressed his hope for the emergence of a similar document at the international level in the form of an additional protocol to the ICERD, so that more states can adopt legal measures to combat the use of the Internet for racist or xenophobic purposes.[480] There was support for such a consideration from the UN General Assembly in 2004.[481] However, as mentioned previously, disagreements (especially between the United States and certain European countries) on the most appropriate strategy for preventing the dissemination

---

474. Ibid. at para. 147.

475. Secretary-General, Measures to combat contemporary forms of racism, racial discrimination, xenophobia and related intolerance, UN GA, 57th Sess., UN Doc. A/57/204 (2002).

476. See Report of the World Conference against Racism, Racial Discrimination, Xenophobia and Related Intolerance, Durban, 31 August to 8 September 2001, UN Doc. A/CONF.189/12 (2002), at www.un.org/WCAR/aconf189_12.pdf, at c. I, paras. 143-147.

477. Secretary-General, The fight against racism, racial discrimination, xenophobia and related intolerance and the comprehensive implementation of and follow-up to the Durban Declaration and Programme of Action, UN GA, 58th Sess., UN Doc. A/58/313 (2003).

478. Note the change in Special Rapporteur: Mr Doudou Diène (Senegal) replaced Mr Maurice Glélé-Ahanhanzo (Benin) (1993-2002) as of August 2002 (E/CN.4/RES/2002/68).

479. Secretary-General, The fight against racism, racial discrimination, xenophobia and related intolerance and the comprehensive implementation of and follow-up to the Durban Declaration and Programme of Action, UN GA, 58th Sess., UN Doc. A/58/313 (2003).

480. Ibid.

481. Secretary-General, The fight against racism, racial discrimination, xenophobia and related intolerance and the comprehensive implementation of and follow-up to the Durban Declaration and Programme of Action, UN GA, 59th Sess., UN Doc. A/59/329 (2004).

of racist content on the Internet, including the need to adopt regulatory measures to that end, remain and these differences were highlighted by the Secretary-General's report in September 2004.[482] These differences were also evident during the fourth session meetings of the UN Intergovernmental Working Group on the effective implementation of the Durban Declaration and Programme of Action in Geneva in January 2006.[483] However, in the absence of global consensus and agreement on the limits of interference with freedom of expression, such an international instrument will be difficult to develop and implement.

According to an October 2008 UN General Assembly report, many UN member states have demonstrated commitment to combating racism, racial discrimination, xenophobia and related intolerance since the adoption of the 2001 Durban Declaration and Programme of Action.[484] The report states that "at the national level, nearly all constitutions guarantee the principle of equality and many countries have carried out reforms of their laws to eliminate those that are discriminatory."[485] The Durban Review Conference will take place in April 2009[486] and will offer an opportunity for all stakeholders to assess the successes and shortcomings in the implementation of the Durban Programme of Action and will create opportunities to facilitate the adoption of specific preventive and remedial measures.

---

482. Ibid. at para. 31.

483. See Report of the Intergovernmental Working Group on the effective implementation of the Durban Declaration and Programme of Action on its fourth session, UN ESCOR, 62nd Sess., UN Doc. E/CN.4/2006/18 (2006), at http://daccessdds. un.org.

484. UN General Assembly, Global efforts for the total elimination of racism, racial discrimination, xenophobia and related intolerance and the comprehensive implementation of and follow-up to the Durban Declaration and Programme of Action: Report of the Secretary-General, A/63/366, 19 October 2008.

485. Ibid., paras. 76-77.

486. See Durban Review Conference 2009 at www.ohchr.org/english/.

7. Effectiveness of regional and international regulatory efforts

This chapter will provide a critique of the effectiveness of regional and international regulatory efforts assessed so far in this book.

Substantial international efforts such as the Council of Europe's Additional Protocol concerning the criminalisation of acts of a racist and xenophobic nature committed through computer systems carry political significance but it remains to be seen whether such legislative initiatives will have an impact in terms of reducing the problem of racist content on the Internet. Owing to the global and decentralised nature of the Internet, government regulation and even the prosecution of individuals who publish racist content on the Internet may have limited effect and application especially if the content is published and transmitted from outside the jurisdiction in which it is considered illegal.

The steps taken by a number of governments at the national level have shown their limitations, and a regional international regulatory initiative such as the Council of Europe additional protocol aimed at punishing racism on the Internet will have limited effect unless every state hosting racist content or messages is a party to it, as rightly stated by Council of Europe Recommendation 1543 (2001) on racism and xenophobia in cyberspace.[487] The ratification process is a drawn-out affair and it took over three years to bring the protocol into force in March 2006 with only 13 member states ratifying it since January 2003 as of December 2008. A considerable amount of time will be required to reach a substantial number of ratifications. This is not necessarily unusual as the ratification of such instruments is typically a long process at the member states level. It is, however, noteworthy that Germany has yet to ratify despite being one of its main supporters. The additional protocol also lacks the support of non-signing member states which include Hungary, Ireland, Italy, Norway, Russia, Spain, Turkey, Ukraine, and the United Kingdom, in addition to the United States of America (an external member).

Member states may be reluctant to sign and/or ratify the additional protocol as becoming a party to the additional protocol may require substantial changes to national laws. Speech-based restrictions may not be allowed by certain state

---

487. Council of Europe Recommendation 1543 (2001) on racism and xenophobia in cyberspace, 8 November 2001.

constitutions, and the definition provided for "racist and xenophobic material" could conflict with state laws and constitutions. The offences included within the additional protocol, *inter alia*, dissemination of racist and xenophobic material, racist and xenophobic motivated threats, racist and xenophobic motivated insults, and the criminalisation of expressions which deny, grossly minimise, approve or justify acts constituting genocide or crimes against humanity may not all be supported by the non-signing and non-ratifying member states. However, the success of such a regional instrument will depend upon the co-operation of all Council of Europe member states.

Furthermore, the reservations present in Articles 3, 5, and 6 could result in disparities between the parties to the additional protocol and harmonisation may never take place in relation to "racist and xenophobic motivated insults" (Article 5), and "denial, gross minimisation, approval or justification of genocide or crimes against humanity" (Article 6) as these two articles allow the parties to the additional protocol to reserve the right not to apply in whole or in part the offences provided within these articles. For example, within the Council of Europe region, only Austria, Belgium, the Czech Republic, France, Germany, Lithuania, the Netherlands, Poland, Romania, Slovakia, Spain and Switzerland have laws criminalising the denial of genocide committed by the Nazis.[488] Yet, "the proliferation of Holocaust denial websites dramatically underscores the limitations of any national laws, or even international conventions, to eliminate or punish any form of hate speech".[489] There may, however, be European Union-wide agreement on the "denial, gross minimisation, approval or justification of genocide or crimes against humanity" following the finalisation of the European Union Council Framework Decision on combating certain forms and expressions of racism and xenophobia by means of criminal law in November 2008. However, as mentioned previously, it remains to be seen how the EU member states will implement the framework decision and whether any states will reserve their right not to implement certain provisions.

A reservation is also provided in relation to the "dissemination of racist and xenophobic material through computer systems" (Article 3) within the Council of Europe additional protocol but only as far as the dissemination is related to material which advocates, promotes or incites discrimination that is not associated with hatred or violence, provided that other effective remedies are available. It is also provided that a party may reserve the right not to apply the dissemination offence provided in Article 3 to those cases of discrimination for which, due to established principles in its national legal system concerning freedom of expression, it cannot provide for effective remedies.

---

488. See generally ECRI, "Legal instruments to combat racism on the Internet", report prepared by the Swiss Institute of Comparative Law (Lausanne), CRI (2000) 27, Strasbourg, August 2000.
489. Cooper, A. and Brackman, H., "Punishing Religious Defamation and Holocaust Denial: Is There a Double Standard?" (2006) *Equal Voices*, Issue 18, EUMC, at www.eumc.europa.eu.

It is therefore difficult to speculate how effective a regional international effort such as the Council of Europe additional protocol will be. States with strong constitutional protection for freedom of expression such as the USA will not rush to sign and ratify such international agreements and conventions. In fact, the US Government is highly unlikely to sign and ratify the additional protocol based on its constitutional values despite the recent changes in its administration with the Obama presidency. In other words, there may always be safe havens to host and carry content deemed to be illegal by certain national laws or under the terms of international agreements, protocols, and conventions.

Nevertheless, the signing and ratification of both the Convention on Cybercrime and more specifically the additional protocol have the potential to improve and harmonise procedural provisions within state laws in the fight against cybercrimes and racist Internet content and facilitate cross-border police operations. Criticism of some governments for their slow response is therefore not unwarranted. It is also predicted that further harmonisation will be achieved within the European Union region through the European Council Framework Decision on combating certain forms and expressions of racism and xenophobia by means of criminal law.

At the same time, even if all member states of the Council of Europe sign and ratify the additional protocol, the problems associated with racist Internet content may not quickly disappear. Certain websites will continue to be hosted in the United States and elsewhere in which the transmission of racist content is not criminalised. Racist organisations will continue to abuse the services offered by popular Web 2.0 applications and services including YouTube and Facebook. This, in a sense, reflects the true nature of the Internet, which carries inherent risks. The key question is how to manage these risks given the increasingly evident limitations of traditional legal responses at a national and international level. The next chapter will assess the additional and alternative methods of regulation which could be relied upon in the fight against hate speech and racist Internet content.

8.   Alternatives to state legislation (self- and co-regulatory initiatives)

This chapter will assess the alternative and additional measures to state legislation in the fight against racist content on the Internet. Therefore, self-regulatory and co-regulatory measures will be critically assessed.

Legal regulation is often designed to reduce risk but alternative methods can be less costly, more flexible, and quicker to adopt than prescriptive government legislation. Hence, alternative or additional options include the option of "doing nothing", social norms, self-regulation, co-regulation, and technical means, information, education and awareness campaigns.

It was growing concerns over the availability of racist content over the Internet that triggered the Council of Europe to develop the Additional Protocol to the Convention on Cybercrime. Therefore, "doing nothing" is not a viable option given the extent and expanding nature of the problem of racist content on the Internet. At the same time relying on social norms, customs and "netiquette" is also not a viable option as these will not be enforceable nor effective in a borderless multinational, and multicultural environment.[490] However, in the past few years companies that offer Web 2.0 services such as Google, YouTube, Facebook, Blogger, and others have adopted acceptable use policies[491] and community guidelines[492] and report abuse policies[493] to tackle the problem of racist content and hate speech that is uploaded to their systems by their users. Such policies and guidelines trigger these companies to remove or block access to content if the content in question is in breach of such guidelines and rules. For example, in the case of YouTube, users can flag inappropriate content or they can comment on the video files on the pages they are published.

However, the effectiveness of these self-regulatory policies has also shown their limitations, and companies like Facebook and YouTube have faced criticism from the media, international organisations, state-level regulators, as well as from non-governmental organisations. Christopher Wolf, Chair of the Anti-Defamation

---

490. See Gelbstein, E. and Kurbalija, J., *Internet Governance: Issues, Actors, and Divide*, DIPLO report, 2005, at www.diplomacy.edu/isl/ig/, p. 71.
491. See, for example, Facebook's Terms of Use and User Conduct Policy at www.facebook.com/.
492. See YouTube Community Guidelines at http://youtube.com/.
493. See Blogger Report Abuse pages at http://help.blogger.com/.

League Internet Task Force, recently stated that "YouTube, MySpace and Facebook prohibit content that is harmful, offensive or illegal or that violates the rights or threatens the safety of any person. On all three sites users have the right to report material violating the Terms of Use. However, such reports often are ignored and the content proliferates faster than conscientious users can report it."[494] For example, when US Senator Joseph Lieberman called in May 2008 for YouTube to take down al-Qaeda videos and all material from US designated terror groups that users had posted, YouTube did not remove them, and stated that most of the videos complained about did not contain material that violated YouTube's community guidelines and rejected Lieberman's request.[495] However, subsequently in September 2008 YouTube modified its community guidelines, and Lieberman stated that "Google's community guidelines for YouTube will now bar videos that incite violence, in addition to videos that contain hate speech and gratuitous violence".[496] However, YouTube will not impose a blanket ban on any groups or persons, and will only remove content from its servers if there is a breach of its community guidelines.

Other potential additional or alternative regulatory measures lie predominantly in the field of self- and co-regulation. The Declaration on Freedom of Communication on the Internet adopted by the Committee of Ministers of the Council of Europe on 28 May 2003 notably encouraged self-regulation and co-regulatory initiatives regarding Internet content. Similar recommendations were made in Council of Europe Recommendation Rec(2001)8 on self-regulation concerning cyber-content.[497] The European Union's Action Plan on promoting safer use of the Internet[498] also supports and encourages self-regulatory solutions especially in terms of protecting children from harmful content. One recognised benefit of self- and co-regulatory initiatives is that states and international organisations are encouraged to co-operate with NGOs and the private sector. This in turn promotes a socially responsible private sector which "can help realise an

---

494. See Remarks by Christopher Wolf, Chair, ADL Internet Task Force and Chair, International Network Against Cyber-Hate (INACH) to the Commission on Security and Cooperation in Europe (US Helsinki Commission): Briefing on Hate in the Information Age, Washington, DC, 15 May 2008, at www.adl.org.
495. Waterman, S., "Analysis: Should YouTube censor al-Qaida?" UPI, 20 May 2008. Note further US Senate Committee on Homeland Security and Governmental Affairs, *Violent Extremism, the Internet, and the Homegrown Terrorist Threat*, Majority & Minority Staff Report, 8 May 2008, at http://hsgac.senate.gov.
496. Fox News, "YouTube Yanks Radical Islamist Videos After Lieberman's Complaint", 11 September 2008, at www.foxnews.com/story/0,2933,420861,00.html.
497. Council of Europe Rec(2001)8, 5 September 2001.
498. Decision No. 854/2005/EC of the European Parliament and of the Council establishing a Multiannual Community Programme on promoting safer use of the Internet and new online technologies, PE-CONS 3688/1/04 REV1, Strasbourg, 11 May 2005.

Information Society that respects human rights".[499] This multi-actor approach is also supported by the United Nations' Durban Programme of Action[500] which encouraged the private sector to promote the development of voluntary ethical codes of conduct and self-regulatory measures, and policies and practices aimed at combating racism, racial discrimination, xenophobia and related intolerance.[501] Multi-actor partnership is also favoured at the UN Internet Governance Forum level to "help to find solutions to the issues arising from the use and misuse of the Internet, of particular concern to everyday users".[502]

ISPs and blocking access to illegal content

In terms of the role that can be played by ISPs it is recognised that the ISPs can contribute to the development of self-regulatory mechanisms such as industry-wide codes of conduct as well as hotlines to report illegal content. In terms of liability, a general monitoring obligation has not been imposed on ISPs within the Council of Europe or within the European Union region.

However, although no ISP controls third-party content or all of the backbones of the Internet, the role they play in providing access has made them visible targets for the control of content on the Internet, and their responsibility as gateways to communication for the mass public has been brought into question especially in relation to the availability of such illegal content as child pornography, pirated digital content such as music, movies, and TV episodes, and with regard to racist content. While ISPs are not directly part of the chain of liability in terms of offending behaviour, they are considered by many states, as well as international agreements and conventions, to be part of the chain which contributes to the distribution of illegal content on the Internet. Policy makers often consider whether ISPs should be compelled to block access to certain websites or whether they should be compelled to remove certain types of content from their servers.

Within the context of developing its revised Action Plan on Terrorism,[503] which includes the development of policies and measures to detect misuse of the Internet by extremist websites, and to enhance co-operation of states against terrorist use of the Internet, the European Union considered "adopting legal

---

499. Office of the High Commissioner for Human Rights, Background Note on the Information Society and Human Rights, WSIS/PC-3/CONTR/178-E, October 2003.

500. See generally the Report of the World Conference against Racism, Racial Discrimination, Xenophobia and Related Intolerance, Durban, 31 August to 8 September 2001, A/CONF.189/12, GE.02-10005 (E) 100102, 25 January 2002 at www.un.org/WCAR/aconf189_12.pdf.

501. Ibid., para. 144.

502. See generally Internet Governance Forum at www.intgovforum.org/.

503. Council of the European Union, Revised Action Plan on Terrorism, 10043/06, Brussels (31 May 2006).

measures obliging Internet service providers to remove or disable access to the dissemination of terrorist propaganda they host".[504] However, this policy option has been ruled out during the impact assessment work done by the European Commission with regard to the proposal for a Council framework decision amending Framework Decision 2002/475/JHA on combating terrorism.[505] The European Commission also ruled out "encouraging blocking through the industry's self-regulation or through agreements with industry, without the previous adoption of legal measures outlawing the dissemination of terrorist propaganda and terrorist expertise".[506]

The European Commission cited "the issue of the speedy re-apparition of websites that have been closed down" as the main reason for not recommending a blocking policy. The Commission argued that blocking policies are ineffective as in most cases blocked websites reappear under another name outside the jurisdiction of the European Union in order to avoid the eventuality of being closed down or blocked once more.[507] The Commission also acknowledged that existing methods of filtering can be circumvented,[508] and they are designed specifically for websites and are not capable of blocking the distribution of objectionable content through other Internet services such as P2P networks. The Commission within this context concluded that "the removal or disablement of access to terrorist propaganda or terrorist expertise by Internet service providers hosting such information, without the possibility to open an investigation and prosecute the one responsible behind such content, appears inefficient".[509] The Commission reached the conclusion that the dissemination of such content would only be hindered rather than eliminated.[510] The Commission expressed the opinion that:

> the adoption of blocking measures necessarily implies a restriction of human rights, in particular the freedom of expression and therefore, it can only be imposed by law, subject to the principle of proportionality, with respect to the legitimate aims pursued and to their necessity in a democratic society, excluding any form of arbitrariness or discriminatory or racist treatment.[511]

---

504. European Commission Staff Working Document, Accompanying document to the proposal for a Council Framework Decision amending Framework Decision 2002/475/JHA on combating terrorism: Impact Assessment, 14960/07 ADD1, Brussels, 13 November 2007, para. 4.2, pp. 29-30.
505. Ibid.
506. Ibid.
507. See ibid. See further Communication from the Commission to the European Parliament, the Council and the Committee of the Regions "Towards a general policy on the fight against cyber crime" of 22 May 2007 COM(2007) 267.
508. Ibid., p. 41.
509. Ibid.
510. See further ibid., section 5.2, pp. 41-42.
511. Ibid., p. 29.

Furthermore, the Commission expressed concern with regard to the cost of implementing blocking and filtering systems by ISPs and concluded that the implementation of such a system would have direct economic impact not only on ISPs but also on consumers.[512] The Commission, however, proposed to criminalise the public provocation to commit terrorist offences, recruitment for terrorism and training for terrorism by amending the Framework Decision on combating terrorism. It is expected that the amendments will take place during 2009.[513] Furthermore, partially declassified documents in relation to the EU Check the Web Project, which monitors the use of the Internet for terrorist purposes through Europol, suggest that "Member States will not be obliged to monitor, interrupt or shut down specific Internet sites" in the fight against terrorist use of the Internet.[514] Therefore, blocking access to websites is not a common policy adopted within the EU, and there are no EU policies actively encouraging blocking access to websites.

With regard to the deployment and use of blocking systems the Council of Europe Convention on Cybercrime Committee (T-CY) also recognised the legal difficulties which could arise when attempting to block certain sites with illegal content.[515] More importantly, a Council of Europe Committee of Ministers Recommendation, CM/Rec(2007)16 of November 2007, called upon the member states to promote freedom of communication and creation on the Internet regardless of frontiers, in particular by not subjecting individuals to any licensing or other requirements having a similar effect, nor any general blocking or filtering measures by public authorities, or restrictions that go further than those applied to other means of content delivery.[516] More recently, the Committee of Ministers in Recommendation CM/Rec(2008)6 of March 2008[517] recalled the Declaration of the Committee of Ministers on freedom of communication on the

---

512. Ibid., pp. 42-45.

513. See Proposal for a Council Framework Decision amending Framework Decision 2002/475/JHA on combating terrorism, 2007/0236 (CNS), COM(2007) 650 final, Brussels, 6.11.2007, at http://ec.europa.eu/commission_barroso/.

514. Council of the European Union, document No. 13930/06 RESTREINT UE, 13930/06, EXT 2, ENFOPOL 169, Brussels, 10 November 2008, Conclusions of the Kick-off conference "Check the Web", Berlin, 26-27 September 2006: this is a partially declassified document following a request to access the document made by Yaman Akdeniz.

515. Council of Europe Convention on Cybercrime Committee (T-CY), 2nd Multilateral Consultation of the Parties, Strasbourg, 13 and 14 June 2007, Strasbourg, 15 June 2007, T-CY (2007) 03, para. 29.

516. Recommendation CM/Rec(2007)16 of the Committee of Ministers to member states on measures to promote the public service value of the Internet: adopted by the Committee of Ministers on 7 November 2007 at the 1010th meeting of the Ministers' Deputies.

517. Recommendation CM/Rec(2008)6 of the Committee of Ministers to member states on measures to promote the respect for freedom of expression and information with regard to Internet filters: adopted by the Committee of Ministers on 26 March 2008 at the 1022nd meeting of the Ministers' Deputies.

Internet of 28 May 2003,[518] which stressed that public authorities should not, through general blocking or filtering measures, deny access to the public information and other communication on the Internet regardless of frontiers.[519] The Committee of Ministers stated that "there is a tendency to block access to the population to content on certain foreign or domestic web sites for political reasons. This and similar practices of prior State control should be strongly condemned."[520]

While a general blocking policy does not exist, and a general monitoring obligation cannot be imposed upon ISPs through Article 15 of the EU e-Commerce Directive, this does not stop states issuing "blocking orders". In early 1996, Deutsche Telekom blocked users of its subsidiary T-Online computer network from accessing Internet sites used to spread anti-Semitic propaganda. Deutsche Telekom was responding to demands by Mannheim prosecutors who were investigating Ernst Zündel and his Toronto-based Zundelsite.[521] This initial attempt to block access to Zündel's website resulted in the controversial material being copied and mirrored all over the Internet.[522] During 2002, North Rhine-Westphalia, Germany's most populous state, issued a blocking order to prevent German-based ISPs from providing access to websites based outside Germany (mainly in the US) if those sites host racist and neo-Nazi content.[523] The blocking order affected approximately 76 ISPs within that region.[524] Although there have been legal cases and appeals surrounding the blocking orders, a number of administrative courts have ruled that German authorities can continue to ask ISPs to block such websites. Prior to the issuing of the blocking order, the Düsseldorf District Authority President Jurgen Bussow wrote to four US ISPs in August 2000 requesting that they prevent access to four websites containing racist neo-Nazi material. As this action was unsuccessful, Bussow issued the blocking order to German ISPs within the North Rhine-Westphalia region.[525] Between 2002 and 2004 the Düsseldorf District

---

518. Freedom of communication on the Internet, Declaration adopted by the Council of Europe Committee of Ministers on 28 May 2003 at the 840th meeting of the Ministers' Deputies.

519. Ibid., Principle 3.

520. Recommendation CM/Rec(2008)6.

521. See "German Service Cuts Net Access", *San Jose Mercury News* (27 January 1996).

522. See further Akdeniz, Y., "To Link or Not to Link: Problems with World Wide Web Links on the Internet" (1997) 11:2 *Int'l Rev. L. Comp. & Tech* 281. See further Institute for Jewish Policy Research and American Jewish Committee, *Antisemitism World Report 1997*.

523. *National Journal's Technology Daily*, "Ban On Neo-Nazi Web Content In German State: Upheld", 22 December 2004.

524. See US Bureau of Democracy, Human Rights and Labor, "Report on Global Anti-Semitism", January 2005, at www.state.gov/g/drl/rls/40258.htm. Note also Combating racism, racial discrimination, xenophobia and related intolerance and comprehensive implementation of and follow-up to the Durban Declaration and Programme of Action Note by the UN Secretary-General, A/59/330, 4 October 2004.

525. See generally Eberwine, E. T., "Note & Comment: Sound and Fury Signifying Nothing?: Jurgen Bussow's Battle Against Hate-speech on the Internet" (2004) 49 *N.Y.L. Sch. L. Rev.* 353; and Van Blarcum, C. D., "Internet Hate Speech: The European Framework and the Emerging American Haven" (2005) 62 *Wash & Lee L. Rev.* 781.

Administration issued 90 ordinances against Internet providers in North Rhine-Westphalia, forcing them to block access to certain websites with right-wing extremist content. More recent statistics are not available, but the German authorities continue to issue blocking orders. However, as highlighted above, the effectiveness of such orders is questioned by the European Commission.

A similar attempt in France to block access to the Front14.org portal[526] and the racist sites it hosted for free was unsuccessful in 2001. J'accuse!, an association aimed at eradicating racism on the Internet, sued 14 major French ISPs[527] and although the court agreed that the racist portal violated French law, it did not require ISPs to block access to the portal.[528] But in June 2005, a Paris court ordered French ISPs to block access of French viewers to the website of the French revisionist organisation Association of Former Connoisseurs of War and Holocaust Stories (AAARGH).[529] Two US-based ISPs have since also agreed to stop hosting AAARGH's website.

Furthermore, some governments and state regulators may not always agree with blocking, and in August 2006, the Canadian Radio-Television and Telecommunications Commission (CRTC) refused to authorise the blocking by Canadian ISPs of two US neo-Nazi websites that published the personal contact information of Canadian lawyer and human rights activist Richard Warman.[530] The publication of Warman's personal details resulted in death threats which in turn led him to ask the Canadian ISPs to block access to the websites; they refused to do so in the absence of an order from the CRTC. The commission published its decision in a letter stating that it would be inappropriate to order blockage

---

526. The Front14.org website had the following disclaimer:
"Only front 14 offers free web hosting and e-mail exclusively to racialists. Join today. Many White people don't have the time and energy to put into hosting their own domain, so they join Geocities, Angelfire, etc, in an attempt to get their voices heard. But these 'free' services (who bombard you with ads) have adopted an aggressive anti-White policy. We decided to provide an alternative to proud White men and women, one that would be for our White interests only. Join."
527. In the course of 1996, the four principal network providers in France (Imaginet, Calvacon, Internetway and Internet France) blocked access to 14 discussion forums of French antisemitic and Holocaust-denying propaganda, advertisements for Nazi memorabilia and banned literature. In March 1997, the UEJF took out a court injunction against nine network providers guilty of transmitting Holocaust-denial material. It was the country's first Internet trial. No penalty has been announced, but the network providers have been ordered to revise contracts to ensure that racist and Holocaust-denial propaganda is removed from the sites on which they appear. See Institute for Jewish Policy Research and American Jewish Committee, *Antisemitism World Report 1997*.
528. Trib. gr. inst. Paris, ordonnance de référé, 30 October 2001, online : www.foruminternet.org. See generally Benoit Frydman and Isabelle Rorive, "Regulating Internet Content through Intermediaries in Europe and the USA" (2002) 23 *Zeitschrift für Rechtssoziologie* Heft 1, S. 41-59, at www.isys.ucl.ac.be/e.
529. See US Bureau of Democracy, Human Rights, and Labor, International Religious FreedomReport 2005 – France, at www.state.gov/g/drl/rls/irf/2005/51552.htm.
530. See "Ottawa lawyer loses CRTC bid to block access to US website: Neo-Nazis calling for man's death" *Ottawa Citizen* (27 August 2006). The websites in question were www. overthrow.com and http://dossiernoir.blogspot.com.

of the particular websites without affording Canadian ISPs and all other interested parties an opportunity for comment.[531]

As racist websites and organisations seem to find refuge in the United States, where they benefit from the protection offered by the First Amendment, the utility and effectiveness of various blocking or removal orders around the globe remains to be seen. However, in the case of Redwatch.info, the website of the Polish wing of the neo-fascist Blood and Honour organisation, the Federal Bureau of Investigation (FBI) contacted the hosting company in Arizona which decided to remove the website from its server.[532] Redwatch.info published blacklists of Polish gays, feminists and left-wing sympathisers, including personal information such as their names, photos, and in some cases their addresses, phone numbers, and car registration numbers. Polish police asked the FBI for assistance in May 2006, following a knife attack in Warsaw on a Jewish human rights activist who was named on the website. Several journalists with left-leaning political affiliations who were named on the website were also threatened.

Nevertheless, even when responsible US hosting companies agree to remove racist websites from their servers, hosting for those sites is still available through specialised companies such as NSM88 Network, a design network initiated and maintained by America's Nazi Party. In fact, when nukeisrael.com was removed from the servers of a Toronto-based Canadian ISP called Canaca.com in May 2005, the site was simply moved to the NSM88 Network.[533]

Notice-based liability for ISPs and takedown procedures

In terms of ISP liability, in most instances liability will only be imposed upon ISPs if there is "knowledge and control" over the information which is transmitted or stored by an ISP. Based on the "knowledge and control theory" notice-based takedown procedures have been developed in Europe. For example, the EU Directive on Electronic Commerce[534] provides a limited and notice-based liability with takedown procedures for illegal content.

The EU directive suggested that "it is in the interest of all parties involved in the provision of information society services to adopt and implement procedures"[535]

---

531. Letter from Canadian Radio-television and Telecommunications Commission to J. Edward Antecol (24 August 2006), CRTC File No. 8622-P49-200610510, at www.crtc.gc.ca/. See further Michael Geist, "Content blocking a can of worms that must be opened", *The Toronto Star* (28 August 2006).

532. See "Polish police, US FBI block neo-Nazi website", Agence France Presse (6 July 2006).

533. See League for Human Rights of B'nai Brith Canada, 2005 *Audit of Antisemitic Incidents 2005* (2006), at www.bnaibrith.ca/audit2005.html.

534. Directive 2000/31/EC of the European Parliament and of the Council of 8 June 2000 on certain legal aspects of information society services, in particular electronic commerce, in the Internal Market, Official Journal of the European Communities, vol. 43, OJ L 178 17 July 2000, p. 1.

535. Ibid.

to remove and disable access to illegal information. As far as hosting issues by ISPs or information society service providers are concerned, Article 14(1) of the e-Commerce Directive requires member states to:

> ensure that the service provider is not liable for the information stored at the request of a recipient of the service, on condition that:
>
> (a) the provider does not have actual knowledge of illegal activity or information and, as regards claims for damages, is not aware of facts or circumstances from which the illegal activity or information is apparent; or
>
> (b) the provider, upon obtaining such knowledge or awareness, acts expeditiously to remove or to disable access to the information.

Therefore, there is no absolute protection provided within the directive for ISPs and the European ISPs are required to act expeditiously "upon obtaining actual knowledge" of illegal activity or content "to remove or to disable access to the information concerned".[536] Such removal or disabling of access "has to be undertaken in the observance of the principle of freedom of expression and of procedures established for this purpose at national level"[537] according to the directive. Under the directive, "notice" has to be specific and may be given by an individual complainant or by a self-regulatory hotline. In some states the notice may be given by law-enforcement agencies or provided through court orders.

Termination or prevention of an infringement is also possible by a court or administrative authority order. Article 14(3) also states that the provisions of Article 14 do not "affect the possibility for Member States of establishing procedures governing the removal or disabling of access to information". It was decided that the notice and takedown procedures would not be regulated in the directive itself.[538] Rather, the directive, through Recital 40 and Article 16, encourages self-regulatory solutions and procedures to be developed by the Internet industry to implement and bring into action notice and takedown procedures.[539]

In addition to the notice-based limited liability exceptions, the directive prevents member states from imposing a monitoring obligation on service providers only with respect to obligations of a general nature but "this does not concern monitoring obligations in a specific case, and in particular, does not affect orders by national authorities in accordance with national legislation".[540] Under Article 15,

---

536. Ibid., para. 46.
537. Ibid.
538. See Report from the Commission to the European Parliament, the Council and the European Economic and Social Committee – First report on the application of Directive 2000/31/EC on electronic commerce), COM(2003) 702 final, Brussels, 21 November 2003, section 4.7.
539. Of those member states which have transposed the directive, only Finland has included a legal provision setting out a notice and takedown procedure concerning copyright infringements only. This information has been taken from the above-mentioned Commission Report: COM(2003) 702 final.
540. Ibid., para. 47.

the directive specifically requires member states not to "impose a general obligation on providers, when providing the services covered by Articles 12, 13 and 14, to monitor the information which they transmit or store, nor impose a general obligation actively to seek facts or circumstances indicating illegal activity". However, member states "may establish obligations for information society service providers promptly to inform the competent public authorities of alleged illegal activities undertaken or information provided by recipients of their service or obligations to communicate to the competent authorities, at their request".[541]

Overall, the e-Commerce Directive provides limited and notice-based liability with takedown procedures for illegal content and requires member states and the Commission to encourage the development of codes of conduct.[542] A European Commission analysis of work on notice and takedown procedures published in 2003 claimed that "though a consensus is still some way off, agreement would appear to have been reached among stake holders in regards to the essential elements which should be taken into consideration".[543] However, various studies so far showed that ISPs based in Europe tend to remove and take down content without challenging the notices they receive. A Dutch study claimed that "it only takes a Hotmail account to bring a website down, and freedom of speech stands no chance in front of the cowboy-style private ISP justice".[544]

Furthermore, although primarily developed to combat child pornography, the concept of notice-based liability is expanding to other types of content including pirated content, racist content, and terrorism-related materials over the Internet.[545] An example is the British Government's proposed criminalisation of the encouragement of terrorism and the dissemination of terrorist material through the Internet following the July 2005 terrorist attacks in London.[546] The Terrorism Act 2006, which came into force in March 2006, contains provisions

---

541. Article 14(2).

542. Ibid., para. 49.

543. See report from the Commission to the European Parliament, the Council and the European Economic and Social Committee – First report on the application of Directive 2000/31/EC on electronic commerce, COM(2003) 702 final, Brussels, 21.11.2003, at http://europa.eu.int/, section 4.7.

544. Nas, S., (Bits of Freedom), "The Multatuli Project: ISP notice & take down", (2004), at www.bof.nl/docs/researchpaperSANE.pdf. Note also Ahlert, C., Marsden, C. and Yung, C., "How 'Liberty' Disappeared from Cyberspace: The Mystery Shopper Tests Internet Content Self-Regulation", at http://pcmlp.socleg.ox.ac.uk/.

545. See, for example, Brynjar Lia, "Al-Qaeda online: understanding jihadist internet infrastructure", in *Jane's Intelligence Review* (1 January 2006).

546. But note the human rights considerations, especially in relation to freedom of expression: ODIHR, *Background Paper on Human Rights Considerations in Combating Incitement to Terrorism and Related Offences* (2006), at www.osce.org.

criminalising the encouragement of terrorism[547] and the dissemination of terrorist publications.[548] The Act also includes notice and takedown provisions if the encouragement or dissemination takes place over the Internet.[549] Hazel Blears, the Minister of State for the Home Office, explained that the intention behind section 3 is "to provide a method by which webmasters could be made aware of content on their websites, thus ensuring that they could not claim not to have known about it if they were subsequently prosecuted".[550]

Contrasting approach adopted in the USA

It is important to note the different approach adopted in the United States to ISP liability. While a notice-based liability policy seems to be preferred in Europe, American ISPs have more protection from liability for third party content regardless of their "knowledge" of it. In the United States, section 230(c)(1) of the Communications Decency Act provides that "no provider or user of an interactive computer service shall be treated as the publisher or speaker of any information provided by another information content provider".[551] Section 230 was considered and tested by the Fourth Circuit Court of Appeals in *Zeran v. America Online Inc.*, a defamation case where the court held that "by its plain language, section 230 created a federal immunity to any cause of action that would make service providers liable for information originating with a third-party user of the service".[552]

---

547. Terrorism Act 2006 (UK), 2006, c. 11, s. 1: "This section applies to a statement that is likely to be understood by some or all of the members of the public to whom it is published as a direct or indirect encouragement or other inducement to them to the commission, preparation or instigation of acts of terrorism …".

548. Ibid., s. 2(2): dissemination of terrorist publications includes: distributing or circulating a terrorist publication; giving, selling, or lending such a publication; offering such a publication for sale or loan; providing a service to others that enables them to obtain, read, listen to or look at such a publication, or to acquire it by means of a gift, sale or loan; transmitting the contents of such a publication electronically.

549. Ibid. ss. 3, 4.

550. UK HC, *Parliamentary Debates*, vol. 442, col. 1471 (15 February 2006).

551. Communications Decency Act, 47 U.S.C. (1996). Section 230(e)(2) defines "interactive computer service" as "any information service, system, or access software provider that provides or enables computer access by multiple users to a computer server, including specifically a service or system that provides access to the Internet and such systems operated or services offered by libraries or educational institutions". Section 230(e)(3) defines "information content provider" as "any person or entity that is responsible, in whole or in part, for the creation or development of information provided through the Internet or any other interactive computer service". See however, the different policy established for copyright infringement with the passage of the *Digital Millenium Copyright Act of 1998*, Pub. L. No. 105-304, 112 Stat. 2860.

552. *Zeran v. America Online Inc.*, 129 F.3d 327 at 330 (4th Cir. 1997), certiorari denied, 48 S. Ct. 2341 (1998). The plaintiff's claim, which arose out of a false bulletin board posting that the plaintiff was selling t-shirts with offensive messages about the Oklahoma City bombing, was framed as one for negligence in failing to remove the posting, but the court said that the allegations were in substance indistinguishable from a "garden variety defamation action": 129 F.3d 327 at 332.

Nor did the fact that the provider had notice of the transmission of wrongful material prevent the operation of this immunity in Zeran. However, it should be noted that the Zeran decision is often criticised[553] and in his dissent in *Doe v. America Online, Inc.* Lewis J wrote that "the so-called 'Decency Act' has, contrary to well-established legal principles, been transformed from an appropriate shield into a sword of harm and extreme danger which places technology buzz words and economic considerations above the safety and general welfare of our people".[554] Yet, in *Batzel v. Smith*,[555] the US Court of Appeals for the Ninth Circuit re-emphasised that "in insulating Internet service providers from liability for certain content published on their sites, [Congress] recognised the importance of protecting the unfettered and unregulated development of free speech on the Internet".[556] Although the Zeran decision remains the authority on ISP liability, "whether or not that is a desirable state of affairs is of course a matter for debate".[557] Section 230 and the protection it offers to US ISPs remains the current law in the United States,[558] and its protection also extends to obscene and other types of content.[559]

Despite such protection being granted to ISPs, US regulators have introduced provisions for legal responsibility for the reporting of child pornography by electronic communication service providers in 2004 under 42 USC 13032. This provision includes a "duty to report" when an electronic communication service provider "obtains knowledge of facts or circumstances from which a violation of sections 2251, 2251A, 2252, 2252A, 2252B, or 2260 of title 18, United States Code, involving child pornography (as defined in section 2256 of that title), or a violation of section 1466A of that title is apparent".[560] The Digital Millennium Copyright Act 1998 (DMCA) is the only US legislation which provides notice-based liability for ISPs within the context of intellectual property infringements.

Finally, with regard to the effectiveness of notice and takedown orders, the Canadian Human Rights Tribunal in *Warman v. Kyburz* assessed that "the unique nature of

---

553. See, for example, *Doe v. GTE Corp.*, 347 F.3d. 655 (7th Cir. 2003) (held, Zeran was flawed). See also *Barrett v. Rosenthal*, 9 Cal. Rptr. 3d 142 at 154 (C.A. 2004). See further David A. Myers, "Defamation and the Quiescent Anarchy of the Internet: A Case Study of Cyber Targeting" (2006) 110 *Penn St. L. Rev.* 667.
554. *Doe v. America Online Inc.*, 783 So. 2d 1010 (Fla. Sup. Ct. 2001), Lewis J dissenting.
555. *Batzel v. Smith*, 333 F.3d 1018 at 1027 (9th Cir. 2003) quoted in *Yahoo! Inc. v. La Ligue Contre le Racisme et l'Antisémitisme*, 433 F.3d 1199 (9th Cir. 2006).
556. Ibid.
557. See generally Akdeniz, Y. and Rogers, H., "Defamation on the Internet" in Akdeniz et al., eds., *The Internet, Law and Society* (Essex: Longman, 2000) pp. 294-317.
558. Note further cases such as *Nemet Chevrolet, Ltd. v. Consumeraffairs.com, Inc.*, 564 F. Supp. 2d 544 (E.D. Va. 2008); and *Universal Communication Systems, Inc. v. Lycos*, Inc., 478 F.3d 413, 35 *Media L. Rep.* (BNA) 1417 (1st Cir. 2007).
559. *Langdon v. Google Inc.*, D.Del. (2007), 474 F.Supp.2d 622.
560. 42 USCS para. 13032 (b)(1). See generally Akdeniz, Y., *Internet Child Pornography and the Law: National and International Responses* (Ashgate, 2008), pp. 93-141.

Internet technology, including the jurisdictional challenges arising from the borderless world of cyberspace, as well as the 'moving targets' created by the use of mirror sites raise real concerns as to the efficacy of cease and desist orders in relation to hate messages disseminated on the Internet".[561] Despite these difficulties and technical challenges, a "cease and desist order can have both a practical and symbolic effect".[562] Such a decision can prevent (albeit not always successfully) the individuals or organisations concerned from continuing to publish material of a racist nature. Apart from trying to prevent and eliminate discriminatory practices, such a decision also has a significant symbolic value in the public denunciation of such actions.

Internet hotlines for reporting illegal content

Notice-based liability systems have been developed hand to hand in Europe with hotlines to report illegal Internet content. While most Internet hotlines do have expertise in terms of content involving indecent photographs of children under the age of 18 (child pornography), the same may not be said for content involving racist material on the Internet. This type of content is predominantly text-based and in most cases assessing the racist nature of a Web-based publication may not be as straightforward as in the case of content involving child pornography.

However, expertise and specialised hotlines do exist in Europe, and it is worth mentioning the International Network Against Cyber Hate (INACH)[563] which acts as an umbrella organisation for hotlines specialised in racist content. INACH was set up in 2002[564] by the Magenta Foundation, the Dutch Complaints Bureau for Discrimination on the Internet and by Jugendschutz.net in Germany. The work of both the Dutch and the German hotlines are noteworthy in this field. The Dutch hotline received a total of 5 825 complaints about racist content between 1997 and 2003.[565] In 2002, of the 1 798 reported expressions, 1 619 originated in the Netherlands, and 1 238 were deemed illegal following the hotline's own assessment. In 881 cases, the Dutch hotline asked that the content in question be removed, and was successful in 557 instances.[566] In 2003 alone, the hotline dealt with 1 496

---

561. *Warman v. Kyburz* (9 May 2003) 2003 CHRT 18, at para. 81. For Canadian Human Rights Tribunal decisions in Internet-related cases see further: *Warman v. Harrison* (15 August 2006) 2006 CHRT 30; *Warman v. Kulbashian* (10 March 2006) 2006 CHRT 11; *Warman v. Winnicki* (13 April 2006) 2006 CHRT 20.

562. *Warman v. Harrison* (15 August 2006) 2006 CHRT 30, at paras. 71-72.

563. See www.inach.net. Note the INACH reports, "Antisemitism on the Internet", April 2004, and "Hate on the Net – Virtual nursery for In Real Life crime", June 2004.

564. Note the INACH Annual Report for 2005 which was published during 2006 at www.inach.net/.

565. Ibid.

566. Magenta Foundation, Complaints Bureau for Discrimination on the Internet, *Meldpunt Discriminatie Internet, Annual Report 2002* (Amsterdam: Stichting Magenta, 2003), at www. inach.net/.

reported expressions; 797 of these were deemed illegal and the hotline was successful in the removal of 624 expressions of the 655 instances reported to the authorities.[567]

In Germany, Jugendschutz.net's activities resulted in action against 184 illegal extreme right-wing websites in 2003.[568] In 154 instances, websites were blocked by German ISPs or relevant parts removed from the Internet in cases where they were hosted within Germany, and 107 of these were considered to be illegal websites based in Germany, while 47 were based on foreign servers.[569] During 2004, the hotline asked German hosting companies and service providers to block access or remove 131 further websites.[570] During 2007 Jugendschutz.net contacted service and content providers 252 times and was successful in the closure of websites and takedown of content on 232 occasions.[571]

In May 2008, in the United States, the Simon Wiesenthal Center launched a new web-based initiative to combat the growing wave of hate and terror sites. The initiative will act as a hotline to report hate-, racism-, and terrorism-related content and an e-mail address (ireport@wiesenthal.com) has been set up for this purpose.[572]

However, reporting to the hotlines seems to be low, and users seem to prefer to report illegal content they come across to the police rather than to the hotlines. According to a EuroBarometer Survey 2008 which was conducted in October 2008 with approximately 12 750 randomly selected parents of children aged 6-17 years old who were interviewed in the 27 EU member states, 92% "thought of the police when asked how they would report illegal or harmful content seen on the Internet".[573] Only four out of 10 parents (38%) said they would report such content to a hotline set up for this purpose and one-third mentioned non-profit or other associations. The survey results seem to challenge the self-claimed success of some of the hotlines operating in the European region as under-reporting seems to be a huge problem.

Although hotlines could potentially play an important role in relation to illegal Internet content there remain significant question marks in terms of their operation. Hotlines are often criticised as there remain serious concerns regarding

---

567. Magenta Foundation, Complaints Bureau for Discrimination on the Internet, *Meldpunt Discriminatie Internet, Annual Report 2003* (Amsterdam: Stichting Magenta, 2004), at www.inach.net/.

568. Jugendschutz.net, *Annual Report 2003: Right-Wing Extremism on the Internet*, at www.inach.net/.

569. See further Jugendschutz.net, *Chart of illegal and blocked websites containing right-wing extremism 01.01.-31.12.2003*, 2003, at www.inach.net/.

570. Jugendschutz.net, *Right-Wing Extremism on the Internet – successful strategies against Online-Hate*, 2004 Annual Report, at www.inach.net/.

571. Jugendschutz.net, *Annual Report 2007, Right-Wing Extremism on the Internet*, 15 June 2008.

572. Press Release: Wiesenthal Center Launches New Web-Based Initiative At Capitol Hill Hearing, iREPORT@wiesenthal.com to be clearing house for Hate postings, 16 May 2008, at www.wiesenthal. com/. Note further Stone, B., "Tracking Hate 2.0 on the Web", *The New York Times*, 20 May 2008.

573. EuroBarometer Survey 2008, Summary Report, available through http://ec.europa.eu/.

the "policing" role such organisations play. Many maintain that decisions involving illegality should remain a matter for courts of law rather than hotline operators and "these hotlines violate due process concepts that are also enshrined in international, regional, and national guarantees around the world".[574] Whilst it may be tempting to identify and attempt to block content posted to particular newsgroups, websites, or other Internet forums that seem devoted to illegal material there is concern that such measures could set dangerous precedents if hotlines assume the role of the courts. Such an approach could result in an act of privatised censorship that would come to be applied too broadly over time. This danger was recognised in the Martabit report to the UN which stated "while encouraging these initiatives, States should ensure that the due process of law is respected and effective remedies remain available in relation to measures enforced".[575]

Self-regulation through code: rating and filtering systems

The development of rating and filtering systems has been encouraged since the mid-1990s to deal with harmful Internet content as a means of user empowerment. Such tools are "promoted in order to enable users to make their own decisions on how to deal with unwanted and harmful content".[576] Rating systems, such as the Platform for Internet Content Selections (PICS),[577] work by embedding electronic labels into web documents to vet their content before a computer displays them.[578] The vetting system could include political, religious, advertising or commercial topics that can be added either by the publisher of the material or by a third party (for example, an ISP or an independent vetting body).

In addition to the rating systems, several filtering software tools have been developed to prevent children from deliberately or accidentally accessing illegal and harmful content such as racist materials. These stand-alone tools are available in response to the wishes of parents making decisions about what their children can access at home. The type of harmful, offensive, disturbing, shocking, unwanted or undesirable content that is blocked by various filtering software usually includes: sexually explicit material; graphically violent material; content advocating hate;

---

574. Per Professor Nadine Strossen, from an ACLU Press Release, "ACLU Joins International Protest Against Global Internet Censorship Plans", 9 September 1999, at www.aclu.org/.

575. Report of the Intergovernmental Working Group on the effective implementation of the Durban Declaration and Programme of Action on its fourth session (Chairperson-Rapporteur: Juan Martabit (Chile)), E/CN.4/2006/18, 20 March 2006, at http://daccessdds.un.org/, at para. 47.

576. The EU Safer Internet Plus programme, from Decision No. 854/2005/EC.

577. Note also the ICRA (Internet Content Rating Association) system which follows from the RSACi system; see www.icra.org/.

578. See Computer Professionals for Social Responsibility, "Filtering FAQ" http://cpsr.org/. Note that most filtering systems based on third-party rating, such as CyberPatrol, are compliant with the PICS labelling system.

and content advocating illegal activity such as drug use, bomb-making, or under-age drinking and gambling.

The market for filtering software is blooming, and there are currently around 50 filtering products (mainly US-based),[579] and approximately 40 of these block content that advocate or promote hatred and discrimination. A specific filtering software to restrict access to websites that may encourage endorsement of or participation in acts of terrorism was developed in the UK following joint work between the Internet industry and government, and it was announced in November 2008 by the Home Office that this tool would be freely available for parents, schools, businesses and Web users to download.[580]

For a long time, filtering software was seen as a preferable alternative to government legislation including at the US Supreme Court level,[581] and it has been stated that "promoting filter use does not condemn as criminal any category of speech, and so the potential chilling effect is eliminated, or at least much diminished".[582] It was argued that filters might well be more effective than certain legislation and impose selective restrictions on speech at the receiving end, and would prevent universal restrictions at the source level. It has since been acknowledged by the Supreme Court that "filtering software is not a perfect solution because it may block some materials not harmful to minors and fail to catch some that are".[583]

Filtering software use in Europe

A EuroBarometer survey was conducted in October 2008 to study parents' views about their children's use of the Internet, to determine parents' strategies to supervise their child's Internet usage and their own awareness of safety measures.[584] Approximately 12 750 randomly selected parents of children aged 6-17 years old were interviewed in the 27 EU member states. Half of the parents – with a child who accessed the Internet at home – answered that they had installed filtering software on the computer that their children used at home as 45% of the parents interviewed were very worried that their children might see sexually or violently explicit images on the Internet. However, there was considerable variation across countries in the use of monitoring and filtering software, and

---

579. See http://kids.getnetwise.org/tools/index.php.

580. See Home Office press release, "Industry and government work together to tackle internet terror", 18 November 2008, at http://press.homeoffice.gov.uk/press-releases/.

581. *Reno v. ACLU*, 117 S. Ct. 2329 (1997).

582. *Ashcroft, Attorney General v. American Civil Liberties Union et al.*, certiorari to the United States Court of Appeals for the Third Circuit, No. 03–218. Argued 2 March 2004 – Decided 29 June 2004, at http://supct.law.cornell.edu/supct/html/03-218.ZS.html. See further *ACLU v. Reno II*, No. 99-1324. For the full decision see http://pacer.ca3.uscourts.gov:8080/.

583. Ibid.

584. See EuroBarometer Survey 2008, Summary Report, available through http://ec.europa.eu.

more than half of the British parents used such software compared to only 5% of the parents in Romania and Bulgaria. More than six out of 10 parents – who did not use filtering or monitoring software – simply saw no need for such software since they trusted their children on the Internet. In Greece, 53%, in Hungary, 80% and in Ireland, Cyprus, Romania, the UK and Malta between 36% and 48% of the parents provided this as the reason for not using the filtering software. Only a minority (3%) did not use such software because they did not believe in its efficiency.

Apart from usage-related issues, it is important to note the limitations and criticisms related to rating and filtering systems. Neither system offers total protection to citizens or addresses content-related problems in full. The key limitations are highlighted below.

Limited functionality of rating systems

Although various governments have welcomed the use and development of rating systems, the capacity of these tools is limited to certain parts of the Internet. Rating systems are designed for websites while excluding other Internet-related communication forums such as chat environments,[585] file transfer protocol (ftp) servers,[586] peer-to-peer (p2p) networks, Usenet discussion groups, real-audio and real-video systems (which can include live sound and image transmissions), and finally the ubiquitous e-mail communication. These cannot be rated with the systems that are currently available and therefore the assumption that rating systems would make the Internet a "safer environment" is false as World Wide Web content represents only a fraction of the whole of the Internet; it may be argued that it is the most fanciful and rapidly growing fraction, but problems such as racism are not unique to the World Wide Web. The development of rating systems has been gradual and it does not seem realistic to expect that they will ever be widely used.

Third-party systems and problems with accountability

If the duty of rating is handed to third parties, this could cause problems for freedom of speech and with few third-party rating products currently available, the potential for arbitrary censorship increases. This would leave no scope for argument and dissent because the ratings would be done by private bodies without any "direct" government involvement. So far this has not been the case, but as self-rating is not booming, from time to time third-party rating systems are considered.

---

585. Interactive environments, like chat channels, cannot be rated as the exchange and transmission of information takes place live and spontaneously.

586. It is estimated there are nearly a million ftp servers accessible via the Internet; some of these online libraries may have offensive content or legal content that may be considered harmful for children.

Defective filtering systems

Another downside of relying on such technologies is that these systems can lead to restrictions on access to socially useful websites and information.[587] It has been reported many times that filtering systems and software can be over-inclusive, limiting access to and censoring inconvenient websites,[588] as well as filtering potentially educational materials regarding AIDS, drug abuse prevention and teenage pregnancy. According to the report on Internet filters by the National Coalition Against Censorship:

–   I-Gear blocked an essay on "Indecency on the Internet: Lessons from the Art World", the United Nations report "HIV/AIDS: The Global Epidemic", and the home pages of four photography galleries.

–   Net Nanny, SurfWatch, Cybersitter, and Bess, among other products, blocked House Majority Leader Richard "Dick" Armey's official website upon detecting the word "dick".

–   SmartFilter blocked the Declaration of Independence, Shakespeare's complete plays, *Moby Dick*, and *Marijuana: Facts for Teens*, a brochure published by the National Institute on Drug Abuse (a division of the National Institute of Health).

–   SurfWatch blocked human rights sites like the Commissioner of the Council of the Baltic Sea States and Algeria Watch, as well as the University of Kansas' Archie R. Dykes Medical Library (upon detecting the word "dykes").

–   X-Stop blocked the National Journal of Sexual Orientation Law, Carnegie Mellon University's Banned Books page, "Let's Have an Affair" catering company, and, through its "foul word" function, searches for *Bastard Out of Carolina* and *The Owl and the Pussy Cat.*[589]

At the same time some filtering software has been criticised for under-blocking.[590] In general, there is too much reliance on mindless mechanical blocking through identification of key words and phrases. Moreover, this is usually based on the morality to which a particular company or organisation is committed in devel-

---

587. See Electronic Privacy Information Center, "Faulty Filters: How Content Filters Block Access to Kid-Friendly Information on the Internet" (Washington, 1997), at www.epic.org/. See generally www.peacefire.org as well as Seth Finkelstein, "Anticensorware Investigations – Censorware Exposed", at http://sethf.com/ anticensorware/.
588. Gay & Lesbian Alliance Against Defamation, *Access Denied: The Impact of Internet Filtering Software on the Lesbian and Gay Community* (New York, 1997), at www.glaad.org/.
589. Marjorie Heins and Christina Cho, *Internet Filters: A Public Policy Research* (2001), at www.ncac.org.
590. At one time, WebSENSE published a daily list of sexually explicit websites to show which websites its competitors did not block. Anybody – including students from schools that were using SmartFilter and SurfControl – could access the list, however, simply by clicking a button on the WebSENSE site agreeing that they were over the age of 18. See Peacefire's report on WebSENSE at http://peacefire.org.

oping their filtering criteria and databases. Broad and varying concepts of offensiveness, inappropriateness, or disagreement with the political viewpoint of the manufacturer are seen in the use of such tools. Most of the companies creating this kind of software provide no appeal mechanism[591] to content providers who are banned or blocked, thereby "subverting the self-regulating exchange of information that has been a hallmark of the Internet community".[592]

In the framework of the EU Safer Internet Plus programme, Deloitte Enterprise Risk Services has been performing a Study on Benchmarking of Filtering software and services in collaboration with the Katholieke Universiteit Leuven and DLA Piper since 2006.[593] This study involved 26 tools for parental control, and the benchmark analyses how effectively these technical solutions protect children aged 6 to 16 against harmful content on the Internet. About 140 parents and teachers from various European countries were involved in the study. During their 2008 study, although the researchers observed a very positive trend in filter accuracy, they also detected certain products that unduly over-blocked harmless content.

The researchers also found out that the filtering products they tested struggle with user-driven Web 2.0 based services and sites such as YouTube, Flickr, MySpace and Hyves (popular in the Netherlands). According to the study, the filtering solutions benchmarked had great difficulty in distinguishing innocent content from harmful in these highly dynamic environments. The researchers found that the traditional methods of blacklisting or whitelisting are not suitable to address the availability of harmful content through Web 2.0 based services. The benchmarking study reported that most of the tested filtering solutions need further improvement before they successfully filter non-obvious, non-pornographic content for youngsters aged 11-16 years.

Circumvention is possible

Apart from the worrying defects explained above, circumvention of such tools is also relatively easy. There is not only the often-cited example of children uninstalling or removing such software from their computers, but also a piece of software known as Circumventor, developed by Peacefire.org, which bypasses any content-blocking attempts including those by the likes of CyberSitter and

---

591. Some companies provide a review mechanism and others let their databases be searched online, but in most cases, without testing the software itself, an online content provider would not know if its webpage was being blocked by the filtering software. Considering the number of such software products, it is an impossible task to find out whether one blocks a certain website and for what reason.
592. Letter from Computer Professionals for Social Responsibility to Solid Oak, makers of CyberSitter (18 December 1996) at www.cpsr.org.
593. Deloitte Enterprise Risk Services, SIP-Bench Synthesis Report 2008, available through www.sip-bench.eu/.

NetNanny.[594] One of the main motivations for developing Circumventor was Peacefire.org's desire to bypass censorship of political websites. It is a well-known fact that almost all Internet users in China[595] and the Middle East[596] are prevented from accessing a considerable number of political websites. Technologies like Circumventor can help Internet users in censored countries to access such websites. In addition to Circumventor, websites providing anonymous proxy services and anonymous web surfing (such as anonymizer.com, the Electronic Frontier Foundation's (EFF) TOR network[597] and onion routers) can also be used to bypass filtering. It is, however, often the case that the filters block such well-known websites and proxy servers, which is why Circumventor, accessed through an unknown IP address (or one known to a limited number of users), provides better success in circumvention and avoids possible unintended risks associated with circumvention technologies.[598]

Freedom of expression and censorship

Problems associated with rating and filtering systems were also acknowledged at the European Union level. As the Economic and Social Committee of the European Commission pointed out in its report on the European Commission's Action Plan on promoting safe use of the Internet,[599] it is highly unlikely that the proposed measures will result in a safe Internet in the long term, with the task of rating and classification of all information on the Internet being "impracticable".[600] More importantly, the committee was worried that the possibility of ISPs using filtering and rating systems at the level of entry would render these systems, dubbed as "user empowering", an instrument of control, "actually taking choice out of citizens' hands". The committee concluded that there was "little future in the active promotion of filtering systems based on rating".[601]

An important and more recent Council of Europe Recommendation CM/Rec(2008)6 of March 2008 stated that any intervention by member states that forbids access to specific Internet content may constitute a restriction on freedom

---

594. For further information about Peacefire.org's Circumventor, see www.peacefire.org.

595. See OpenNet Initiative, *Probing Chinese search engine filtering* (August 2004), at www.opennet.net/.

596. See generally Jonathan Zittrain and Benjamin Edelman, *Documentation of Internet Filtering Worldwide* (Berkman Center for Internet & Society, 2003), at http://cyber.law.harvard.edu/filtering/.

597. See http://torproject.org/.

598. See further OpenNet Initiative, *Unintended Risks and Consequences of Circumvention Technologies: The IBB's Anonymizer Service in Iran* (May 2004), at www. opennet.net.

599. EC Commission, Opinion of the Economic and Social Committee on the "Proposal for a Council Decision adopting a Multiannual Community Action Plan on promoting safe use of the Internet", [1998] OJ C 214/29.

600. Ibid. at para. 4.1.1.

601. Ibid. See further Akdeniz, Y., "The Regulation of Internet Content in Europe: Governmental Control versus Self-Responsibility" (1999) 5(2) *Swiss Political Science Review* 123.

of expression and access to information in the online environment and that such a restriction would have to fulfil the conditions in Article 10(2) of the European Convention on Human Rights and the relevant case law of the European Court of Human Rights. The recommendation noted that the voluntary and responsible use of Internet filters (products, systems and measures to block or filter Internet content) can promote confidence and security on the Internet for users, in particular children and young people, while also noting that the use of such filters can seriously impact on the right to freedom of expression and information as protected by Article 10 of the Convention.

The March 2008 Guidelines provided within Recommendation CM/Rec(2008)6[602] stated that Internet users should have the possibility to challenge the blocking decisions or filtering of content and be able to seek clarifications and remedies.[603] The guidelines called upon the member states to refrain from filtering Internet content in electronic communications networks operated by public actors for reasons other than those laid down in Article 10(2) of the Convention as interpreted by the European Court of Human Rights.

Blocking rather than removal

As highlighted in this book, racist Internet content is often difficult to categorise and accordingly is not always categorised as illegal content. If such content does not pass the illegality threshold, then it must always be recognised that such speech or content will not be prohibited at its source where the server is located. Although the content could be regarded as harmful and offensive to some audiences, it is a matter for those audiences to decide whether they want to access the expression or content in question. Filtering software can help audiences make that decision and block access to certain types of Internet content. This can prevent the removal of offensive, objectionable but legal content from public networks, an action that would be inconsistent with fundamental human rights such as freedom of expression.

The Council of Europe March 2008 Guidelines provided within Recommendation CM/Rec(2008)6 called upon the member states to guarantee that nationwide general blocking or filtering measures are only introduced by the states if the conditions of Article 10(2) of the Convention are fulfilled. According to the guidelines such action by the state should only be taken if the filtering concerns specific and clearly identifiable content, a competent national authority has taken a decision on its illegality and the decision can be reviewed by an independent and impartial tribunal or regulatory body in accordance with the requirements

---

602. Recommendation CM/Rec(2008)6 of the Committee of Ministers to member states on measures to promote the respect for freedom of expression and information with regard to Internet filters: adopted by the Committee of Ministers on 26 March 2008 at the 1022nd meeting of the Ministers' Deputies.
603. Ibid., Guideline I.

of Article 6 of the Convention. The guidelines also called upon the member states to ensure that all filters are assessed both before and during their implementation to ensure that the effects of the filtering are proportionate to the purpose of the restriction and thus necessary in a democratic society, in order to avoid unreasonable blocking of content.

According to the guidelines the universal and general blocking of offensive or harmful content for users who are not part of a specific vulnerable group (such as children) which a filter has been activated to protect should be avoided. Within this context the controversial recent Australian plans[604] to introduce a mandatory filtering system for all users to block access to allegedly illegal Internet content must be criticised. Opponents of the proposed system argue that the government has not demonstrated a need for such an online censorship system. If the system is implemented, there will be concern for its potential "domino effect" and consideration for the implementation of similar filtering systems elsewhere. It is submitted that filters should only be used by individuals on their home computers if their use is deemed necessary to protect vulnerable groups of people such as children.

Information, education and awareness campaigns

Finally, it should not be forgotten that the Internet itself can be an effective tool in the fight against racism.[605] The need to promote the use of new information and communication technologies, including the Internet, to contribute to the fight against racism, racial discrimination, xenophobia and related intolerance[606] is recognised by the previously mentioned UN Durban Declaration. According to the declaration, "new technologies can assist the promotion of tolerance and respect for human dignity, and the principles of equality and non-discrimination."[607] As noted by an April 2000 UN report leading into the Durban World Conference "governments, intergovernmental organizations, national human rights institutions and non-governmental organizations are using the Internet to inform the public about their work and to spread positive messages of equality and non-discrimination".[608] More recently, the UN Special Rapporteur on Racism, Racial

---

604. Foley, M., "Proposed Web Filter Criticized in Australia", *The New York Times*, 11 December 2008; Foley, M., "Australia to Test Web Filter to Block Banned Content", *The New York Times*, 13 December 2008.

605. Reports, studies and other documentation for the Preparatory Committee and the World Conference: Consultation on the use of the Internet for the purpose of incitement to racial hatred, racial propaganda and xenophobia, A/CONF.189/PC.1/5, 5 April 2000.

606. See Report of the World Conference against Racism, Racial Discrimination, Xenophobia and Related Intolerance, Durban, 31 August to 8 September 2001, A/CONF.189/12, 25 January 2002, para. 92.

607. Ibid.

608. Reports, studies and other documentation for the Preparatory Committee and the World Conference: Consultation on the use of the Internet for the purpose of incitement to racial hatred, racial propaganda and xenophobia, A/CONF.189/PC.1/5, 5 April, 2000.

Discrimination, Xenophobia, and all forms of Discrimination also highlighted the "importance on the intellectual front of efforts to combat racism and thus of combating, through education and information, ideas and concepts likely to incite or legitimise racism, racial discrimination or xenophobia, in particular on the Internet".[609]

A number of initiatives aim to assist parents and teachers in preparing children for safer use of the Internet,[610] and within this context a recent Partners Against Hate initiative report highlights critical thinking skills as "one of the most effective tools to provide young people with protection against hate on the Internet".[611] A similar approach has been taken at the OSCE level with recommendations that "Internet users should be educated about tolerance and that cooperation should be promoted among all actors, particularly nongovernmental organisations and associations working to combat racist, anti-Semitic and xenophobic propaganda on the Internet".[612]

Another good example of this approach is a pilot study of websites in English conducted by the European Monitoring Centre on Racism and Xenophobia to be used for intercultural training by children, young adults, teachers and trainers.[613] A total of 273 good websites which deal with and promote cultural diversity were identified in the first half of 2002 by the pilot study.

In summary, there are currently a limited number of specific self-and co-regulatory measures, including codes of conduct aimed at combating racist Internet content. However, there remain significant question marks[614] over the effectiveness and efficacy of the various mechanisms and tools presently offered by the private sector. Self- and co-regulatory measures may yet play an important role in the fight against racist Internet content, and their development is

---

609. Racism, Racial Discrimination, Xenophobia, and all forms of Discrimination: Annual Report submitted by Mr Doudou Diène, Special Rapporteur on contemporary forms of racism, racial discrimination, xenophobia and related intolerance, E/CN.4/2006/16, 18 January 2006 (Economic and Social Council of the UN), para. 63.

610. Note particularly Partners Against Hate initiative report entitled *Hate on the Internet: A Response Guide for Educators and Parents*, ADL, December 2003, at www.partnersagainsthate.org/.

611. Ibid., at page 30.

612. The fight against racism, racial discrimination, xenophobia and related intolerance and the comprehensive implementation of and follow-up to the Durban Declaration and Programme of Action, Note by the Secretary-General, A/59/329, 7 September 2004. See further OSCE meeting on the relationship between racist, xenophobic, and anti-Semitic propaganda on the Internet and hate crimes, Consolidated Summary, PC.DEL/918/04/Corr.1, 27 September 2004, at www.osce.org/.

613. Hieronymus, A., "Using the Internet for Intercultural Training! A pilot study of web sites in English for children, young adults, teachers and trainers", EUMC, Vienna, September 2003, at http://eumc.europa.eu.

614. Note European Parliament Report A6-0244/2005 on the proposal for a recommendation of the European Parliament and of the Council on the protection of minors and human dignity and the right of reply in relation to the competitiveness of the European audiovisual and information services industry, 19 July 2005 (Rapporteur: Marielle de Sarnez).

constantly recommended as witnessed by a recent UN level report on Complementary International Standards which stated that "the emerging approach of self-regulatory governance of the Internet offers an important opportunity that needs to be further explored".[615] At Council of Europe level, the Committee of Ministers adopted a recommendation on promoting freedom of expression and information in the new information and communications environment (CM/Rec(2007)11) in September 2007[616] which encouraged member states, the private sector and civil society to develop various forms of multi-stakeholder co-operation and partnerships, taking into account their respective roles and responsibilities.[617]

Ultimately, this will be dependent upon substantial improvement of existing systems or the devising of less problematic alternatives.

615. See UN General Assembly, Complementary International Standards: Report on the study by the five experts on the content and scope of substantive gaps in the existing international instruments to combat racism, racial discrimination, xenophobia and related intolerance, A/HRC/4/WG.3/6, 27 August 2007, at www.ohchr.org, para. 151.
616. See Recommendation CM/Rec(2007)11 of the Committee of Ministers to member states on promoting freedom of expression and information in the new information and communications environment (adopted by the Committee of Ministers on 26 September 2007 at the 1005th meeting of the Ministers' Deputies). The text of the recommendation is at https://wcd.coe.int/.
617. Note that civil liberties organisations have been critical of this Council of Europe recommendation on the grounds that the recommendation is promoting opaque "self-regulation" and other soft law instruments driven by private interests and implemented through technical mechanisms. As a result, EDRI has great concern that the recommendation will fail to uphold respect for freedom of expression and information in the online world: see EDRI, "New Council of Europe Recommendation fails to uphold online freedom of expression, European Digital Rights Statement and Call for Action – 10 October 2007", at www.edri.org/coerec200711.

Conclusion

This book has focused on legal and policy initiatives to address the problem, availability, and distribution of racist content and hate speech through the Internet in recognition that governments and international organisations have a compelling interest to encounter the global phenomenon of racism. A summary of main conclusions reached from legal and policy perspectives is set out below where remaining issues of concern are also highlighted.

In the last few years we have witnessed an exponential growth of racist content and hate speech on the Internet. Currently there are almost 8 000 problematic websites containing hate- and terrorism-related content according to the Simon Wiesenthal Center. Once within the strict boundaries and control of individual states, whether through paper-based publications (such as pamphlets, local papers, and even books), or audio-visual transmissions limited to a particular area (such as local radio, or TV), or public demonstrations and talks, currently with its digital transmission and availability through the Internet such content respects neither national rules nor boundaries. The increasing popularity of user-driven interactive Web 2.0 applications and services seem to eliminate virtual Internet borders even further. Web 2.0 services such as YouTube, Facebook, and the popular blogging services such as Blogger and Blogspot, user-driven multilingual, web-based, free content encyclopaedia project Wikipedia, and the popular digital social networking game Second Life are used by racist organisations to disseminate content and their views. Racism, racist content, and hate speech therefore become more visible and accessible through the Internet.

As has been seen in this book, eliminating racist content and hate from the Internet is a challenging task,[618] and there is no single solution to this multidimensional problem in the information age. However, "the intractability of the problem does not absolve us of the responsibility to engage in its resolution. The very size of the problem requires us to pursue multiple approaches for partnership with government, police services, schools, community groups and service providers".[619] US Senator Cardin, who co-chairs the United States Commission on Security and Cooperation in Europe (Helsinki Commission), recently expressed

---

618. ECRI, "Legal Instruments to Combat Racism on the Internet", Report prepared by the Swiss Institute of Comparative Law (Lausanne), CRICRI (2000) 27. See ECRI's general conclusions, No. 1.
619. Farber, B., "The Internet and Hate Promotion: The 21st Century Dilemma," Canadian Human Rights Commission, *Hate on the Net*, Spring 2006, at www.chrc-ccdp.ca/pdf/hateoninternet_bil.pdf, pp. 12-15.

deep concern over the growing hate crimes on both sides of the Atlantic and stated that "winning also includes finding ways to fight old hatreds expressed in new ways. Cyberspace is increasingly becoming a new platform for the purveyors of hate to swell their ranks and plan their assaults on the innocent."[620] As highlighted by ECRI almost eight years ago, "the real cause for concern is not so much that there is an absence of relevant legal provisions, as the fact that the very nature of the Internet may block their full implementation. In particular, the diffused structure of the Internet, its pervasiveness and the possibility it affords for anonymity, may render difficult the enforcement of legal provisions."[621]

Looking to the future, one can expect a trend towards "governance" rather than "government", where the role of the nation state is not exclusive and where more varied forms of regulation come into play. The governance of the Internet will continue to evolve at the national and international levels[622] "regardless of frontiers",[623] and therefore policy initiatives need to reflect the decentralised nature of the Internet. Although legal regulation will doubtless continue to form the most important part of future efforts to tackle the problem of online racism it will only ever form part of the solution. Ratification and state-level implementation of international and regional-international treaties such as the Council of Europe Convention on Cybercrime and the Additional Protocol to the Convention on Cybercrime concerning the Criminalisation of Acts of a Racist and Xenophobic Nature Committed Through Computer Systems have been extremely slow, and their true impact on the fight against the dissemination of racist content over the Internet remains to be seen. Such treaties also allow the signing and ratifying member states to include reservations with regard to certain provisions, and inevitably there may be variations in terms of state-level response. Therefore, rather than a harmonised response, we might witness a "fragmented approach" in the near future in terms of legal responses at state level.

This undoubtedly does not mean that certain states do not take seriously the problem of racist content or hate speech on the Internet but agreements may not be easy to reach in terms of how the criminal provisions are drafted and

---

620. Press Release: Wiesenthal Center Launches New Web-Based Initiative At Capitol Hill Hearing, iREPORT@wiesenthal.com to be clearing house for Hate postings, 16 May 2008, at www.wiesenthal. com. See further United States Commission on Security and Cooperation in Europe (Helsinki Commission) Holds Briefing: "Hate In The Information Age", 15 May 2008, at http://csce.gov/.

621. ECRI, Legal Instruments to Combat Racism on the Internet, Report prepared by the Swiss Institute of Comparative Law (Lausanne), CRICRI (2000) 27. See ECRI's general conclusions, No. 2.

622. Note the World Summit on the Information Society, Tunis Commitment 2005, Doc. WSIS-05/ TUNIS/DOC/7, 18 November 2005.

623. Article 10(1) of the European Convention on Human Rights; Article 19 of the Universal Declaration of Human Rights. See further Global Internet Liberty Campaign, *Regardless Of Frontiers: Protecting The Human Right to Freedom of Expression on the Global Internet* (Washington DC: CDT, 1998), at www.cdt.org/.

defined, and whether these provisions would be compatible with state constitutions and freedom of expression.

Ultimately, until wider agreement and consensus at an international level is reached, it will prove necessary to rely on additional measures in the form of self- and co-regulatory initiatives. The success of these measures will, in turn, depend upon substantial improvement of existing systems including the development of ISPs' codes of conduct, complaint and other mechanisms aimed at combating racist Internet content. If successful, these measures would potentially be more flexible and could be more effective than prescriptive government legislation. However, these systems should also respect fundamental human rights such as freedom of expression and privacy of electronic communications by design. Striking the right balance will be increasingly difficult but the success of such mechanisms will depend upon whether and how normative standards such as Article 10 of the European Convention on Human Rights are respected.

Ryan[624] suggested a user-driven strategy to promote the articulation of moderate opinions, rebuttals and refutations to violent radicalisation on the Internet by Internet users themselves as he believes that "censorship is impractical and should not be pursued".[625] According to Ryan, "the user driven Internet is well suited to a countermovement against the mass-mobilisation of violent radicals for the same reason that it accommodated the call to violence in the same place: the Internet is a venue where individuals do not passively receive messages delivered vertically, top-down from authority. Rather, users on the Internet contribute to, adapt, and delete content horizontally."[626] According to Ryan's theory users themselves "are the ideal agents to present moderate alternatives to their peers".[627] This obviously recalls John Stuart Mill's "free market of ideas"[628] in which good ideas would multiply and bad ideas would die out if all ideas were allowed expression. Although interesting and worth pursuing in the name of free speech and to avoid censorship, such a theory may not have strong support from the relevant stakeholders to combat racist content and hate speech. Many will continue to argue that strong laws to combat racial hatred on the Internet is the only way forward and such laws have a significant symbolic value in the public denunciation of such actions despite various limitations attached to enforcement as shown in this book.

Consistent with Recommendation 141 of the Durban Programme of Action, education about racist content on the Internet and how to foster tolerance is argu-

---

624. Ryan, J., "Countering Militant Islamist Radicalisation on the Internet: A User Driven Strategy to Recover the Web" (Dublin: Institute of European Affairs, 2007), at p. 125.
625. Ibid., at p. 142.
626. Ibid., at p. 129.
627. Ibid.
628. John Stuart Mill, *On Liberty*, at http://etext.library.adelaide.edu.au/m/mill/john_stuart/m645o/. Derived from the "Harvard Classics" Volume 25, published in 1909 by P. F. Collier & Son.

ably the single most effective way of combating racist content.[629] The importance of education to promote respect and fight intolerance is highlighted in other broader forums especially following the events of 11 September 2001 with the rise of Islamophobia, religious intolerance[630] as well as anti-Semitism.[631] It is often argued that the development of good practice initiatives to reduce prejudice and "cultural, academic and educational initiatives, supplemented by a range of inter-religious and intercultural awareness events" is the best way to address such problems.[632] State, international and specialised[633] organisations should continue to invest in education[634] and awareness-raising[635] campaigns to "provide users, particularly young people, with accurate information on the dangers of racism and anti-Semitism so as to counter the influence of racist organizations".[636] Information, education, and awareness campaigns should be a "crucial component in any initiative or programme to combat racism".[637] As stressed by the UN Intergovernmental Working Group, "States should increase awareness about the possibilities offered by new information technologies and continually develop tools to promote, among civil society, in particular parents, teachers and children

---

629. See review of reports, studies and other documentation for the Preparatory Committee and the World Conference: Report of the High Commissioner for Human Rights on the use of the Internet for purposes of incitement to racial hatred, racist propaganda and xenophobia, and on ways of promoting international cooperation in this area, A/CONF.189/PC.2/12, 27 April 2001.

630. Note Council of Europe Parliamentary Assembly Recommendation 1805 (2007) on Blasphemy, religious insults and hate speech against persons on grounds of their religion. Text adopted by the Assembly on 29 June 2007 (27th Sitting). See http://assembly.coe.int. See further Doc. 11296, report of the Committee on Culture, Science and Education, rapporteur: Mrs Hurskainen; Doc. 11319, opinion of the Committee on Legal Affairs and Human Rights, rapporteur: Mr Bartumeu Cassany; and Doc. 11322, opinion of the Committee on Equal Opportunities for Women and Men, rapporteur: Mr Dupraz).

631. Note ODIHR (OSCE), *Education on the Holocaust and on Anti-Semitism: An Overview and Analysis of Educational Approaches*, April 2006, at www.osce.org/.

632. Allen, C. and Nielsen, J. S., *Summary Report on Islamophobia in the EU after 11 September 2001*, European Monitoring Centre on Racism and Xenophobia (EUMC), Vienna, May 2002, at http://eumc. europa.eu/. Note further EUMC, *The fight against Anti-Semitism and Islamophobia – Bringing Communities together*, Vienna/Brussels, Fall 2003, at http://eumc.europa.eu/.

633. ECRI, Specialised bodies to combat racism, xenophobia, antisemitism and intolerance, CRI(2006)5, January 2006, at www.coe.int.

634. Note within this context Canada's Action Plan Against Racism, 2005, available through www.pch.gc.ca/.

635. Note, for example, the Turn it Down initiative, a campaign against white power music and their Resource Kit at http://turnitdown.newcomm.org/.

636. Implementation of the Programme of Action for the Third Decade to Combat Racism and Racial Discrimination, Report of the United Nations seminar to assess the implementation of the International Convention on the Elimination of All Forms of Racial Discrimination with particular reference to Articles 4 and 6 (Geneva, 9-13 September 1996), E/CN.4/1997/68/Add.1, 5 December 1996, para. 71.

637. Reports, studies and other documentation for the Preparatory Committee and the World Conference: Consultation on the use of the Internet for the purpose of incitement to racial hatred, racial propaganda and xenophobia, A/CONF.189/PC.1/5, 5 April 2000.

on the use of the information networks".[638] There are no quick and easy solutions to resolve the problem of racist content and hate on the Internet, but the role the Internet can play as a powerful instrument to combat racism should not be underestimated.

---

638. Report of the Intergovernmental Working Group on the effective implementation of the Durban Declaration and Programme of Action on its fourth session (Chairperson-Rapporteur: Juan Martabit (Chile)), E/CN.4/2006/18, 20 March 2006, at http://daccessdds.un.org/, para. 103(c).

Appendix I

Council of Europe Additional Protocol to the Convention on Cybercrime, concerning the criminalisation of acts of a racist and xenophobic nature committed through computer systems ETS No. 189

Strasbourg, 28.01.2003

Preamble

The member States of the Council of Europe and the other States Parties to the Convention on Cybercrime, opened for signature in Budapest on 23 November 2001, signatory hereto;

Considering that the aim of the Council of Europe is to achieve a greater unity between its members;

Recalling that all human beings are born free and equal in dignity and rights;

Stressing the need to secure a full and effective implementation of all human rights without any discrimination or distinction, as enshrined in European and other international instruments;

Convinced that acts of a racist and xenophobic nature constitute a violation of human rights and a threat to the rule of law and democratic stability;

Considering that national and international law need to provide adequate legal responses to propaganda of a racist and xenophobic nature committed through computer systems;

Aware of the fact that propaganda to such acts is often subject to criminalisation in national legislation;

Having regard to the Convention on Cybercrime, which provides for modern and flexible means of international co-operation and convinced of the need to harmonise substantive law provisions concerning the fight against racist and xenophobic propaganda;

Aware that computer systems offer an unprecedented means of facilitating freedom of expression and communication around the globe;

Recognising that freedom of expression constitutes one of the essential foundations of a democratic society, and is one of the basic conditions for its progress and for the development of every human being;

Concerned, however, by the risk of misuse or abuse of such computer systems to disseminate racist and xenophobic propaganda;

Mindful of the need to ensure a proper balance between freedom of expression and an effective fight against acts of a racist and xenophobic nature;

Recognising that this Protocol is not intended to affect established principles relating to freedom of expression in national legal systems;

Taking into account the relevant international legal instruments in this field, and in particular the Convention for the Protection of Human Rights and Fundamental Freedoms and its Protocol No. 12 concerning the general prohibition of discrimination, the existing Council of Europe conventions on co-operation in the penal field, in particular the Convention on Cybercrime, the United Nations International Convention on the Elimination of All Forms of Racial Discrimination of 21 December 1965, the European Union Joint Action of 15 July 1996 adopted by the Council on the basis of Article K.3 of the Treaty on European Union, concerning action to combat racism and xenophobia;

Welcoming the recent developments which further advance international understanding and co-operation in combating cybercrime and racism and xenophobia;

Having regard to the Action Plan adopted by the Heads of State and Government of the Council of Europe on the occasion of their Second Summit (Strasbourg, 10-11 October 1997) to seek common responses to the developments of the new technologies based on the standards and values of the Council of Europe;

Have agreed as follows:

Chapter I – Common provisions

Article 1 – Purpose

The purpose of this Protocol is to supplement, as between the Parties to the Protocol, the provisions of the Convention on Cybercrime, opened for signature in Budapest on 23 November 2001 (hereinafter referred to as "the Convention"), as regards the criminalisation of acts of a racist and xenophobic nature committed through computer systems.

Article 2 – Definition

1   For the purposes of this Protocol:

"racist and xenophobic material" means any written material, any image or any other representation of ideas or theories, which advocates, promotes or incites hatred, discrimination or violence, against any individual or group of individuals, based on race, colour, descent or national or ethnic origin, as well as religion if used as a pretext for any of these factors.

2   The terms and expressions used in this Protocol shall be interpreted in the same manner as they are interpreted under the Convention.

Chapter II – Measures to be taken at national level

Article 3 – Dissemination of racist and xenophobic material through computer systems

1   Each Party shall adopt such legislative and other measures as may be necessary to establish as criminal offences under its domestic law, when committed intentionally and without right, the following conduct:

distributing, or otherwise making available, racist and xenophobic material to the public through a computer system.

2   A Party may reserve the right not to attach criminal liability to conduct as defined by paragraph 1 of this article, where the material, as defined in Article 2, paragraph 1, advocates, promotes or incites discrimination that is not associated with hatred or violence, provided that other effective remedies are available.

3   Notwithstanding paragraph 2 of this article, a Party may reserve the right not to apply paragraph 1 to those cases of discrimination for which, due to established principles in its national legal system concerning freedom of expression, it cannot provide for effective remedies as referred to in the said paragraph 2.

Article 4 – Racist and xenophobic motivated threat

1   Each Party shall adopt such legislative and other measures as may be necessary to establish as criminal offences under its domestic law, when committed intentionally and without right, the following conduct:

threatening, through a computer system, with the commission of a serious criminal offence as defined under its domestic law, (i) persons for the reason that they belong to a group, distinguished by race, colour, descent or national or ethnic origin, as well as religion, if used as a pretext for any of these factors, or (ii) a group of persons which is distinguished by any of these characteristics.

Article 5 – Racist and xenophobic motivated insult

1   Each Party shall adopt such legislative and other measures as may be necessary to establish as criminal offences under its domestic law, when committed intentionally and without right, the following conduct:

insulting publicly, through a computer system, (i) persons for the reason that they belong to a group distinguished by race, colour, descent or national or ethnic origin, as well as religion, if used as a pretext for any of these factors; or (ii) a group of persons which is distinguished by any of these characteristics.

2   A Party may either:

a   require that the offence referred to in paragraph 1 of this article has the effect that the person or group of persons referred to in paragraph 1 is exposed to hatred, contempt or ridicule; or

b   reserve the right not to apply, in whole or in part, paragraph 1 of this article.

Article 6 – Denial, gross minimisation, approval or justification of genocide or crimes against humanity

1   Each Party shall adopt such legislative measures as may be necessary to establish the following conduct as criminal offences under its domestic law, when committed intentionally and without right:

distributing or otherwise making available, through a computer system to the public, material which denies, grossly minimises, approves or justifies acts constituting genocide or crimes against humanity, as defined by international law and recognised as such by final and binding decisions of the International Military Tribunal, established by the London Agreement of 8 August 1945, or of any other international court established by relevant international instruments and whose jurisdiction is recognised by that Party.

2   A Party may either

a   require that the denial or the gross minimisation referred to in paragraph 1 of this article is committed with the intent to incite hatred, discrimination or violence against any individual or group of individuals, based on race, colour, descent or national or ethnic origin, as well as religion if used as a pretext for any of these factors, or otherwise

b   reserve the right not to apply, in whole or in part, paragraph 1 of this article.

Article 7 – Aiding and abetting

Each Party shall adopt such legislative and other measures as may be necessary to establish as criminal offences under its domestic law, when committed intentionally and without right, aiding or abetting the commission of any of the offences established in accordance with this Protocol, with intent that such offence be committed.

Chapter III – Relations between the Convention and this Protocol

Article 8 – Relations between the Convention and this Protocol

1   Articles 1, 12, 13, 22, 41, 44, 45 and 46 of the Convention shall apply, *mutatis mutandis*, to this Protocol.

2   The Parties shall extend the scope of application of the measures defined in Articles 14 to 21 and Articles 23 to 35 of the Convention, to Articles 2 to 7 of this Protocol.

Chapter IV – Final provisions

Article 9 – Expression of consent to be bound

1   This Protocol shall be open for signature by the States which have signed the Convention, which may express their consent to be bound by either:

a   signature without reservation as to ratification, acceptance or approval; or

b   subject to ratification, acceptance or approval, followed by ratification, acceptance or approval.

2   A State may not sign this Protocol without reservation as to ratification, acceptance or approval, or deposit an instrument of ratification, acceptance or approval, unless it has already deposited or simultaneously deposits an instrument of ratification, acceptance or approval of the Convention.

3   The instruments of ratification, acceptance or approval shall be deposited with the Secretary General of the Council of Europe.

Article 10 – Entry into force

1   This Protocol shall enter into force on the first day of the month following the expiration of a period of three months after the date on which five States have expressed their consent to be bound by the Protocol, in accordance with the provisions of Article 9.

2   In respect of any State which subsequently expresses its consent to be bound by it, the Protocol shall enter into force on the first day of the month following the expiration of a period of three months after the date of its signature without reservation as to ratification, acceptance or approval or deposit of its instrument of ratification, acceptance or approval.

Article 11 – Accession

1   After the entry into force of this Protocol, any State which has acceded to the Convention may also accede to the Protocol.

2   Accession shall be effected by the deposit with the Secretary General of the Council of Europe of an instrument of accession which shall take effect on the first day of the month following the expiration of a period of three months after the date of its deposit.

Article 12 – Reservations and declarations

1   Reservations and declarations made by a Party to a provision of the Convention shall be applicable also to this Protocol, unless that Party declares

otherwise at the time of signature or when depositing its instrument of ratification, acceptance, approval or accession.

2   By a written notification addressed to the Secretary General of the Council of Europe, any Party may, at the time of signature or when depositing its instrument of ratification, acceptance, approval or accession, declare that it avails itself of the reservation(s) provided for in Articles 3, 5 and 6 of this Protocol. At the same time, a Party may avail itself, with respect to the provisions of this Protocol, of the reservation(s) provided for in Article 22, paragraph 2, and Article 41, paragraph 1, of the Convention, irrespective of the implementation made by that Party under the Convention. No other reservations may be made.

3   By a written notification addressed to the Secretary General of the Council of Europe, any State may, at the time of signature or when depositing its instrument of ratification, acceptance, approval or accession, declare that it avails itself of the possibility of requiring additional elements as provided for in Article 5, paragraph 2.*a*, and Article 6, paragraph 2.*a*, of this Protocol.

Article 13 – Status and withdrawal of reservations

1   A Party that has made a reservation in accordance with Article 12 above shall withdraw such reservation, in whole or in part, as soon as circumstances so permit. Such withdrawal shall take effect on the date of receipt of a notification addressed to the Secretary General of the Council of Europe. If the notification states that the withdrawal of a reservation is to take effect on a date specified therein, and such date is later than the date on which the notification is received by the Secretary General, the withdrawal shall take effect on such a later date.

2   The Secretary General of the Council of Europe may periodically enquire with Parties that have made one or more reservations in accordance with Article 12 as to the prospects for withdrawing such reservation(s).

Article 14 – Territorial application

1   Any Party may at the time of signature or when depositing its instrument of ratification, acceptance, approval or accession, specify the territory or territories to which this Protocol shall apply.

2   Any Party may, at any later date, by a declaration addressed to the Secretary General of the Council of Europe, extend the application of this Protocol to any other territory specified in the declaration. In respect of such territory, the Protocol shall enter into force on the first day of the month following the expiration of a period of three months after the date of receipt of the declaration by the Secretary General.

3   Any declaration made under the two preceding paragraphs may, in respect of any territory specified in such declaration, be withdrawn by a notification addressed to the Secretary General of the Council of Europe. The withdrawal

shall become effective on the first day of the month following the expiration of a period of three months after the date of receipt of such notification by the Secretary General.

Article 15 – Denunciation

1   Any Party may, at any time, denounce this Protocol by means of a notification addressed to the Secretary General of the Council of Europe.

2   Such denunciation shall become effective on the first day of the month following the expiration of a period of three months after the date of receipt of the notification by the Secretary General.

Article 16 – Notification

The Secretary General of the Council of Europe shall notify the member States of the Council of Europe, the non-member States which have participated in the elaboration of this Protocol as well as any State which has acceded to, or has been invited to accede to, this Protocol of:

a any signature;

b the deposit of any instrument of ratification, acceptance, approval or accession;

c any date of entry into force of this Protocol in accordance with its Articles 9, 10 and 11;

d any other act, notification or communication relating to this Protocol.

In witness whereof the undersigned, being duly authorised thereto, have signed this Protocol.

Done at Strasbourg, this 28th day of January 2003, in English and in French, both texts being equally authentic, in a single copy which shall be deposited in the archives of the Council of Europe. The Secretary General of the Council of Europe shall transmit certified copies to each member State of the Council of Europe, to the non-member States which have participated in the elaboration of this Protocol, and to any State invited to accede to it.

Appendix II

European Commission against Racism and Intolerance, General Policy Recommendation No. 6

Combating the dissemination of racist, xenophobic and antisemitic material via the Internet, adopted by ECRI on 15 December 2000

The European Commission against Racism and Intolerance:

Recalling the Declaration adopted by the Heads of State and Government of the member States of the Council of Europe at their first Summit held in Vienna on 8-9 October 1993;

Recalling that the Plan of Action on combating racism, xenophobia, antisemitism and intolerance set out as part of this Declaration invited the Committee of Ministers to establish the European Commission against Racism and Intolerance with a mandate, *inter alia*, to formulate general policy recommendations to member States;

Recalling also the Final Declaration and Action Plan adopted by the Heads of State and Government of the member States of the Council of Europe at their second Summit held in Strasbourg on 10-11 October 1997;

Recalling Article 4 of the International Convention on the Elimination of All Forms of Racial Discrimination;

Recalling Recommendation No. R(92)19 of the Committee of Ministers to member States on video games with a racist content and Recommendation No. R(97)20 of the Committee of Ministers to member States on "Hate Speech";

Recalling that, in its general policy recommendation No. 1, ECRI called on the governments of Council of Europe member States to ensure that national criminal, civil and administrative law expressly and specifically counters racism, xenophobia, antisemitism and intolerance;

Stressing that, in the same recommendation, ECRI asked for the aforementioned law to provide in particular that oral, written, audio-visual expressions and other forms of expression, including the electronic media, inciting to hatred, discrimination or violence against racial, ethnic, national or religious groups or against their members on the grounds that they belong to such a group are legally categorised as a criminal offence, which should also cover the production, the distribution and the storage for distribution of the material in question;

Taking full account of the General Conclusions of the European Conference against racism held in Strasbourg on 11-13 October 2000 as the European regional contribution to the World Conference against racism, racial discrimination, xenophobia and related intolerance, which will be held on 31 August – 7 September 2001 in Durban, South Africa;

Noting that the European Conference against racism urged participating States to make every effort to prosecute those responsible for incitement to racial hatred on the Internet and their accomplices;

Welcoming the fact that, in the Political Declaration adopted on 13 October 2000 at the closing session of the European Conference, the member States of the Council of Europe committed themselves to combating all forms of expression which incite racial hatred as well as to take action against the dissemination of such material in the media in general and on the Internet in particular;

Aware of actions and initiatives taken in this field by the United Nations, the OECD, the Council of Europe and the European Union;

Welcoming the progress made by the Council of Europe in suppressing cybercrime, notably the work on the draft Convention on cybercrime, and hoping for a prompt finalisation of this first international instrument for suppressing cybercrime;

Regretting nevertheless that, for the time being, the draft Convention does not include provisions on racist, xenophobic and antisemitic crimes committed via the Internet;

Aware of the positive contribution that the Internet can make to combating racism and intolerance on a world scale;

Recognising that the Internet offers unprecedented means of facilitating the cross-border communication of information on human rights issues related to anti-discrimination;

Stressing that the use of the Internet to set up educational and awareness-raising networks in the field of combating racism and intolerance is a good practice which should be supported and further developed;

Deeply concerned by the fact that the Internet is also used for disseminating racist, xenophobic and antisemitic material, by individuals and groups aiming to incite to intolerance or racial and ethnic hatred;

Convinced of the determination of the member States of the Council of Europe to combat the phenomena of racism, xenophobia, antisemitism and intolerance which destroy democracy, and thus to act efficiently against the use of the Internet for racist, xenophobic and antisemitic aims;

Aware that the very nature of the Internet calls for solutions at international level, and thus a willingness on the part of all States to combat incitement to racial hatred, enabling the fundamental principle of respect for human dignity to prevail;

Recommends that the Governments of the member States:

–   include the issue of combating racism, xenophobia and antisemitism in all current and future work at international level aimed at the suppression of illegal content on the Internet;

–   reflect in this context on the preparation of a specific protocol to the future Convention on cybercrime to combat racist, xenophobic and antisemitic offences committed via the Internet;

–   take the necessary measures for strengthening international co-operation and mutual assistance between law enforcement authorities across the world, so as to take more efficient action against the dissemination of racist, xenophobic and antisemitic material via the Internet;

–   ensure that relevant national legislation applies also to racist, xenophobic and antisemitic offences committed via the Internet and prosecute those responsible for this kind of offences;

–   undertake sustained efforts for the training of law enforcement authorities in relation to the problem of dissemination of racist, xenophobic and antisemitic material via the Internet;

–   reflect, in this context, on the setting up of a national consultation body which might act as a permanent monitoring centre, mediating body and partner in the preparation of codes of conduct;

–   support existing anti-racist initiatives on the Internet as well as the development of new sites devoted to the fight against racism, xenophobia, antisemitism and intolerance;

–   clarify, on the basis of their respective technical functions, the responsibility of content host and content provider and site publishers as a result of the dissemination of racist, xenophobic and antisemitic messages;

–   support the self-regulatory measures taken by the Internet industry to combat racism, xenophobia and antisemitism on the net, such as anti-racist hotlines, codes of conduct and filtering software, and encourage further research in this area;

–   increase public awareness of the problem of the dissemination of racist, xenophobic and antisemitic material via the Internet while paying special attention to awareness-raising among young Internet-users – particularly children – as to the possibility of coming upon racist, xenophobic and antisemitic sites and the potential risk of such sites.

Bibliography

Cases

Australian cases

Jones v. Töben, Federal Court of Australia, [2002] FCA 1150. The decision can be accessed at www.austlii.edu.au/au/cases/cth/federal_ct/2002/1150.html

Töben v. Jones [2003] FCAFC 137 (27 June 2003)

Jones v. Töben (5 October 2000), Australian Human Rights and Equal Opportunity Commission, Case No. H97/120

Canadian cases

Canada (Human Rights Commission) v. Heritage Front [1994] F.C.J. No. 2010 (T.D.) (QL)

Canada (Human Rights Commission) v. Canadian Liberty Net [1998] 1 S.C.R. 626

Canada (Human Rights Commission) v. Taylor [1990] 3 S.C.R. 892

Citron and Toronto Mayor's Committee v. Zündel, 2002 CanLII 23557

Citron v. Zündel (18 January 2002), T.D. 1/02, Canadian Human Rights Tribunal

Citron v. Zündel (2000), 189 D.L.R. (4th) 131 (F.C.A.); and 195 D.L.R. (4th) 399 (F.C.A.).

R. v. Zündel [1992] 2 S.C.R. 731

Re Zündel (2005), 251 D.L.R. (4th) 511, 2005 FC 295 (T.D.)

Sabina Citron Toronto Mayor's Committee on Community and Race Relations and Canadian Human Rights Commission v. Ernst Zündel, Canadian Human Rights Tribunal, T.D. ½ 2002/01/18

Schnell v. Machiavelli and Associates Emprize Inc. (20 August 2002) T.D. 11/02 (CHRT)

Töben v. Jones [2003] FCAFC 137

Warman v. Guille & Canadian Heritage Alliance, 2008 CHRT 40, decided on 30 September 2008

Warman v. Harrison (15 August 2006) 2006 CHRT 30

Warman v. Kouba, 2006 CHRT 50

Warman v. Kulbashian (10 March 2006) 2006 CHRT 11

Warman v. Kyburz (9 May 2003) 2003 CHRT 18

Warman v. Warman (23 September 2005) 2005 CHRT 36

Warman v. Winnicki (13 April 2006) 2006 CHRT 20

Zündel v. Canada (Attorney General) (T.D.), [1999] 4 F.C. 289 (T.D.)

French cases

Trib. gr. inst. Paris, 20 November 2000, *League Against Racism and Anti-Semitism (LICRA), French Union of Jewish Students v. Yahoo! Inc. (USA), Yahoo! France* (Interim Court Order)

UK cases

District Court of Mannheim Germany v. Töben (2008), Latham LJ, Blair J, Case No. CO/8582/2008, date: 24/11/2008

R. v. Malik [2008] All ER (D) 201 (Jun)

US cases

ACLU v. Reno II, No. 99-1324

Ashcroft, Attorney General v. American Civil Liberties Union et al., certiorari to the United States Court of Appeals for the Third Circuit, No. 03–218. Argued 2 March 2004, Decided 29 June 2004

Barrett v. Rosenthal, 9 Cal. Rptr. 3d 142 at 154 (C.A. 2004)

Batzel v. Smith, 333 F.3d 1018 at 1027 (9th Cir. 2003)

Beauharnais v. Illinois, 343 U.S. 250, 72 S.Ct. 725, 96 L.Ed. 919 (1952)

Brandenburg v. Ohio, 395 U.S. 444, 447 (1969)

Chaplinsky v. New Hampshire, 315 U.S. 568

Cohen v. California, 403 U.S. 15, 20 (1971)

Doe v. America Online Inc., 783 So. 2d 1010 (Fla. Sup. Ct. 2001)

Doe v. GTE Corp., 347 F.3d. 655 (7th Cir. 2003)

Gertz v. Robert Welch, Inc., 418 U.S. 323, 94 S.Ct. 2997, 41 L.Ed.2d 789 (1974)

Langdon v. Google, Inc., D.Del. (2007), 474 F.Supp.2d 622

Miller v. California, 413 U.S. 15, 93 S.Ct. 2607, 37 L.Ed.2d 419 (1973)

Nemet Chevrolet, Ltd. v. Consumeraffairs.com, Inc., 564 F. Supp. 2d 544 (E.D. Va. 2008)

New York Times Co. v. Sullivan, 376 U.S. 254, 84 S.Ct. 710, 11 L.Ed.2d 686 (1964)

New York v. Ferber 458 U.S. 747 (1982)

Planned Parenthood of the Colombia/Willamette, Inc. v. American Coalition of Life Activists, 290 F. 3d 1058 (9th Cir. 2002), cert denied, 539 U.S. 958 (2003)

R.A.V. v. City of St. Paul, 505 U.S. 377, at 392; 112 S.Ct. 2538, 120 L.Ed.2d 305 (1992)

Reno v. ACLU, 117 S. Ct. 2329 (1997)

Roth v. United States, 354 U.S. 476, 77 S.Ct. 1304, 1 L.Ed.2d 1498 (1957)

Texas v. Johnson, 491 U.S. 397, 406, 109 S.Ct. 2533, 2540, 105 L.Ed.2d 342 (1989)

United States v. Viefhaus, 168 F.3d 392, 395 (10th Cir.1999)

Universal Communication Systems, Inc. v. Lycos, Inc., 478 F.3d 413, 35 Media L. Rep. (BNA) 1417 (1st Cir. 2007)

Virginia v. Black, 538 U.S. 343, 123 S.Ct. 1536, 155 L.Ed.2d 535 (2003)

Watts v. United States, 394 U.S. 705

Yahoo! Inc. v. La Ligue Contre Le Racisme et L'antisemitisme, 169 F.Supp.2d 1181 (N.D. Cal. 2001)

Yahoo! Inc. v. La Ligue Contre Le Racisme et L'antisemitisme, 379 F.3d 1120 (9th Cir. 2004)

Yahoo! Inc. v. La Ligue Contre Le Racisme et L'antisemitisme, 399 F.3d 1010 (9th Cir. 2005)

Yahoo! Inc. v. La Ligue Contre Le Racisme et L'antisemitisme, 433 F.3d 1199 (9th Cir. 2006)

Zeran v. America Online Inc., 129 F.3d 327 at 330 (4th Cir. 1997), certiorari denied, 48 S. Ct. 2341 (1998)

European Court of Human Rights cases

Alinak and Others v. Turkey, judgment of 4 May 2006

Autronic AG v. Switzerland, Series A No. 178, 22 May 1990

B.H., M.W., H.P. and G.K. v. Austria, Application No. 12774/87, Commission decision of 12 October 1989, DR 62, p. 216

Başkaya and Okçuoğlu, judgment of 8 July 1999, Reports 1999

Bladet Tromsø and Stensaas, judgment of 20 May 1999, Reports 1999

Castells v. Spain (1992), Application No. 11798/85, Series A vol. 236

De Haes and Gijsels v. Belgium, 24 February 1997, para. 46, Reports 1997-I

Erbakan v. Turkey, 6 July 2006, para. 56

Erdoğdu and İnce v. Turkey, 8 July 1999, Application Nos. 25067/94 and 25068/94

Ergin v. Turkey, judgment of 4 May 2006

Garaudy v. France (dec.), Application No. 65831/01, ECHR 2003-IX

Giniewski v. France, Application No. 64016/00, judgment of 31 January 2006

Glimmerveen and J. Hagenbeek v. the Netherlands, Application Nos. 8348/78 and 8406/78, Commission decision of 11 October 1979, Decisions and Reports (DR) 18, p. 187

Groppera Radio AG and Others v. Switzerland, Application No. 00010890/84, Series A No. 173, 28 March, 1990

Gündüz v. Turkey, Application No. 35071/97 judgment of 4 December 2003, para. 40

Han v. Turkey, judgment of 13 September 2005

Handyside v. the United Kingdom (1976), Application No. 5493/72, Series A vol. 24

Honsik v. Austria, No. 25062/94, Commission decision of 18 October 1995, DR 83-A, p. 77

İ.A. v. Turkey, No. 42571/98, para. 29, ECHR 2005-VIII

Jersild v. Denmark, judgment of 23 September 1994, Series A No. 298, p. 25, para. 35

Kühnen v. the Federal Republic of Germany, D.R. 56, p. 205 and No. 19459/92, Dec. of 29.3.93 unpublished

Lawless v. Ireland, judgment of 14 November 1960

Lehideux and Isorni v. France, judgment of 23 September 1998

Leroy v. France, Application No. 36109/03, Chamber judgment of 2 October 2008

Lingens v. Austria, 8 July 1986, Series A No. 103, p. 26, para. 41

Nationaldemokratische Partei Deutschlands, Bezirksverband München-Oberbayern v. Germany, No. 25992/94, Commission decision of 29 November 1995, DR 84, p. 149

Nachtmann v. Austria, No. 36773/97, Commission decision of 9 September 1998

Norwood v. the United Kingdom, No. 23131/03, decision of 15 November 2004

Ochsenberger v. Austria, No. 21318/93, Commission decision of 2 September 1994

Okçuoğlu v. Turkey, No. 24246/94, 8.7.1999

Otto-Preminger-Institut v. Austria, 20 September 1994, Series A No. 295-A, para. 49

Rebhandel v. Austria, No. 24398/94, Commission decision of 16 January 1996

Remer v. Germany, No. 25096/94, Commission decision of 6 September 1995, DR 82, p. 117

Sacchi v. Italy, Case No. 6452/74, decision of 12 March 1976, D.R. 5

Schimanek v. Austria (dec.), No. 32307/96, 1 February 2000

Sener v. Turkey, 18 July 2000, Application No. 26680/95

Seurot v. France, No. 57383/00, decision of 18 May 2004

Sunday Times *v. the United Kingdom* (No. 2), Series A No. 217, 26.11.1991

Sürek v. Turkey (No. 1) (Application No. 26682/95), judgment of 8 July 1999, Reports 1999

Sürek v. Turkey (No. 1) No. 26682/95, para. 62, ECHR 1999-IV

Sürek v. Turkey (No. 3) judgment of 8 July 1999

Sürek v. Turkey (No. 4) (Application No. 24762/94), judgment of 8 July 1999

Udo Walendy v. Germany, No. 21128/92, decision of 11 January 1995, European Commission of Human Rights

W.P. v. Poland, No. 42264/98, decision of 2 September 2004

Walendy v. Germany, No. 21128/92, Commission decision of 11 January 1995, DR 80, p. 94

Witzsch v. Germany (dec.), No. 41448/98, 20 April 1999

Witzsch v. Germany, No. 7485/03, decision of 13 December 2005

Books, academic articles, reports, official documents

Ahlert, C., Marsden, C. and Yung, C., "How 'Liberty' Disappeared from Cyberspace: The Mystery Shopper Tests Internet Content Self-Regulation", at http://pcmlp.socleg.ox.ac.uk/text/liberty.pdf.

Akdeniz, Y., "Anonymous Now", *Index on Censorship*, The Privacy Issue (2000)3, June, pp. 57-62.

Akdeniz, Y., "Case Analysis of *League Against Racism and Antisemitism (LICRA), French Union of Jewish Students v. Yahoo! Inc. (USA), Yahoo! France*" (2001) *Electronic Business Law Reports* 1(3), p. 110.

Akdeniz, Y., "The Regulation of Internet Content in Europe: Governmental Control versus Self-Responsibility" (1999) 5(2) *Swiss Political Science Review* 5(2), p. 123.

Akdeniz, Y., "To Link or Not to Link: Problems with World Wide Web Links on the Internet" (1997) 11:2 *Int'l Rev. L. Comp. & Tech* p. 281.

Akdeniz, Y. and Altiparmak, K., *Internet: Restricted Access: A Critical Assessment of Internet Content Regulation and Censorship in Turkey,* Ankara: IHOP, November 2008, at http://privacy.cyber-rights.org.tr/?page_id=256.

Akdeniz, Y. and Rogers, H., "Defamation on the Internet", in Akdeniz et al., eds, *The Internet, Law and Society* (Essex: Longman, 2000) at 294-317.

Akdeniz, Y., *An Advocacy Handbook for the Non Governmental Organisations: The Council of Europe's Cyber-Crime Convention 2001 and the additional protocol on the criminalisation of acts of a racist or xenophobic nature committed through computer systems,* Cyber-Rights & Cyber-Liberties, December 2003 (revised and updated in May 2008), at www.cyber-rights.org/cybercrime/coe_handbook_crcl.pdf.

Akdeniz, Y., *Internet Child Pornography and the Law: National and International Responses* (Ashgate, 2008).

Allen, C., and Nielsen, J. S., *Summary Report on Islamophobia in the EU after 11 September 2001,* European Monitoring Centre on Racism and Xenophobia (EUMC), Vienna, May 2002 at http://eumc.europa.eu/eumc/material/pub/anti-islam/Synthesis-report_en.pdf.

Annan, K., Global Forum on Internet Governance, 24 March 2004 (*Internet Governance: A Grand Collaboration*, March 2004).

Anti-Defamation League, Report, "Computerized Networks of Hate" (January 1985).

Australian Human Rights and Equal Opportunity Commission, *Change and Continuity: Review of the Federal Unlawful Discrimination Jurisdiction: Supplement September 2002 – August 2003* (Sydney, 2003), Carr J at 2.

Australian Human Rights Commission, Cyber-Racism, 2008, at www.humanrights.gov.au/racial_discrimination/publications/cyberracism_factsheet.html.

Australian Human Rights Commission, *Racial Vilification Law in Australia*, Race Discrimination Unit, HREOC, October 2002, at www.humanrights.gov.au/racial_discrimination/cyberracism/vilification.html.

Australian Race Discrimination Commissioner, *Racism and the Internet: Review of the operation of Schedule 5, Broadcasting Services Act 1992* (November 2002), at www.dcita.gov.au/.

B'Nai Brith Canada, *Hate on the Internet: 3rd International Symposium, Taking Action Against Hate on the Internet: A Legal Analysis report,* "No charges have ever been laid under section 318 or 319(1) of the *Criminal Code*" (2007, at www.hateontheinternet.com.

Barlow, J. P., "Thinking Locally, Acting Globally" (1996), *Cyber-Rights Electronic List*, 15 January.

Canada's Action Plan Against Racism, 2005, available through www.pch.gc.ca/multi/index_e.cfm.

Canadian Human Rights Commission, *Hate on the Net* (Ottawa: Association for Canadian Studies, Spring 2006), at www.chrc-ccdp.ca/pdf/HateOnInternet_bil.pdf.

Castells, M., *The Power of Identity* (Volume II of *The Information Age: Economy, Society and Culture*) (Oxford: Blackwell Publishers, 1997).

Cleaver, H., "The Zapatistas and the Electronic Fabric of Struggle", at www.utexas.edu/.

Cohn, N., *Warrant for Genocide: The Myth of the Jewish World Conspiracy and the Protocols of the Elders of Zion* (Serif Publishing, 2005).

Cooper, A. and Brackman, H., "Punishing Religious Defamation and Holocaust Denial: Is There a Double Standard?" (2006) *Equal Voices*, Issues 18, EUMC, at www.eumc.europa.eu/.

Council of Europe – ECRI General Policy Recommendation No. 1: Combating Racism, Xenophobia, Antisemitism and Intolerance, adopted by ECRI on 4 October 1996, CRI (96) 43 rev.

Council of Europe – ECRI General Policy Recommendation No. 7: National legislation to combat racism and racial discrimination, CRI (2003) 8, adopted by ECRI on 13 December 2002, at www.coe.int.

Council of Europe – ECRI Third Report on Germany, June 2004, CRI (2004) 23.

Council of Europe – ECRI, Expert Seminar: Combating Racism while Respecting Freedom of Expression, Proceedings, Strasbourg, 16-17 November 2006, published in July 2007.

Council of Europe – ECRI, "Legal Instruments to combat racism on the Internet", report prepared by the Swiss Institute of Comparative Law (Lausanne), CRI(2000)27, Strasbourg, August 2000.

Council of Europe – ECRI, Specialised bodies to combat racism, xenophobia, anti-Semitism and intolerance, CRI(2006)5, January 2006, at www.coe.int.

Council of Europe – ECRI, Third Report on France, CRI (2005) 3, adopted on 25 June 2004 and made public on 15 February 2005, at www.coe.int, para 106.

Council of Europe – ECRI, General Policy Recommendation No. 6: Combating the Dissemination of Racist, Xenophobic and Antisemitic Material via the Internet, CRI(2001)1, adopted by ECRI on 15 December 2000.

Council of Europe – Explanatory Report of the Additional Protocol to the Convention on Cyber-Crime, concerning the criminalisation of acts of a racist and xenophobic nature committed through computer systems, as adopted by the Committee of Ministers on 7 November 2002, at http://conventions.coe.int/.

Council of Europe – Freedom of communication on the Internet, Declaration adopted by the Council of Europe Committee of Ministers on 28 May 2003 at the 840th meeting of the Ministers' Deputies.

Council of Europe – Recommendation CM/Rec(2007)11 of the Committee of Ministers to member states on promoting freedom of expression and information in the new information and communications environment (adopted by the Committee of Ministers on 26 September 2007 at the 1005th meeting of the Ministers' Deputies). The text of the recommendation is at https://wcd.coe.int/.

Council of Europe – Recommendation CM/Rec(2007)16 of the Committee of Ministers to member states on measures to promote the public service value of the Internet (adopted by the Committee of Ministers on 7 November 2007 at the 1010th meeting of the Ministers' Deputies).

Council of Europe – Recommendation CM/Rec(2008)6 of the Committee of Ministers to member states on measures to promote the respect for freedom of expression and information with regard to Internet filters (adopted by the Committee of Ministers on 26 March 2008 at the 1022nd meeting of the Ministers' Deputies).

Council of Europe – Recommendation on Hate Speech, No. R (97) 20, adopted by the Committee of Ministers of the Council of Europe on 30 October 1997.

Council of Europe Convention on Cybercrime Committee (T-CY), 2nd Multilateral Consultation of the Parties, Strasbourg, 13 and 14 June 2007, Strasbourg, 15 June 2007, T-CY (2007) 03.

Council of Europe Parliamentary Assembly Recommendation 1805 (2007) on Blasphemy, religious insults and hate speech against persons on grounds of their religion, Text adopted by the Assembly on 29 June 2007 (27th Sitting). See http://assembly.coe.int/.

Council of Europe Recommendation 1543(2001) on Racism and xenophobia in cyberspace, 8 November 2001.

Council of Europe Steering Committee for Human Rights (CDDH), Committee of Experts for the Development of Human Rights (DH-DEV), Working Group A, Report on "hate speech", document GT-DH-DEV A(2006)008, Strasbourg, 9 February 2007, at www.coe.int/.

Council of Europe Committee of Ministers, Recommendation No. R(89)9 of the Committee of Ministers to Member States on Computer-Related Crime (adopted by the Committee of Ministers on 13 September 1989 at the 428th meeting of the Ministers' Deputies), at http://cm.coe.int/.

Council of Europe Committee of Ministers, Recommendation No. R(95)13 of the Committee of Ministers to Member States Concerning Problems of Criminal Procedural Law Connected with Information Technology (adopted by the

Committee of Ministers on 11 September 1995 at the 543rd meeting of the Ministers' Deputies), at: http://cm.coe.int/.

Council of Europe, Committee of Ministers, Explanatory Report of the Additional Protocol to the Convention on Cybercrime, concerning the criminalisation of acts of a racist and xenophobic nature committed through computer systems (2002) at http://conventions.coe.int/.

Council of Europe, Octopus Programme, *Organised Crime in Europe: The Threat of Cybercrime: Situation Report 2004* (Strasbourg: Council of Europe Publishing, 2005) p. 138.

Council of Europe, PA, 2003 Ordinary Sess. (Fourth Part) Racist, xenophobic and intolerant discourse in politics, Texts Adopted, Res. 1345 (2003) at http://assembly.coe.int/.

Council of Europe, PA, 2003 Ordinary Sess. (Fourth Part) Report of the Committee on Legal Affairs and Human Rights, Documents, Doc. 9904 (2003), at http://assembly.coe.int/.

Drake, W. J., ed., *Reforming Internet Governance: Perspectives from the Working Group on Internet Governance (WGIG)*, United Nations ICT Task Force, 2005, at http://www.wgig.org/docs/book/WGIG_book.pdf.

Eberwine, E. T., "Note & Comment: Sound and Fury Signifying Nothing?: Jurgen Bussow's Battle Against Hate-speech on the Internet" (2004) 49 *N.Y.L. Sch. L. Rev.*, p. 353.

EDRI, "New Council of Europe Recommendation fails to uphold online freedom of expression, European Digital Rights Statement and Call for Action", 10 October 2007, at www.edri.org/coerec200711.

Eisner, W., *The Plot: The Secret Story of the Protocols of the Elders of Zion* (New York: W. W. Norton & Company, 2005).

Electronic Privacy Information Center, *Faulty Filters: How Content Filters Block Access to Kid-Friendly Information on the Internet* (Washington, 1997), at www.epic. org/.

EU – ADRI, *National Analytical Study on Racist Violence and Crime: RAXEN Focal Point for France* (2004), compiled for the National Focal Point of the European Monitoring Centre on Racism and Xenophobia (EUMC).

EU – Communication from the Commission to the European Parliament, the Council and the Committee of the Regions "Towards a general policy on the fight against cyber crime" of 22 May 2007, COM(2007) 267.

EU – Communication from the European Commission to the European Parliament and the Council concerning Terrorist recruitment: addressing the factors contributing to violent radicalisation, Brussels, 21.9.2005, COM(2005) 313 final.

EU – Council Framework Decision on combating certain forms and expressions of racism and xenophobia by means of criminal law, 2001/0270 (CNS), 16771/07, DROIPEN 127, Brussels, 26 February 2008.

EU – Council Joint Action 96/443/JHA of 15 July 1996 concerning action to combat racism and xenophobia.

EU – Council of the European Union, document No. 13930/06 RESTREINT UE, 13930/06, EXT 2, ENFOPOL 169, Brussels, 10 November 2008, Conclusions of the Kick-off conference "Check the Web", Berlin, 26-27 September 2006.

EU – Council of the European Union, Proposal for a Council Framework Decision on combating certain forms and expressions of racism and xenophobia by means of criminal law, 14904/01 DROIPEN 105 COM(2001) 664 final, 15699/1/08, REV 1, Brussels, 25 November 2008.

EU – Council of the European Union, *Revised Action Plan on Terrorism*, 10043/06, Brussels (31 May 2006).

EU – Council of the European Union, *The European Union Strategy for Combating Radicalisation and Recruitment to Terrorism*, 14347/05 JAI 414 ENFOPOL 152 COTER 69, Brussels (25 November 2005).

EU – Decision No. 854/2005/EC of the European Parliament and of the Council establishing a Multiannual Community Programme on promoting safer use of the Internet and new online technologies, PE-CONS 3688/1/04 REV1, Strasbourg, 11 May 2005.

EU – Directive 2000/31/EC of the European Parliament and of the Council of 8 June 2000 on certain legal aspects of information society services, in particular electronic commerce, in the Internal Market, Official Journal of the European Communities, vol. 43, OJ L 178 17 July 2000, p. 1.

EU – Documentation and Advisory Centre on Racial Discrimination (DACoRD), *National Analytical Study on Racist Violence and Crime: RAXEN Focal Point for Denmark* (2003), compiled for the National Focal Point of the European Monitoring Centre on Racism and Xenophobia (EUMC), at www.eumc.at/.

EU – Draft Framework Decision: Council of the European Union, Proposal for a Council Framework Decision on combating certain forms and expressions of racism and xenophobia by means of criminal law, Document No. 11522/07, 19 July 2007.

EU – EC Decision No. 854/2005/EC of the European Parliament and of the Council establishing a Multiannual Community Programme on promoting safer use of the Internet and new online technologies [2005] OJ L 149/1 at http://ec.europa.eu/.

EU – EC Follow-up to the Multiannual Community action plan on promoting safer use of the Internet by combating illegal and harmful content on global networks:

Proposal for a decision of the European Parliament and of the Council amending Decision No. 276/1999/EC adopting a Multiannual Community Action Plan on promoting safer use of the Internet by combating illegal and harmful content on global networks, COM (2002) 152, Brussels.

EU – EUMC working paper, *Antisemitism: Summary overview of the situation in the European Union 2001-2005* (May 2006), online EUMC http://eumc.europa.eu/.

EU – European Commission Staff Working Document, Accompanying document to the proposal for a Council Framework Decision amending Framework Decision 2002/475/JHA on combating terrorism: Impact Assessment, 14960/07 ADD1, Brussels, 13 November 2007, para 4.2, pp. 29-30.

EU – European Commission, First Report on the application of Directive 2000/31/EC of the European Parliament and of the Council of 8 June 2000 on certain legal aspects of information society services, in particular electronic commerce, in the Internal Market (Directive on electronic commerce), COM(2003) 702 final.

EU – European Commission, Interim report on Initiatives in EU Member States with respect to Combating Illegal and Harmful Content on the Internet, Version 7 (4 June 1997).

EU – European Commission, Opinion of the Economic and Social Committee on the Proposal for a Council Decision adopting a Multiannual Community Action Plan on promoting safe use of the Internet [1998] OJ C 214/29.

EU – European Forum for Migration Studies (EFMS), Institute at the University of Bamberg, *National Analytical Study on Racist Violence and Crime: RAXEN Focal Point for Germany* (2004), written by Rühl, S. and Will, G., compiled for the National Focal Point of the European Monitoring Centre on Racism and Xenophobia (EUMC).

EU – European Parliament legislative resolution of 22 October, 2008 on the proposal for a decision of the European Parliament and of the Council establishing a Multiannual Community Programme on protecting children using the Internet and other communication technologies (COM(2008)0106 – C6-0092/2008 – 2008/0047(COD)).

EU – European Parliament Report A6-0244/2005 on the proposal for a recommendation of the European Parliament and of the Council on the protection of minors and human dignity and the right of reply in relation to the competitiveness of the European audiovisual and information services industry, 19 July 2005 (Rapporteur: Marielle De Sarnez).

EU – European Parliament Resolution of 13 December 2007 on combating the rise of extremism in Europe, P6_TA(2007)0623.

EU – "FRA welcomes new EU Framework Decision on combating racism and xenophobia", 28 November 2008, at www.ue2008.fr/.

EU – Ludwig Boltzmann Institute of Human Rights Research Association (BIM-FV), in co-operation with the Department of Linguistics (University of Vienna) and the Institute of Conflict Research (IKF), *National Analytical Study on Racist Violence and Crime: RAXEN Focal Point for Austria* (2003), report compiled for the National Focal Point of the European Monitoring Centre on Racism and Xenophobia (EUMC), at www.eumc.at/.

EU – Proposal for a Council Framework Decision amending Framework Decision 2002/475/JHA on combating terrorism, 2007/0236 (CNS), COM(2007) 650 final, Brussels, 6.11.2007, at http://ec.europa.eu/.

EU – Proposal for a Directive of the European Parliament and of the Council amending Council Directive 89/552/EEC on the coordination of certain provisions laid down by law, regulation or administrative action in Member States concerning the pursuit of television broadcasting activities (Television without frontiers), COM(2005) 646 final.

EU – Report from the Commission to the European Parliament, the Council and the European Economic and Social Committee – First report on the application of Directive 2000/31/EC on electronic commerce), COM(2003) 702 final, Brussels, 21 November, 2003, at http://europa.eu.int/.

EU – *Safer Internet Action Plan: Work Programme 2003-2004* at http://ec.europa.eu/.

EU Annual Report on Human Rights – 2005, 12416/05, Brussels, 28 September 2005.

EUMC, *The fight against Anti-Semitism and Islamophobia—Bringing Communities together*, Vienna/Brussels, Fall 2003, at http://eumc.europa.eu/.

European Commission for Democracy through Law (Venice Commission), Report on the relationship between freedom of expression and freedom of religion: the issue of regulation and prosecution of blasphemy, religious insult and incitement to religious hatred adopted by the Venice Commission at its 76th Plenary Session (Venice, 17-18 October 2008), CDL-AD(2008)026, at www.venice.coe.int/.

European Commission for Democracy through Law (Venice Commission), Annexe II: Analysis of the Domestic Law concerning blasphemy, religious insult and inciting religious hatred in Albania, Austria, Belgium, Denmark, France, Greece, Ireland, Netherlands, Poland, Romania, Turkey, United Kingdom on the basis of replies to a questionnaire, CDL-AD(2008)026add2, Study No. 406/2006, 22 October 2008, at www.venice.coe.int/.

European Commission for Democracy through Law (Venice Commission), Report on the relationship between freedom of expression and freedom of religion: the issue of regulation and prosecution of blasphemy, religious insult and incitement to religious hatred adopted by the Venice Commission at its 76th Plenary Session (Venice, 17-18 October 2008), CDL-AD(2008)026, at www.venice.coe.int/.

Farber, B., "The Internet and Hate Promotion: The 21st Century Dilemma", Canadian Human Rights Commission, *Hate on the Net*, Spring 2006, at www.chrc-ccdp.ca/pdf/hateoninternet_bil.pdf, pp. 12-15.

Federal Research Division of the Library of Congress, *Romania – A Country Study*, 1989, at http://memory.loc.gov/frd/cs/rotoc.html.

Finkelstein, S., *Anticensorware Investigations – Censorware Exposed*, at http://sethf.com/anticensorware/.

Framework Decision 2008/913/JHA on combating certain forms and expressions of racism and xenophobia by means of criminal law of 28 November 2008, Official Journal of the European Union L 328/55, 6 December 2008.

Francis Harry Hinsley, *Sovereignty*, 2nd edn (Cambridge: Cambridge University Press, 1986).

Freedom of Expression and the Internet in China, a Human Rights Watch Backgrounder, August 2001, at www.hrw.org/backgrounder/asia/china-bck-0701.htm.

Frydman, B. and Rorive, I., "Regulating Internet Content through Intermediaries in Europe and the USA" (2002) *Zeitschrift für Rechtssoziologie* 23 Heft 1, S. 41-59, at www.isys.ucl.ac.be/etudes/cours/linf2202/Frydman_&_Rorive_2002.pdf.

Gay & Lesbian Alliance Against Defamation, *Access Denied: The Impact of Internet Filtering Software on the Lesbian and Gay Community* (New York, 1997), at www.glaad.org/.

Gelbstein, E. and Kurbalija, J., "Internet Governance: Issues, Actors, and Divide", DIPLO report, 2005, at www.diplomacy.edu/isl/ig/.

Glaser, J., Dixit, J. and Green, D. P., "Studying Hate Crime with the Internet: What Makes Racists Advocate Racial Violence?" (2002) *Journal of Social Issues* 58(1) spring, pp. 177-193.

Goldsmith, J., "Unilateral Regulation of the Internet: A Modest Defence", (2000) *European Journal of International Law* 11, pp. 135-148.

Hadassa, Ben-Itto, *The Lie That Wouldn't Die: The Protocols of the Elders of Zion*, (Mitchell Vallentine & Company, 2005).

Heins, M. and Cho, C., *Internet Filters: A Public Policy Research* (2001), National Coalition Against Censorship, at www.ncac.org/.

Held, D., *Democracy and the Global Order* (Cambridge: Polity, 1995).

Hieronymus, A., Using the Internet for Intercultural Training! A pilot study of web sites in English for children, young adults, teachers and trainers, EUMC, Vienna, September 2003, at http://eumc.europa.eu/.

Hirst P. and Thompson, G., "Globalization and the Future of the Nation State" (1995) *Economy and Society*, 24(3), 408-442, at 419.

House of Commons, *The Racial and Religious Hatred Bill*, Research Paper 05/48, 16 June 2005.

Hudson, H. E, *Global Connections: International Telecommunications Infrastructure and Policy* (New York: Van Nostrand Reinhold, 1997).

INACH Annual Report for 2005, published during 2006 at www.inach.net/.

INACH reports, *Antisemitism on the Internet*, April 2004, at www.inach.net/content/INACH – Antisemitism on the Internet.pdf, and *Hate on the Net – Virtual nursery for In Real Life crime*, June 2004, at www.inach.net/.

JIHAD Online: Islamic Terrorists and the Internet (2002), Anti-Defamation League, at www.adl.org/.

Jugendschutz.net Annual Report 2007, *Right-Wing Extremism on the Internet*, 15 June 2008.

Jugendschutz.net, *'Right-wing Extremism on the Internet' – successful strategies against Online-Hate*, 2004 Annual Report, at www.inach.net/.

Jugendschutz.net, *Annual Report 2003: Right-Wing Extremism on the Internet*, at www.inach.net/.

Jugendschutz.net, *Chart of illegal and blocked websites containing right-wing extremism 01.01.-31.12.2003*, 2003, at www.inach.net/.

Kahin, B. and Nesson, C., eds, *Borders in Cyberspace: Information Policy and Global Information Infrastructure* (Cambridge, Mass.: MIT Press, 1997).

Kahn, R. A., "Rebuttal versus Unmasking: Legal Strategy in *R. v. Zündel*" (2000) *Institute for Jewish Policy Research* 34(3), p. 3.

Kahn, R. A., *Holocaust Denial and the Law: A Comparative Study* (New York: Palgrave Macmillan, 2004).

Laurie, B., "An Expert's Apology", 21 November 2000, at www.apache-ssl.org/apology.html.

League for Human Rights of B'nai Brith Canada, *2005 Audit of Antisemitic Incidents 2005* (2006), at www.bnaibrith.ca/audit2005.html.

Lia, B., "Al-Qaeda online: understanding jihadist internet infrastructure" in *Jane's Intelligence Review* (1 January 2006).

Long, A., "Forgetting the Fuhrer: The recent history of the Holocaust denial movement in Germany" (2002) 48(1) *Australian Journal of Politics & History* 48(1), p. 72.

Maastricht Ministerial Council, Decision No. 4/03 on Tolerance and Non-Discrimination (2003).

MacDonald, A., *The Turner Diaries: A Novel* (Fort Lee, N.J.: Barricade Books, 1996).

Magenta Foundation, Complaints Bureau for Discrimination on the Internet, *Meldpunt Discriminatie Internet, Annual Report 2002* (Amsterdam: Stichting Magenta, 2003), at www. inach.net/.

Magenta Foundation, Complaints Bureau for Discrimination on the Internet, *Meldpunt Discriminatie Internet, Annual Report 2003* (Amsterdam: Stichting Magenta, 2004), at www.inach.net/.

Maillet, M., "Hate Message Complaints and Human Rights Tribunal Hearings" in *Hate on the Net*, Ottawa: Association for Canadian Studies, spring 2006, 78, Canadian Human Rights Commission, at www.chrc-ccdp.ca/pdf/hateoninternet_bil.pdf.

Martin, W. J., *The Global Information Society* (Aslib Gower, Guildford: 1995), pp. 9-10.

Mill, J. S., *On Liberty*, at http://etext.library.adelaide.edu.au/m/mill/john_stuart/m645o/. Derived from the "Harvard Classics" Vol. 25, published in 1909 by P. F. Collier & Son.

Myers, D. A., "Defamation and the Quiescent Anarchy of the Internet: A Case Study of Cyber Targeting" (2006) *Penn St. L. Rev.* 110, p. 667.

Nas, S., (Bits of Freedom), The Multatuli Project: ISP Notice & take down, 2004, at www.bof.nl/docs/researchpaperSANE.pdf.

Nathwani, N., "Religious cartoons and human rights – a critical legal analysis of the case law of the European Court of Human Rights on the protection of religious feelings and its implications in the Danish affair concerning cartoons of the Prophet Muhammad,"(2008) *E.H.R.L.R.* 4, pp. 488-507.

Nilus, S., The Protocols of the Meetings of the Learned Elders of Zion With Preface and Explanatory Notes (Honolulu: University Press of the Pacific, 2003).

OpenNet Initiative, *Probing Chinese search engine filtering* (August 2004), at www. opennet.net/.

OpenNet Initiative, *Unintended Risks and Consequences of Circumvention Technologies: The IBB's Anonymizer Service in Iran* (May 2004), at www. opennet.net/.

OSCE – ODIHR, *Background Paper on Human Rights Considerations in Combating Incitement to Terrorism and Related Offences* (2006), at www.osce.org/.

OSCE – ODIHR, *Challenges and Responses to Hate-Motivated Incidents in the OSCE Region*, (October 2006), at www.osce.org/.pdf.

OSCE – ODIHR, *Combating Hate Crimes in the OSCE Region: An Overview of statistics, legislation, and national initiatives* (June 2005), at www.osce.org/.

OSCE – ODIHR, *Education on the Holocaust and on Anti-Semitism: An Overview and Analysis of Educational Approaches*, April 2006, at www.osce.org/.

OSCE – ODIHR, *Hate Crimes in the OSCE Region: Incidents and Responses, Annual Report for 2006*, OSCE/ODIHR (2007).

OSCE Cordoba Declaration, CIO.GAL/76/05/Rev.2, 9 June 2005, at www.osce.org/.

OSCE Maastricht Ministerial Council, *Decision No. 633: Promoting Tolerance and Media Freedom on the Internet* (2004), at www.osce.org/.

OSCE meeting on the relationship between racist, xenophobic, and anti-Semitic propaganda on the Internet and hate crimes, Consolidated Summary, PC. DEL/918/04/Corr.1, 27 September 2004, at www.osce.org/.

OSCE Ministerial Council Decision No. 12/04 on Tolerance and Non-Discrimination, December 2004, at www.osce.org/.

OSCE Office for Democratic Institutions and Human Rights (ODIHR), *International Action Against Racism, Xenophobia, Anti-Semitism and Tolerance in the OSCE Region: A Comparative Study* (September 2004), at www.osce.org/.

Österreich, Bundesministerium für Inneres (2002) Verfassungsschutzbericht 2001 (Report on the Protection of the Constitution 2000), www.bmi.gv.at/.

Partners Against Hate initiative report entitled *Hate on the Internet: A Response Guide for Educators and Parents*, ADL, December 2003, at www.partnersagainsthate.org/.

Partners Against Hate, Investigating Hate Crimes on the Internet, September 2003, at www.partnersagainsthate.org/.

Pierson, C., *The Modern State* (London: Routledge, 1996).

Pool, I. S., *Technologies without Boundaries* (Cambridge, MA: Harvard University Press, 1990).

Racism, Racial Discrimination, Xenophobia, and all forms of Discrimination: Annual Report submitted by Mr Doudou Diène, Special Rapporteur on contemporary forms of racism, racial discrimination, xenophobia and related intolerance, E/CN.4/2006/16, 18 January 2006 (Economic and Social Council of the UN).

Reidenberg, J. R, "Governing Networks and Cyberspace Rule-Making" (1996) *Emory Law Journal* (45), p. 911.

Report to the Minister of Justice of the Special Committee on Hate Propaganda in Canada (Ottawa: Queen's Printer, 1966).

Rosen, P., *Hate Propaganda* in Current Issue Review 85-6E (Ottawa: Canadian Parliamentary Research Branch, 2000), Government of Canada, at www.parl.gc.ca/.

Ryan, J., *Countering Militant Islamist Radicalisation on the Internet: A User Driven Strategy to Recover the Web* (Dublin: Institute of European Affairs, 2007).

Schauer, F., "Codifying the First Amendment: *New York v. Ferber*" (1982) *Sup. Ct. Rev* 285, p. 317.

Sparks, C., *Communism, Capitalism and the Mass Media* (London: Sage, 1997).

Stern, K. S., *Hate and the Internet* (2004), American Jewish Committee, at www.ajc.org/.

Stern, K. S., *Holocaust Denial* (1993), at www.ajc.org/.

Taylor, G., "Casting the Net Too Widely: Racial Hatred on the Internet" (2001) *Criminal Law Journal*, p. 262.

The Simon Wiesenthal Center, *Digital Terrorism & Hate 2006*, available through www.wiesenthal.com/.

The Simon Wiesenthal Center, *Digital Terrorism & Hate 2007*, available through www.wiesenthal.com/.

The Simon Wiesenthal Center, iReport: *Online Terror and Hate: The First Decade*, May 2008, at www.wiesenthal.com/ireport.

The WGIG Background Report, June 2005, at www.wgig.org/docs/BackgroundReport.doc, para 31. See further the WGIG Report, June 2005, at www.wgig.org/docs/WGIGREPORT.doc.

Third Decade to Combat Racism and Racial Discrimination, GA Res. 51/81, UN GAOR, 51st Sess., UN Doc. A/RES/51/81 (1997) at para. 10.

Tunis Agenda for the Information Society, Second Phase of the WSIS (16-18 November 2005, Tunis), at www.itu.int/.

Tunis Commitment of November 2005 – Second Phase of the WSIS (16-18 November 2005, Tunis), at www.itu.int/.

UK Parliamentary Committee Against Antisemitism, *Report of the All-Party Parliamentary Inquiry into Antisemitism*, London: The Stationery Office Limited, 2006, at http://thepcaa.org/Report.pdf.

UK – Crown Prosecution Service Racist and Religious Crime Prosecution Policy, March 2008, at www.cps.gov.uk/publications/prosecution/rrpbcrbook.html.

UN – Implementation of the Programme of Action for the Third Decade to Combat Racism and Racial Discrimination, Report of the United Nations seminar to assess the implementation of the International Convention on the Elimination of All Forms of Racial Discrimination with particular reference to Articles 4 and 6, Commission on Human Rights, 53rd Sess., UN Doc. E/CN.4/1997/68/Add.1 (1996).

UN – General Assembly, Global efforts for the total elimination of racism, racial discrimination, xenophobia and related intolerance and the comprehensive implementation of and follow-up to the Durban Declaration and Programme of Action: report of the Secretary-General, A/63/366, 19 October 2008.

UN – Maurice Glélé-Ahanhanzo, Implementation of the Programme of Action for the Second Decade to Combat Racism and Racial Discrimination – Report of the UN Special Rapporteur on contemporary forms of racism, racial discrimination, xenophobia and related intolerance, CHR Res. 1994/64, UN ESCOR, 51st Sess., UN Doc. E/CN.4/1995/78 (1995).

UN – Maurice Glélé-Ahanhanzo, Implementation of the Programme of Action for the Second Decade to Combat Racism and Racial Discrimination – Report of the UN Special Rapporteur on contemporary forms of racism, racial discrimination, xenophobia and related intolerance, CHR Res. 1996/21, UN ESCOR, 53rd Sess., UN Doc. E/CN.4/1997/71 (1997).

UN – Maurice Glélé-Ahanhanzo, Racism, racial discrimination, xenophobia and related intolerance: Report of the UN Special Rapporteur on Contemporary Forms of Racism, Racial Discrimination, Xenophobia and Related Intolerance, CHR Res. 1997/73, Commission on Human Rights, 54th Sess., UN Doc. E/CN.4/1998/79 (1998).

UN – Office of the High Commissioner for Human Rights, Background Note on the Information Society and Human Rights, WSIS/PC-3/CONTR/178-E, October 2003.

UN – Progress report of the Office of the United Nations High Commissioner for Human Rights (OHCHR Report 2006), Implementation of relevant recommendations of the third session of the Intergovernmental Working Group on the Effective Implementation of the Durban Declaration and Programme of Action, United Nations Economic and Social Council, E/CN.4/2006/15, 16 February 2006.

UN – Promotion and protection of the right to freedom of opinion and expression, Report of the Special Rapporteur, Mr Abid Hussain, E/CN.4/1998/40, 28 January 1998.

UN – Racism, racial discrimination, xenophobia and related intolerance: Report of the Expert Seminar on the role of the Internet in the light of the provisions of the International Convention on the Elimination of All Forms of Racial Discrimination, Commission on Human Rights, 54th Sess., UN Doc. E/CN.4/1998/77/Add.2 (1998).

UN – Report of the Committee on the Elimination of Racial Discrimination, Sixty-fourth session (23 February to 12 March 2004) Sixty-fifth session (2-20 August 2004), No. A/59/18, 1 October 2004.

UN – Report of the Intergovernmental Working Group on the effective implementation of the Durban Declaration and Programme of Action on its fourth session (Chairperson-Rapporteur: Juan Martabit (Chile)), E/CN.4/2006/18, 20 March 2006, at http://daccessdds.un.org/.

UN – Report of the World Conference against Racism, Racial Discrimination, Xenophobia and Related Intolerance, Durban, 31 August to 8 September 2001, A/CONF.189/12, GE.02-10005 (E) 100102, 25 January 2002 at www.un.org/WCAR/aconf189_12.pdf.

UN – Report of the World Conference against Racism, Racial Discrimination, Xenophobia and Related Intolerance, Durban, 31 August to 8 September 2001, UN Doc. A/CONF.189/12 (2002), at www.un.org/WCAR/aconf189_12.pdf.

UN – Report of the World Conference against Racism, Racial Discrimination, Xenophobia and Related Intolerance, Durban, 31 August to 8 September 2001, A/CONF.189/12, 25 January 2002.

UN – Reports, studies and other documentation for the Preparatory Committee and the World Conference: Consultation on the use of the Internet for the purpose of incitement to racial hatred, racial propaganda and xenophobia, A/CONF.189/PC.1/5, 5 April 2000.

UN – Review of reports, studies and other documentation for the Preparatory Committee and the world conference: Report of the High Commissioner for Human Rights on the use of the Internet for purposes of incitement to racial hatred, racist propaganda and xenophobia, and on ways of promoting international cooperation in this area, A/CONF.189/PC.2/12, 27 April 2001.

UN – Rights of the Child: Report submitted by Mr Juan Miguel Petit, Special Rapporteur on the sale of children, child prostitution and child pornography, E/CN.4/2005/78, 23 December 2004. Note also the Addendum to this report: E/CN.4/2005/78/Add.3, 8 March 2005.

UN – Secretariat, Efforts by the Office of the United Nations High Commissioner for Human Rights for universal ratification of the International Convention on the Elimination of All Forms of Racial Discrimination, E/CN.4/2006/13, 15 February 2006.

UN – Secretary-General, *Elimination of Racism and Racial Discrimination*, UN GA, 49th Sess., UN Doc. A/49/677 (1994).

UN – Secretary-General, Elimination of Racism and Racial Discrimination: Measures to combat contemporary forms of racism, racial discrimination, xenophobia and related intolerance, UN GA, 51st Sess., UN Doc. A/51/301 (1996).

UN – Secretary-General, Elimination of Racism and Racial Discrimination: Measures to combat contemporary forms of racism, racial discrimination, xenophobia and related intolerance, UN GA, 52nd Sess., UN Doc. A/52/471 (1997).

UN – Secretary-General, Measures to combat contemporary forms of racism, racial discrimination, xenophobia and related intolerance, UN GA, 54th Sess., UN Doc. A/54/347 (1999).

UN – Secretary-General, Measures to combat contemporary forms of racism, racial discrimination, xenophobia and related intolerance, UN GA, 57th Sess., UN Doc. A/57/204 (2002).

UN – Secretary-General, Report of the Special Rapporteur of the Commission on Human Rights on contemporary forms of racism, racial discrimination, xenophobia and related intolerance, UN GA, 55th Sess., UN Doc. A/55/304 (2000).

UN – Secretary-General, The fight against racism, racial discrimination, xenophobia and related intolerance and the comprehensive implementation of and follow-up to the Durban Declaration and Programme of Action, UN GA, 58th Sess., UN Doc. A/58/313 (2003).

UN – Secretary-General, The fight against racism, racial discrimination, xenophobia and related intolerance and the comprehensive implementation of and follow-up to the Durban Declaration and Programme of Action, UN GA, 59th Sess., UN Doc. A/59/329 (2004).

UN – The fight against racism, racial discrimination, xenophobia and related intolerance and the comprehensive implementation of and follow-up to the Durban Declaration and Programme of Action, Note by the Secretary-General, A/59/329, 7 September 2004.

UN Committee on the Elimination of Racial Discrimination (CERD), 18th Periodic Report submitted by Germany under Article 9 of the International Convention on the Elimination of All Forms of Racial Discrimination, submitted on 16 January 2007, CERD/C/DEU/18, 31 January 2008.

UN Committee on the Elimination of Racial Discrimination (CERD), 6th Periodic Report submitted by USA under Article 9 of the International Convention on the Elimination of All Forms of Racial Discrimination, submitted on 24 April 2007, CERD/C/USA/6, 1 May 2007.

UN General Assembly Resolution on Holocaust Remembrance, A/60/L.12, 26 October 2005, at www.hmd.org.uk/. UN General Assembly adopted a resolution No. A/RES/61/255 (GA/10569) condemning any denial of Holocaust (www.un.org/News/Press/docs/2007/ga10569.doc.htm).

UN ICT Task Force Series 5 – Internet Governance: A Grand Collaboration, September 2004, available through www.unicttf.org/.

UN, General Assembly, Complementary International Standards: Report on the study by the five experts on the content and scope of substantive gaps in the existing international instruments to combat racism, racial discrimination, xenophobia and related intolerance, at www.ohchr.org/.

UN, General Assembly, Complementary International Standards: Report on the study by the five experts on the content and scope of substantive gaps in the existing international instruments to combat racism, racial discrimination, xenophobia and related intolerance, 27 August 2007 at www.ohchr.org/, para 151.

United States Commission on Security and Cooperation in Europe (Helsinki Commission) Holds Briefing: "Hate In The Information Age", 15 May 2008, at http://csce.gov/.

US Bureau of Democracy, Human Rights, and Labor, *International Religious FreedomReport 2005 – France*, US Department of State, at www.state.gov.

US Bureau of Democracy, Human Rights, and Labor, *Report on Global Anti-Semitism*, January 2005, at www.state.gov/g/drl/rls/40258.htm. Note also Combating racism, racial discrimination, xenophobia and related intolerance and comprehensive implementation of and follow-up to the Durban Declaration and Programme of Action, Note by the UN Secretary-General, A/59/330, 4 October 2004.

USA – Computer Crime and Intellectual Property Section (CCIPS) of the Criminal Division of the US Department of Justice "Frequently Asked Questions and Answers About the Council of Europe Convention on Cybercrime" (Final Draft, released June 29, 2001), at www.cybercrime.gov.

Van Blarcum, C. D., "Internet Hate Speech: The European Framework and the Emerging American Haven" (2005) 62 *Wash & Lee L. Rev.* 62, p. 781.

Weimann, G., *Terror on the Internet: The New Arena, the New Challenges* (Washington: US Institute of Peace, 2006).

WGIG Background Report, June 2005, at www.wgig.org/.

Wolf, C., To the Commission on Security and Cooperation in Europe (US Helsinki Commission): Briefing on Hate in the Information Age, Washington, DC, 15 May 2008, at www.adl.org/.

World Information Society Report 2007 at www.itu.int/osg/spu/publications/worldinformationsociety/2007/. "Note Implementing the WSIS Outcomes" chapter at www.itu.int.

WSIS Outcome Documents 2003-2005 at www.itu.int.

Zittrain, J. and Edelman, B., *Documentation of Internet Filtering Worldwide* (Berkman Center for Internet & Society, 2003), at http://cyber.law.harvard.edu/filtering/.

Sales agents for publications of the Council of Europe
Agents de vente des publications du Conseil de l'Europe

BELGIUM/BELGIQUE
La Librairie Européenne -
The European Bookshop
Rue de l'Orme, 1
BE-1040 BRUXELLES
Tel.: +32 (0)2 231 04 35
Fax: +32 (0)2 735 08 60
E-mail: order@libeurop.be
http://www.libeurop.be

Jean De Lannoy/DL Services
Avenue du Roi 202 Koningslaan
BE-1190 BRUXELLES
Tel.: +32 (0)2 538 43 08
Fax: +32 (0)2 538 08 41
E-mail: jean.de.lannoy@dl-servi.com
http://www.jean-de-lannoy.be

**BOSNIA AND HERZEGOVINA/
BOSNIE-HERZÉGOVINE**
Robert's Plus d.o.o.
Marka Maruliça 2/V
BA-71000, SARAJEVO
Tel.: + 387 33 640 818
Fax: + 387 33 640 818
E-mail: robertsplus@bih.net.ba

CANADA
Renouf Publishing Co. Ltd.
1-5369 Canotek Road
CA-OTTAWA, Ontario K1J 9J3
Tel.: +1 613 745 2665
Fax: +1 613 745 7660
Toll-Free Tel.: (866) 767-6766
E-mail: order.dept@renoufbooks.com
http://www.renoufbooks.com

CROATIA/CROATIE
Robert's Plus d.o.o.
Marasoviçeva 67
HR-21000, SPLIT
Tel.: + 385 21 315 800, 801, 802, 803
Fax: + 385 21 315 804
E-mail: robertsplus@robertsplus.hr

**CZECH REPUBLIC/
RÉPUBLIQUE TCHÈQUE**
Suweco CZ, s.r.o.
Klecakova 347
CZ-180 21 PRAHA 9
Tel.: +420 2 424 59 204
Fax: +420 2 848 21 646
E-mail: import@suweco.cz
http://www.suweco.cz

DENMARK/DANEMARK
GAD
Vimmelskaftet 32
DK-1161 KØBENHAVN K
Tel.: +45 77 66 60 00
Fax: +45 77 66 60 01
E-mail: gad@gad.dk
http://www.gad.dk

FINLAND/FINLANDE
Akateeminen Kirjakauppa
PO Box 128
Keskuskatu 1
FI-00100 HELSINKI
Tel.: +358 (0)9 121 4430
Fax: +358 (0)9 121 4242
E-mail: akatilaus@akateeminen.com
http://www.akateeminen.com

FRANCE
La Documentation française
(diffusion/distribution France entière)
124, rue Henri Barbusse
FR-93308 AUBERVILLIERS CEDEX
Tél.: +33 (0)1 40 15 70 00
Fax: +33 (0)1 40 15 68 00
E-mail: commande@ladocumentationfrancaise.fr
http://www.ladocumentationfrancaise.fr

Librairie Kléber
1 rue des Francs Bourgeois
FR-67000 STRASBOURG
Tel.: +33 (0)3 88 15 78 88
Fax: +33 (0)3 88 15 78 80
E-mail: librairie-kleber@coe.int
http://www.librairie-kleber.com

**GERMANY/ALLEMAGNE
AUSTRIA/AUTRICHE**
UNO Verlag GmbH
August-Bebel-Allee 6
DE-53175 BONN
Tel.: +49 (0)228 94 90 20
Fax: +49 (0)228 94 90 222
E-mail: bestellung@uno-verlag.de
http://www.uno-verlag.de

GREECE/GRÈCE
Librairie Kauffmann s.a.
Stadiou 28
GR-105 64 ATHINAI
Tel.: +30 210 32 55 321
Fax.: +30 210 32 30 320
E-mail: ord@otenet.gr
http://www.kauffmann.gr

HUNGARY/HONGRIE
Euro Info Service
Pannónia u. 58.
PF. 1039
HU-1136 BUDAPEST
Tel.: +36 1 329 2170
Fax: +36 1 349 2053
E-mail: euroinfo@euroinfo.hu
http://www.euroinfo.hu

ITALY/ITALIE
Licosa SpA
Via Duca di Calabria, 1/1
IT-50125 FIRENZE
Tel.: +39 0556 483215
Fax: +39 0556 41257
E-mail: licosa@licosa.com
http://www.licosa.com

MEXICO/MEXIQUE
Mundi-Prensa México, S.A. De C.V.
Río Pánuco, 141 Delegación Cuauhtémoc
MX-06500 MÉXICO, D.F.
Tel.: +52 (01)55 55 33 56 58
Fax: +52 (01)55 55 14 67 99
E-mail: mundiprensa@mundiprensa.com.mx
http://www.mundiprensa.com.mx

NETHERLANDS/PAYS-BAS
Roodveldt Import BV
Nieuwe Hemweg 50
NE-1013 CX AMSTERDAM
Tel.: + 31 20 622 8035
Fax.: + 31 20 625 5493
Website: www.publidis.org
Email: orders@publidis.org

NORWAY/NORVÈGE
Akademika
Postboks 84 Blindern
NO-0314 OSLO
Tel.: +47 2 218 8100
Fax: +47 2 218 8103
E-mail: support@akademika.no
http://www.akademika.no

POLAND/POLOGNE
Ars Polona JSC
25 Obroncow Street
PL-03-933 WARSZAWA
Tel.: +48 (0)22 509 86 00
Fax: +48 (0)22 509 86 10
E-mail: arspolona@arspolona.com.pl
http://www.arspolona.com.pl

PORTUGAL
Livraria Portugal
(Dias & Andrade, Lda.)
Rua do Carmo, 70
PT-1200-094 LISBOA
Tel.: +351 21 347 42 82 / 85
Fax: +351 21 347 02 64
E-mail: info@livrariaportugal.pt
http://www.livrariaportugal.pt

**RUSSIAN FEDERATION/
FÉDÉRATION DE RUSSIE**
Ves Mir
17b, Butlerova ul.
RU-101000 MOSCOW
Tel.: +7 495 739 0971
Fax: +7 495 739 0971
E-mail: orders@vesmirbooks.ru
http://www.vesmirbooks.ru

SPAIN/ESPAGNE
Mundi-Prensa Libros, s.a.
Castelló, 37
ES-28001 MADRID
Tel.: +34 914 36 37 00
Fax: +34 915 75 39 98
E-mail: libreria@mundiprensa.es
http://www.mundiprensa.com

SWITZERLAND/SUISSE
Planetis Sàrl
16 chemin des Pins
CH-1273 ARZIER
Tel.: +41 22 366 51 77
Fax: +41 22 366 51 78
E-mail: info@planetis.ch

UNITED KINGDOM/ROYAUME-UNI
The Stationery Office Ltd
PO Box 29
GB-NORWICH NR3 1GN
Tel.: +44 (0)870 600 5522
Fax: +44 (0)870 600 5533
E-mail: book.enquiries@tso.co.uk
http://www.tsoshop.co.uk

**UNITED STATES and CANADA/
ÉTATS-UNIS et CANADA**
Manhattan Publishing Co
2036 Albany Post Road
USA-10520 CROTON ON HUDSON, NY
Tel.: +1 914 271 5194
Fax: +1 914 271 5886
E-mail: coe@manhattanpublishing.coe
http://www.manhattanpublishing.com

2935

Council of Europe Publishing/Editions du Conseil de l'Europe
FR-67075 STRASBOURG Cedex
Tel.: +33 (0)3 88 41 25 81 – Fax: +33 (0)3 88 41 39 10 – E-mail: publishing@coe.int – Website: http://book.coe.int